The Cosmic Christ

Hans-Werner Schroeder

The Cosmic Christ

Floris Books

Translated by Jon Madsen

First published in German in 1995 under the title
Der Kosmische Christus by Verlag Urachhaus.
First published in English in 1997 by Floris Books.

This translation © Floris Books, Edinburgh 1997

British Library CIP Data available

ISBN 0–86315–260–0

Printed in Great Britain
by Bookcraft (Bath) Limited

Contents

Introduction

For two millennia human beings have occupied themselves with the question of the nature of the being of Christ. In the spiritual history of mankind there can scarcely be a subject about which so much has been pondered or with which there has been so much struggle as this. How are we to understand and confess the nature and being of Christ and his appearance on earth?

This question, whether directly or indirectly, has often been at the heart of religious disputes, indeed of savage wars of religion. The first Christian centuries were occupied with the search for answers to the problems of understanding which were experienced here. Later, the answers were solidified in ecclesiastical dogmas — as, for instance, in the dogma of the full equality of being of the Father God with the Son God, the Christ.[1]

Such dogmatic answers from the past can no longer satisfy us today: we no longer have easy access to the simple faith which in former times enabled souls to rise above all difficulties of understanding in religious matters; nowadays, faith must be stimulated and supported by understanding and individual experience.

It is on precisely this important point of Christology that modern theology founders. As evidence for this, two Catholic theologians who have reached a wide public can be named, representing various others, namely Hans Küng and Eugen Drewermann. They both represent, to a high degree, the ideals of 'intellectual honesty' and wide learning. But precisely for this reason, they have both come into conflict with traditional Christian teachings about the nature of Christ. For instance, it seems to them not consistent with a sensible attitude of mind to continue to cling to the 'bodily resurrection' of Jesus Christ;[2] and — especially important for our subject — they also depart from the teaching about the original divinity of Christ, his 'pre-existence.' With that, however, the cosmic dimension of Christ has been abandoned: as regards his constitution, Christ is not more than an — admittedly outstanding — human being.[3]

Such examples could be multiplied. To cite just one more, Rudolf Augstein. Some years ago he reduced the religious statements about Christ to absurdity by simply combining the conflicting views of leading modern theologians and the results of 'textual criticism' — the scientific analysis of the Gospels.* The outcome: Jesus Christ as content of the Christian faith is an offspring of pious imagination, a creation of the human mind, that is to say, in this sense — 'son of Man.'

Is our subject relevant?

Contemplating this overall picture as the fruit of the earnest labours of generations of learned theologians, one might despair of the future of Christianity; and then it seems only too understandable that countless people in our day turn away from the Christian tradition, or merely regard religion as a private matter which basically poses moral-ethical demands and maybe offers help in coping with life;[4] or that others incline to the 'fundamentalist' view of Christianity which rejects all scientific criticism of religion. With this kind of contemporary background, does it actually make any sense to write a book about the 'cosmic Christ'?

For two reasons we believe it to be worthwhile: because above all today it is essential to understand Christianity and the nature of Christ anew, if Christianity is to survive; and because there now exist new points of departure for this. Therefore it seems to us not only justified but necessary to attempt to contribute from a wide range of perspectives, so that the Christian truths can be freshly grasped in their full depths. In this respect, the question of the nature and being of Christ is of special significance, in that it touches on the centre of Christianity; this question leads directly to the second, that of the cosmic dimension of the being of Christ, that is, of the significance of Christ for the entire universe, for the earth and the kingdoms of nature, not just for Man.

* *Jesus — Menschensohn.*

However, there is something more. In spite of the clear disinclination of many nowadays to have anything to do with traditional, dogmatic faith, we nonetheless find a widespread and growing inclination, indeed a longing, to accept mystical images of the world which point beyond the merely materialistic. Here there appears to be the beginnings of a backlash against the sterility and spiritual impoverishment of the current world view; the deeper powers of the soul rebel against these superficial interpretations, they demand other experiences than those which materialism and indeed conventional theology have to offer.

This need of the human soul is coming to expression in different directions: in the increase in occult practices and occult literature, also in renewed interest in all types of astrology; in the different trends within the New-Age movement; even, in the field of physics, the attempts to interpret certain facts of physics in conjunction with a mystical experience of the world (best known are the endeavours of Fritjof Capra); finally, this tendency is also present in the sphere of theology — above all in debate about the 'cosmic Christ.'[5]

In recent times, several books have appeared on this subject. In contrast to the usual approach of theology, they attempt to form a view of the 'cosmic dimension' of Christ; however, this attempt remains incomplete — for reasons which are still to be discussed.

Starting point

In considering the cosmic dimension of the being of Christ, we are only touching on one aspect — albeit an essential one — of Christology, that is, everything that can be said about Christ. This Christology consists of three great areas: the being and working of Christ before his becoming man on earth ('pre-existence' of Christ); the event itself of his becoming man: the incarnation of Christ in Jesus of Nazareth and his work on earth until Death, Resurrection, Ascension and Whitsun; and the continued working of Christ after his incarnation until our present time and into the future.

The cosmic dimension of Christ is present, as we shall see, in all three areas of Christology. Initially, we have to consider

Christ only in his cosmic greatness and power. Then, by contrast, that aspect of his being which is close to earth comes into the foreground: that, as a divine being, he could and did become man — the brother of Man; even so, the cosmic background also frequently 'shines through' his work on earth. And finally, we turn to the inter-relationship between the cosmic and the earthly existence of Christ: at the 'Ascension' he returns to his full cosmic power and authority, without, at the same time, leaving the earth; since that time, he is the 'Lord of the heavenly forces upon earth.'

Considerably more than it is possible to achieve in this book would be required in order to make a complete presentation of these three areas of a wide-ranging theology. We must restrict ourselves to highlighting only certain aspects of the cosmic dimension of Christ. In the literature of The Christian Community and in anthroposophical writings there is already a good deal on this subject, so that we may allow ourselves this restriction.[6]

The question of knowledge is fundamental: Is it possible for what previously was only accessible to faith to become available to real knowing? As far as I can see, only the life and work of Rudolf Steiner offers an answer to this question in our time. Through anthroposophy, possibilities of knowledge were opened up which make it permissible to speak with 'intellectual honesty' about spiritual worlds and God, about the life after death, about angelic beings and indeed also about Christ and his cosmic working. We shall have to refer to this frequently, without being able here to elaborate on the answer to the already raised fundamental question.[7]

However, there is also another source which flows into what is set down here: the life and worship of The Christian Community. There, the religious traditions of the Christian past have been renewed and completely opened anew for the consciousness of the present day and of the future. But there the cosmic dimension of Christ is also accessible in a new way to the inner eye, indeed to inner experience. This awareness and experience have flowed into the contents of this book. Together with the insights arising from anthroposophy they form a whole.

1. The overall picture of Christology

To begin with, we will open out the three great areas of Christology before our minds as one overall picture. In order not to burden this with too much detail, we will avoid far-reaching excursions or extensive supporting references to assist further understanding; initially, many questions must remain open.

The pre-existence of Christ

The first step we have to take touches on one of the most difficult and fundamental questions of Christianity, namely the question of the divine Trinity, the threefold and triune nature of God. Elsewhere,* I have shown that it is possible once more to frame sensible thoughts about the view that God is to be conceived of as threefold, that is, as Father, Son and Spirit, and yet also as triune, as One; and this conception can be re-enlivened. Here I will therefore simply summarize.

From the very beginning, Christ holds a 'cosmic' position: he is before the world, before all 'creation,' as 'Son' he is united with 'God the Father' — in the being of the Father he is the heart, the centre. When the world is formed out of the 'being' and the 'substance' of the Father, he (Christ) is the creator.

Without him, nothing would exist. Everything that has come into being has its origin as substance from God the Father, as life from Christ. It is thanks to Christ that every existing being has, as it were, 'sprung' from the being of the Father — which lies in the meaning of the word 'origin,' a spring, a well. This applies to the realms of the angels, who are higher than Man but lower than God;† it applies to the kingdoms of nature and the beings

---

* *Dreieinigkeit und Dreifaltigkeit.* See also Alfred Schütze, *Vom Wesen der Trinität.*

† H.-W. Schroeder, *Mensch und Engel.*

therein; it applies even to the powers of the Adversaries;* and above all it applies to Man since he is the 'image' of God.

The Godhead, the source of all goodness, did not wish to keep its being enclosed to itself and within itself; it desired to unfold itself into a world, to give other beings — outside itself, as it were — a share in the fullness of being. And so the world 'evolved' in the very beginning from unity into multiplicity, from the invisible into the visible, from the static into the movement of forward-striving becoming.

It is as the creator of this 'originating' of beings from the eternal, from non-being into becoming and into the temporal that we see Christ working. It is he who — as the beginning of St John's Gospel witnesses — is the actual creator; who, as it were, takes substance from the being of the Father and out of it forms the earth, Man and the Universe. At the same time, this makes him the proof that the Godhead is not 'sufficient unto itself' but gives space to other beings also; that it wants and recognizes what is outside itself — thereby beings and forces can evolve which otherwise would remain concealed for ever within the Godhead. And Man, in turn, can combine within himself the multiplicity of beings and worlds into which creation tends to fragment; he can reunite into a higher unity what otherwise would be in danger of falling apart.[1] For in Man, the potential is there for fullness, completeness and universality, as is also the power to unite this fullness and universality in the centre of his own being, in his 'I.' In Man, the earthly and the spiritual, the human and the divine, the highest and the lowest are as if bound up together — a tension which challenges his strength and even calls it into question through ever new developments and crises, through defeats and victories, through suffering and joy.

As the second act of creation, that drama unfolded which has to do with the emergence of evil and which leads to the 'Fall' of Man. The creation of Man is for a high purpose: as image of God he is to unite within himself the multiplicity of the created world and so raise it to a new stage. If this aim is to be fulfilled, there is a prerequisite: the creative freedom of Man; for the Godhead

* H.-W. Schroeder, *Der Mensch und das Böse*. Alfred Schütze, *The Enigma of Evil*.

works as a free, creative being in the life of the world. If Man really was to awaken to becoming the image of God, his creation could only be the first act of this development. If God really wanted an image of Himself, then Man must not remain merely a created being, he must himself become a creator, initially a creator of his own self. Therefore he must be given the freedom to grasp his self out of himself, to freely take hold of the forces which are within him and so, himself, find the purpose which is planned for him.

For this, it was necessary for evil, the adversary powers, to emerge and be permitted. They had to exert the power initially to make Man free of God, to make him independent — at the risk of him turning away completely from his origin.[2] In this way, by many stages an earthly world came about, far from God, apparently existing without God, which can be interpreted materialistically and without resource to the spirit — a world in which it is possible to deny God and live totally without Him. What is described in the Bible as the 'Fall' is, therefore, a necessary step towards becoming fully Man.

We see that the high aim and purpose of the becoming of Man make necessary the tremendous risk of allowing evil to become active; it presupposes a God-willed possibility for Man to find and walk the path which makes him a free and creative partner of God — completely out of himself, without any divine 'commands.' The first two acts of the drama have taken place: the creation of Man and his plunge into freedom from his origin, with all the consequences for himself and the world, the Fall. The third act, which alone gives meaning to this sequence of events, the unveiling of the true being of Man, has barely begun; we shall speak of it again when we come to consider the third part of Christology.

With these ideas we are by no means going beyond the truths stated in the Gospel. In the Gospel of John there is a quotation from the Old Testament: 'You are gods!' (John 10:34).

This is what Christ says about human beings — in those days it was certainly no self-evident statement, either. (And Novalis takes this up later, when he calls out: 'God desires gods!').

If the entire cosmos has to do with Christ as creator and life-giver, then the cosmic catastrophe, the fall of all creation into an apparently god-forsaken world in which evil is permitted to triumph, could not leave him untouched. Since the Fall, the evolution of mankind has had the character of ever increasing commitment to the earth and its possibilities. For the earth is, of course, not only a place forsaken and far from God; above all, it is the place where Man can develop and hone his powers through the challenge brought by evil. These possibilities, which are only offered by a life on an earth far from God, were to be active through millennia, in order that mankind should mature thereby. This fact is expressed by St Paul in the words: 'In the fullness of time ...' (Gal.4:4); that is to say: when the capacities and abilities of mankind had matured sufficiently through the sojourn on earth to allow the next act in the drama of human evolution to begin to unfold — at that moment the Christ appeared on earth.

This appearing of Christ as man is the next great mystery we must look at. In his letter to the Philippians, Paul attempted to grasp this mystery:

> Be imbued with the same state of mind which also filled Christ Jesus himself. For although he was of divine nature and form, he chose not to lay claim for himself to be equal to God. Rather, he emptied himself in offering and took on the form of a servant. In human form he took on body, and he showed himself in the form of a man throughout his whole life. Humbly and selflessly he submitted to the laws of earth-existence, even to the experience of death, the death on the cross. (Phil.2:5–8).

So this descent from the standing of a divinity to the human form of existence is a sacrifice of inconceivable magnitude. We can think of this descent as a series of steps or stages through the nine realms of the angel-beings: from the angels and archangels who are nearest to Man, right up to the Thrones, Cherubim and Seraphim to whom it is granted to live in immediate proximity to the Godhead and be able to endure this.*

Christ, as it were, descended through these nine angel stages; at each step he sacrificed something of his almighty cosmic power, finally to live within the narrow confines of a limited

---

* See H.-W. Schroeder, *Mensch und Engel*.

human entity, indeed to become capable of going through suffering and experiencing death, really to be a human being among other human beings; to feel with human beings, to learn about human existence and to enkindle it from within — not as a God standing outside, as it were, but with the love born of his unending sacrifice.

The path of Christ through the angel-spheres is an inner one, but these have their outer correspondences in the spheres of the fixed stars and the planets. Therefore one can just as well say: 'Christ has arrived at a particular angel-sphere' as, for example, 'he is active in the cosmos from the "sun"; for the duration of a world-hour he is a 'sun being'.'[3]

We have now summarized in outline the most important elements which belong to the 'pre-existence' of Christ, that is, his existence before becoming man: Divine origin and creation of the cosmos, suffering the decline of creation through the Fall of Man, and the descent through the cosmic spheres into earthly existence.

Christ's work on earth

We now turn to the work of Christ on earth; as he becomes man, his cosmic existence is changed into an earthly life. Here we will only indicate — later we will develop further — how his cosmic dimension also frequently shines through in his life on earth.

As examples of this, we call to mind four events from the gospels: the appearance of the star at the birth of the child (Matt.1), the 'heavens opening' at the baptism of Jesus of Nazareth in the Jordan (see the description of the baptism in all four gospels, for instance, Mark 1), the 'transfiguration of Christ' on the mountain, where his face 'shines like the sun' and his appearance radiates forth 'like light' (for instance Matt.17); and the earth and the cosmos react at the crucifixion of Christ: the earth quakes and the sun loses its light (Matt.27:52; Luke 23:44f).

Finally, we remember Christ's witnessing about himself, as recorded in John's Gospel: 'I am the light of the world.' (John 8:12) Here his cosmic dimension is stated unequivocally.

So, already by contemplating the Gospel we have ample reason not to forget the cosmic background of Christ, even in view of his earthly-human manifestation.

Christ became man in order to be able fully to feel from within, share from within, in all the suffering, the dangers and the death experiences of human beings on earth. He came to the earth not in order to eliminate earthly suffering and death, but to give human beings the strength to wrest from even the most severe earth-experiences something which can be wrested from them alone: the experience of a power which unites with Man and which is stronger than suffering and death, stronger than evil; and the knowledge that it is only through that experience that a human being truly finds the way to himself and to God.

The work of Christ after his earthly life

Ascension and Whitsun can be regarded as the last stages of Christ's work on earth; they are also the last concrete things which the gospels and the Acts of the Apostles report about Christ. On the other hand, we can reckon both these events as already belonging to the third area of Christology: with the 'Ascension' begins the return of Christ to his cosmic office; the 'descent of the Spirit' upon the disciples at Whitsun shows that human beings are not left behind, alone, but experience the succour of Christ in a new way.

The 'Ascension' is an authentic image for the cosmic ascent which corresponds to the descent of Christ from the cosmos: it shows his return to the cosmic spheres from which he had descended. In returning from the earth, from human beings, into the cosmos, he, as it were, makes ready the way for Man for the future, he prepares for the 'lifting' of the curse of the Fall, for the 'raising' of fallen mankind. Yet he remains united with the earth and mankind. The very utterance of Christ: '... I am with you all the days until the completion of earthly time' indicates that his ascent into the cosmos by no means signifies a turning away from mankind and earth.

In the old Creed, the Ascension is characterized with the words: '... ascended to heaven, sitting at the right hand of God the Father Almighty, from whence he will come ...' This makes it easy to suppose that we have to imagine Christ as a God in the beyond, infinitely far removed from mankind and earth. In reality, he is not infinitely remote but 'infinitely near.' In the

Creed of The Christian Community, the sentence referring to Whitsun goes: 'Since that time he is the Lord of the heavenly forces upon earth, and lives as the fulfiller of fatherly deeds of the Ground of the World.' These words contain both closeness to the earth and cosmic activity.

This is how we see Christ walking the path with mankind. The event of Whitsun, the sending and 'outpouring' of the 'Holy Spirit' is a proof of that. Christ sends 'his spirit,' that is to say, he becomes inwardly present for human beings; he does not overwhelm them with his outer presence, but he fills with spiritual presence the hearts and minds of those human beings who turn to him: giving strength, establishing peace, awakening courage, solace, patience and love.

The Acts of the Apostles, but also the Epistles of the New Testament as well as the Revelation (Apocalypse) of John, they all tell of this ever new inner nearness of the 'ascended' Lord.

And lastly, the entire history of mankind since the turning-point of time is permeated with the traces of him who walks with mankind — and this is by no means true only of the history of the Church, which all too often shows the signature of the adversary powers and yet carries within it the manifold blessing of Christ in its martyrs and saints, its spiritual leaders and in its countless unnamed followers and conquerors.

We see this power of inspiration and blessing — to cite just a few instances — during the first three centuries in the multitude of martyrs, later in the struggle of the knightly and monastic orders to prove themselves and achieve true inwardness; then in the feat of Luther to make a new step possible for Christianity through the Reformation, and at the same time in the inspiration of the modern era to set out for new shores and actually only then begin to discover the earth.

The ideals of the French Revolution, the spiritual achievements of German Idealism in Fichte, Schelling, Hegel, and also Schiller and Goethe and many others: where did they come from? It would be an appealing idea at some point to write the history of mankind of the past two millennia from the point of view of this nearness of Christ, indeed from the point of view of the Christ-inspiration working through this nearness. Admittedly, the working of the opposing powers would then also have to be revealed as, for example, the way in which they distorted the great ideals of the French Revolution into an inferno of hatred and bloodshed.

Looked at like that, history becomes a field of battle between those powers which have led Man away from God and want him to remain far from God, and those inspirations and forces which have rayed forth from Christ since Golgotha. The actual setting for this combat is the human soul itself; the adversary powers unleash their might in such a way that the human being feels as if compulsively attracted by it; he feels himself heightened in passion or experience of self. But Christ exerts no compulsion on the soul; he respects human freedom — that is what he wants to heighten; he needs human beings freely to turn to him in order that he can work within them.*

In our time the conflict between the opposing powers and the forward-leading impulses which proceed from Christ are reaching a climax. In this context, it is not only a matter of humanity itself but also of the earth. It is particularly because of the threat to nature and life on earth that more and more people are waking up to the close mutual relationship between the existence of the earth, mankind and the Godhead, and that this triad is permeated by the working of the cosmic Christ.[4]

If what we have said so far is true — that creation proceeded from the hand of the cosmic Christ; that he remains united with the life of the world and of the earth; that, invisible, he walks with mankind and imparts new impulses from within then the present situation of mankind is an enormously risky one for the divine world: to place the future of mankind and earth in the hands of human beings and not interfere through a divine word of command — what confidence in Man there is in that! Could it be that the divine world, Christ, has such confidence that the power of the Good will, in the end, prove more powerful than all else?

We can go a significant step further: within Christianity, the idea lived from the beginning that the Christ who vanished from mankind's consciousness at Ascension — although, as we have

---

* See H.-W. Schroeder, 'Das Menschheitsschicksal und das Böse,' in *Der Mensch und das Böse*.

seen, he remained present in a deeper sense — would 'come again.' The 'second coming' of Christ, however, is in the first instance the dawning of the omnipresence of Christ within the waking day-consciousness of human beings; it is to lead gradually to a new, concrete experience of his presence and to all the deep experiences of the soul which belong to that; to the encouragement and strengthening of Man and to new inspirations for life on the earth.

This Coming is a growing reality in our time — initially for a few, then increasingly for ever more people. In our age, the cosmic Christ 'takes a step' towards mankind and reveals himself anew; that is the real cause of the 'dawning of a new age,'[5] and all that lives in human souls in the way of presentiment, longing, striving for deeper things — all this is an expression of that fundamental happening.*

The 'Second Coming' of Christ is a first response to the threat to which mankind and earth are exposed in our time. But one could also put it the other way around: in revealing himself anew to mankind, the cosmic Christ calls up the opposing powers all the more: they can do no other than, desperately, try to cancel out and hinder the revelation of Christ.

At the conclusion of this overview, let us venture a glance at the future. By this, we do not mean the next two or three centuries, but the contemplation of how, altogether, the path of mankind and earth is to continue. Maybe further catastrophes are not to be avoided. Yet mankind has not been deserted by God. As long as there is genuine striving on earth for truth and common humanity, for justice and social peace and we can see many instances of sincere efforts in that direction — so long, that is to say, as the powers of the Good are at work in human beings, the spiritual world will also find ways to prevent the extinction of life on the earth.

However, with this prospect we approach the pronouncements and images of the last book of the Bible, namely the Revelation or Apocalypse of John. It describes destruction and catastrophes. Yet its real content is something different; it indicates the reunion of mankind with the cosmic Christ, the 'raising' of Man after the

---

* See H.-W. Schroeder, *Von der Wiederkunft Christi heute.*

'Fall,' and even a new creation of the fallen earth. Both these developments appear at the end of the Apocalypse as the 'new Jerusalem,' the city of peace in which the separation of mankind from the Godhead — from the cosmic Christ — is completely overcome.

This view of the future can only be remotely likely if we now once more recall and think back to the starting point of our considerations: to the condition before the Fall of Man and of the earth into a state of apparent distance from God and absence of God; when human beings, by virtue of being the image of God, were blessed by a special nearness to the reigning cosmic Christ and in which they had — as we said — the potential for universality, fullness and creativity.

If such a condition of mankind ever existed, then it has certainly been eclipsed, distorted and falsified by the consequences of the Fall. Man has become a shadow of himself; everywhere, the adversaries rejoice in major triumphs. And yet, the original status of Man has by no means vanished completely; not every sign of universality, fullness and creativity has departed from Man. Especially in the creations of great art and great spiritual achievements can something of this be seen, but also in unobtrusive deeds of love and common humanity, of forgiveness and understanding, most of which are never reported in public, but about which one may wonder if perhaps their sum within mankind does not exceed cruelty and hatred, or at least balance them.

'You are gods!' This statement of Christ, and Novalis' 'God desires gods,' can only refer to a deeper reality which, however, is still in the future, for: 'what we shall be in the future is not yet manifest.' (1John 3:2).

If that is so, then there still sleep quite other powers within Man than are visible at present; powers which will unfold in the future and which are to experience their initial awakening precisely in the new coming of Christ, in the first experience of the cosmic dimension of our humanity. With the help of the forces that proceed from the new revelation of the cosmic Christ, Man will be able to forge a creative path into the future.

Let it be said once more: it does not seem that this way into the future will be without enormous suffering, even catastrophes and destruction. We are already in the midst of the 'Apocalypse' whose precise images were seen in advance by John, two thousand years ago. But we believe such sufferings can become birth pangs when the deeper human forces arise and begin to live anew in the new presence of Christ; only then would they be apocalyptic sufferings as John saw them — and why should only that part of his prophecy come true which refers to destruction, and not also the portion which concerns the essential thing, the new beginnings of the future?

However, this all involves not only mankind but also the earth. It is even more difficult to grasp how that, too, is to be transformed and spiritualized. Yet if, as we have shown, Man has entangled the earth in his Fall, will he not also be allowed to help 'raise' it again in the course of his own future paths? As we proceed with our description we will return to this question.

And so the circle is complete: Man returns to community with the Godhead, and he brings with him a transformed earth. The images of the Bible speak a clear language about this: at the beginning of history stands the 'garden of Paradise' — an image for nature as created by God, in which Man lived. At the end stands the image of the 'golden city,' a symbol to convey that Man must forge his own future together with Christ who works in the cosmos; for, being a city, the new Jerusalem is the work of Man. So Man does not return to the Godhead empty-handed: as harvest he brings what has ripened in him in the struggle for his own future and that of the earth.

With that, we will conclude this preliminary overview. It has led us through the following stages:

— the very Beginning — the cosmic dimension of Christ — creation of Man and world;
— the 'Fall,' decline — cosmic catastrophe — descent of Christ to earth;
— Christ's work on earth;
— Christ's return to his cosmic office;
— Christ's path with mankind — his return;
— the cosmic future of Man and the earth.

2. Some fundamental concepts

Before we proceed, we need to look more carefully at some basic concepts and to clarify them. Certainly, we will have to limit ourselves within the framework of this book; we will be touching on questions which would demand extensive exploration if dealt with in detail.

Yet this clarifying of concepts seems to me necessary because in the literature surrounding the subject of the 'cosmic Christ,' severe confusion and misjudgments can arise from certain pronouncements by scientists and theologians; it is my intention to set the descriptions in this book against that.

What is meant by 'cosmic'?

This poses already the question: why are we using the expression 'cosmic Christ' with such emphasis? In a sense it would be sufficient if we were to refer to the comprehensive, divine nature of Christ and hold fast to his divinity over against his human appearance as he showed himself during his incarnation in the man Jesus of Nazareth: he is 'very God, and very Man' — as the conventional formulation, laid down by the early Church, puts it. This would, at one and the same time, express the importance and significance of Christ for the world and for the universe.[1] Without a doubt, such a view was held at the beginning of Christianity, for instance, in the Prologue to John's Gospel or by St Paul (Phil.2, quoted on p.16).

On the other hand, it would seem that quite early on this view of the 'cosmic' working of Christ began to be narrowed down. Augustine (354–430) placed the importance of the salvation through Jesus Christ for Man and his innermost soul completely in the foreground. His starting point was the experience of human guilt and divine forgiveness; this approach was to play an influential role for one and a half millennia of Christian theology and religious life.[2] Thereby the significance of Christ for the world and the universe faded into the background. This is also true of the theology of the Reformation. In the eighteenth century, the 'Age of Reason' and Pietism brought a further constriction of the Christian world-view.

Ultimately, this development culminated in the notion of the 'simple man of Nazareth,' 'the carpenter's son,' which has become the widely accepted view since the end of the last century, and which continues to work on in diverse variations, including the explicit rejection of any 'pre-existence' or original divinity of Christ. Not even the new upsurge of interest in the cosmic dimension of the being of Christ can disguise the fact that, fundamentally, the overall view is still dominated today by the effects of centuries of reducing the conception of Christ to the man Jesus.

Nor has the significant work of the Jesuit Teilhard de Chardin, who achieved a view of the cosmic Christ through a path of inner experience, actually changed anything; indeed, he was forbidden by his order to publish his works because of his view of the cosmic Christ and its theological and scientific implications. For this reason his writings only became known in the 1960s when, however, they met with a strong response, and they have probably played a decisive role in stimulating and giving direction to the current discussion about the cosmic working of Christ.

With the commencement of his public work at the beginning of our century, Rudolf Steiner gave a comprehensive description of the nature of Christ, including his cosmic working; this was at a time when the thesis of the 'simple man of Nazareth' dominated the field. It is thanks to this that we have a basis for a view of earth and universe which enables us to understand Christ as a crucial power in world events.[3]

For those who dared to make the step to a fundamental renewal of the religious life with the founding of The Christian Community in 1922, it was a matter of course from the start to include the proclamation about the cosmic Christ as a central declaration.[4] For example, in 1926 two articles by Friedrich Rittelmeyer appeared, entitled 'The cosmic Christ,'* where, in contrast

---

* 'Der kosmische Christus,' in *Die Christengemeinschaft* journal, 1926, p.364.

to the theology of the time, he presented the universal significance of Christ.[5] Later on, we shall be looking further at how
centrally the idea of the cosmic Christ appears in the sacramental
work of The Christian Community.

We see, then, that the formulation 'cosmic Christ' initially
points up the contrast to those theological conceptions which
have limited the idea of Christ to the purely human aspect. But
more than that: it brings to expression something of the fact that
the work of Christ is not only for mankind, that is, for the
salvation of human souls, but also of comprehensive importance
for the earth, indeed for the entire cosmos.

It is precisely at this point that questions arise which we must
put to several theologians who have published on this subject.
For, although these often refer to the 'cosmic' significance of
Christ, yet one looks in vain for a really concrete statement about
it; quite unclear and vague remains the question of what possible
significance the Christ could have for the cosmos, that is to say
the universe, for the fixed stars etc., or indeed whether Christ's
deed of redemption shows any signs of having a cosmic dimension. Certainly we find the idea raised that the kingdoms of
nature on earth are also permeated by Christ and are to partake
of salvation in the future — not least in view of Man's exploita-
tion of nature. But this thought is not given further concrete
development. Less clear still are the statements about Christ's
work in the cosmos: none of the authors is able to convey
anything of substance. Even Teilhard de Chardin falls short of the
claim that is implied in the expression 'cosmic Christ.' Here it
would be more appropriate to speak of an 'earth-embracing,' a
'telluric' working of Christ.[6]

In our presentation we shall attempt to do justice to the
meaning of the word 'cosmic,' and this both in connection
with the creation of the world and with the goal of world
evolution.

For this purpose, however, a different view of the universe is
needed than the one offered by present-day astronomy. It is at
this point that we come up against the already mentioned
problem of method, namely that we cannot, within the framework
of this book, enter into a discussion of the scientific questions
which are bound to arise at once when we begin to speak about

the universe, the sun, the planets and the fixed stars in a different sense to that employed by present-day natural-scientific astronomy. In fact, we are only able to do this here because, in anthroposophy, Rudolf Steiner has developed fully a new insight and new perceptions of the cosmos and its origin, evolution and objective — and, indeed, in such a way that they are not simply to be believed, but can be permeated with one's understanding.[7] In this connection it becomes apparent how much modern research, for all its magnificent discoveries and significant insights, yet clings to the external side of the phenomena, and is not at present able to build a bridge to that which permeates the universe spiritually. For this spiritual entity, what is perceptible to the eye and to instruments is the outer 'garment,' the 'body,' in the same way as our physical body is the 'garment,' the 'body' for our soul and our spirit.

In the descriptions we are presenting here, we therefore intend to follow these insights and perceptions, founded as they are in the anthroposophical theory of knowledge. They, for their part, are in accord with ancient insights into the nature of the universe, as, for example, they have found expression in the Bible. We shall be speaking in more detail about this. And so we may hope also to win through to a genuinely cosmic view of the working of Christ.

In this context, let us recall a detail already touched upon in our earlier summary. We spoke of the 'descent' of Christ out of the cosmos through the nine angel-realms and on to the earth; we also mentioned that, outwardly, these angel-spheres are connected with the 'spheres of the planets,' admittedly including the sun- and the moon-spheres.[8]

About this, too, anthroposophy makes quite concrete, highly differentiated and far-reaching statements which go far beyond what has come down to us by way of descriptions from ancient world views, some of which seem naive to us. In the anthroposophical statements, the relationship becomes clear between spiritual beings and the planets and the domain of the fixed stars, in particular the so-called 'Zodiac.' The 'infinity' of the universe then appears as a sign of the exalted power of the highest spiritual beings who are closest to the 'infinite' Godhead, the 'Cherubim' and 'Seraphim,'[9] and as an image of the infinite greatness of the Godhead itself. Here it is possible to find the beginnings of a view of the world which goes beyond the more usual notions.

Different characteristics and multiplicity of Beings

The vague and unclear use of the concept 'cosmic' which we find in the cited literature extends further into another realm: vague and undifferentiated, too, seems the description of the relationship of Christ to the various beings. Is it sufficient simply to state that all beings and things ultimately have their origin, their fundamental being and their continued existence in God? — a view which, in essence, we share and have established at the outset.

Even though the life of the cosmic Christ permeates the entire world, it does not mean that we can now simply identify all beings in the world with him. Such statements as: 'Jesus Christ as the crucified and resurrected Mother Earth,' or 'we all are the cosmic Christ' (Matthew Fox, 1988); or again, '... now it is rather the globally more appropriate hypothesis that suggests itself: the cosmos as a wonderful organism, or, in our language: the cosmic Christ,' (Günther Schiwy, 1990, p.12) and so on, are misleading in that they equate quite different entities with one another; they obscure important differences.

If we were to pursue narrowly the line indicated by these quotations, we would ultimately have to claim for the adversaries, too, 'that they are the cosmic Christ'! For their existence and being ultimately comes from the divine, which, after all, includes everything — except that they have strayed so far from their origin that now they can be the independently active opposition to the divine.* But it would be blasphemous simply to equate them with Christ.

In a certain respect this is also the case as regards nature, earth and mankind! The earth, mankind, the cosmos are filled with independent beings, each with its own development and history, with its own meaning and right to existence and each with its particular aim and purpose. For that reason they must, in the first

---

* See H.-W. Schroeder, *Der Mensch und das Böse,* the chapter 'Versuch über den Ursprung des Bösen.'

instance, be regarded as something else, something to be distinguished from the being of Christ. It was precisely for this purpose that they were called into being; in order that — originating from the being of God — they should unfold their own existence, so that, in the time to come, they might be able to add their developed fullness to the fullness of the Godhead. The all-embracing power of Christ must, in the first instance, be kept distinct from this independence of beings.

A comparison with something familiar to us in our own human experience suggests itself: initially, a child lives entirely out of the life and substance of the parents; but if the parents understand their task rightly, they will do all that they can to see that their children on growing up will be mature and independent enough to travel their own paths, to develop their own forces and possibilities, which go beyond what was evolved through the parents. Certainly one may say: the child has its origin and its life from father and mother; but it would be completely wrong to say that the child is father, mother — even though the forces of the parents continue to work in the child.

The crucial point is precisely that the Godhead makes it possible for the various beings of the world to have their own existence, whilst at the same time it continues to keep and sustain them. We have seen that in this 'gesture' towards the independence of beings there is even contained the possibility of evil, of the Fall. The earth, mankind, the cosmos are not simply the cosmic Christ; nor are they — as is also claimed — 'the body of the cosmic Christ' as such, for they are all, being 'fallen' creation, also permeated by the adversaries who wage bitter warfare for their possession against the claim of the divine world. Anyone who does not see this, or who plays it down, is too quick to disregard the dramas and tragedies in the world, ending up with illusions which can only lead to confusion.

To mention one more example: it is striking how this forming of illusory concepts also occurs when love and sexuality are being discussed and it is said that '... too many Christians have been led to believe that Christ is not present in physical love. This is nonsense. On the contrary, the cosmic Christ is quite definitely present in sexuality, in all its forms and possibilities. The cosmic Christ rejoices in the great variety within the sphere of sexuality ...' (Fox, 1988). Although the author distances himself in the same context from misuse of sexuality, from pornography, rape etc., the formulation of the concepts is naive and dubious. It has nothing to do with the enmity against all things bodily which dominated Christianity for a long time if one hangs a large question-mark over the sentences just quoted. It is precisely in the sphere of sexuality and love that the highest and the lowest are closely bound together, as every human being knows; a narrowly negative attitude towards the body ought not to be replaced by another biased view which straightaway rates what appertains to the body most highly, albeit within certain limits. Here, too, a dubious way of forming concepts fails to do justice to the dramas which exist particularly in this sphere and which often enough culminate in tragic conflicts.

It is precisely because exalted qualities are given with the bodily nature of Man that it becomes the point of attack for those powers who want to deprive Man of these exalted gifts, and who do not want to allow him to become able to unite with them lastingly. So this very subject — love and sexuality — can serve as a classic example of how one-sided and vague ideas lead to the opposite of clear guidance for our human existence. I have no wish here to score cheap points; what mattered to me was to show even more clearly by this example how necessary it is, also for our subject, to 'distinguish between spirits.' (St Paul, 1Cor.12:10).[10]

The meaning of evil

The great enigma of evil is this: how was it possible for a radical opposition to the Godhead to arise at all? It must, above all, have to do with human freedom, with the possibility for Man to feel himself to be free before the Godhead, in order to 'take hold' of himself in this freedom; in fact, only then to create himself out of himself, as it were. It has already become clear how much this fact shows the magnanimity of the Godhead and its trust in this independent path of Man. However, in the first instance the adversaries have been completely successful in distancing Man from his origin, in alienating him from the divine so that it is possible for him to deny God in thought and deed, and even to bring creation down with him in his alienation.

However true it remains, on the one hand, that ultimately nothing exists outside the divine, it is nevertheless also right to speak of the radical alienation from God and the God-forsakenness of earthly existence as facts of human experience: the divine cannot be experienced as existentially present wherever pleasure is being taken in sadism and torture, in sheer egotism and self-satisfaction — unless it be present in obscurity, and, in obscurity, is supporting and sharing in the suffering. And in the threat to the earth, too, by pollution and poison, in the destructive power of an atomic explosion, the creeping menace of atomic waste — in all this, other than divine powers are at work.

We have already spoken of the important objective behind the creation of Man. Great powers and possibilities have been 'invested' in human beings, which, however, so far have only shown themselves to a very small extent. The threats that emanate from the adversaries now are, at the same time, a challenge permitted by God; it 'calls upon' the deepest forces of Man, it is a 'pro-vocation.' It is only when we 'discover' and confirm the deeper forces which lie hidden within ourselves that Man will be able to create a future.*

We have already mooted the fact that humanity is not left to its own devices with this task. Christ, 'returning,' comes to our aid in our striving, indeed comes to meet us. It is important to see the way in which the adversaries have to play the decisive role of 'provokers,' and how they set about fulfilling it with radical earnestness. Yet ultimately they are to serve the founding of the greatest Good.[11] Whether evil will finally fulfil this purpose, that will, above all, depend on us human beings ourselves.

---

* See H.-W. Schroeder, *Der Mensch und das Böse,* the chapter 'Das Menschheitsschicksal und das Böse.'

The cosmic Christ and matter

Not only Man, but also creation itself became enmeshed in the Fall. This is evident alone through the fact that there is such a thing as 'matter,' that is, material-earthly existence, at all. There are realms of being which seem to exist out of themselves and in which only causal and mechanistic laws appear to hold sway. In this world of atoms and physical structures, the remoteness from God reaches its nadir: a world which is supposed to have evolved 'by itself' from the 'Big Bang' through the simplest forms of life to the highest and most complicated living beings, has no need of any divine power, no need of a cosmic Christ. Such a world could be fully explained by the 'dance of the atoms.'

Nevertheless, there is nowadays a considerable body of scientists who are convinced of the need to 'change the paradigm' of the natural-scientific world-view: natural science ought to move from the Newtonian world-model to a 'holistic,' that is, integrated, experience of the world, which would be able to integrate basic human and even mystical experiences into the scientific world-picture. In fact, the striving of Teilhard de Chardin to fathom the cosmic Christ as the Alpha and the Omega, as creator, mover and aim of the evolution of the world was triggered by a fundamental, mystical experience which deepened by degrees.[12]

Fritjof Capra, who also reaches a wide public through his books and lectures, has similarly arrived at the 'Tao of Physics' via a deeper experience of 'being.'[13] One must agree with Günther Schiwy when he writes:

> In the 1980's, more and more scientists are coming
> forward who increasingly regard evolution as an
> astonishing phenomenon, a kind of revelation: partly on
> the grounds of specialist knowledge, as, for example, Ilya
> Prigogine and the formation of structures in physical and
> chemical systems, partly, as in the case of Klaus Michael
> Meyer-Abich, through reflecting on the need for a change
> of paradigm in science, from physical reductionism, say,
> to biological holism; or, in the case of Rupert Sheldrake
> and others, as a result of individual intuitions.[14]

The disquiet felt about the prevalent scientific world view is caused not least by the ecological catastrophe towards which we are heading and which is evidently a consequence of our one-sided, limited view of nature — a view which is bound to arise from a purely causal-mechanistic approach. In contrast to this, Capra goes so far as to call the 'new' scientific thinking 'ecological holism.'[15]

This interest in the fact that single elements in the world join together to develop from lower to ever higher and more complex 'wholenesses' leads to a search for the underlying forces; in the 'dance of the atoms,' what causes the structures to develop, whence come the connecting 'patterns,'* what makes all life into an evolving unity? But here, too — so it seems to us — the answer is too pat and simplistic: for Capra, 'the principle of self-organization' of all living things, indeed of all being, is enlarged into the experience of 'our being at one with the entire cosmos. This union with the cosmos is, as already mentioned, a spiritual experience.' Capra finds the clue to this experience in oriental mysticism; it is quite consistent with this view that he gives one of his books the title *The Tao of Physics*.[16] Doubtless, ample mystical experience of the spirituality working in the world is contained in the old wisdom — and not only in oriental wisdom; but it is surely a justifiable question when Capra often is asked nowadays whether the leap from scientific analysis to what he calls 'spiritual experience' is as easy to make as that.[17]

The same direction of thought which leads Capra to 'the Tao of physics,' would in a Christian context draw the inner eye to the 'cosmic Christ.' We would certainly fully agree that in him is to be found the unifying thread, the purpose-filled unity of creation, the guiding power of its evolution; but here, too, questions arise if it is made to seem as if this could be immediately deduced from the already mentioned 'change of paradigm.'[18] We should be especially careful in view of our awareness of the tragic breach which runs through creation because of the Fall, which leads to remoteness from God to the extent of death, devastation and ruin. The very fact that, despite the greatness, beauty and astonishing detail of creation, it is based on laws which work in a causal-mechanistic way, devoid of soul and spirit, and that the whole disintegrates into atomistic structures

---

* Gregory Bateson, *Mind and Nature*.

— this betrays a different signature than that of a creative, actively present spirit.

And so it seems to us particularly problematic when the being of Christ is brought into immediate relationship with the atom.[19] The concepts which currently underlie atomic physics must surely lead into quite other realms than those in which the power of the cosmic Christ can reveal itself existentially; rather — here, too — he is concealed: suffering, enduring; once more, we become aware of the need for precise formation of concepts and for more exact distinctions, above all also to include the Fall.

In this context, another thing must be mentioned: when the unity, the 'pattern' upon which everything is based, is under discussion, one ultimately comes close to a 'pantheistic' world-view, that is, a completely undifferentiated concept of the 'universal' divine which is 'somehow' present in all things.[20] However fundamentally true this belief may be, it is surely inadequate in view of the infinite, differentiated wealth of physical beings: a quartz crystal or a ruby, a lily or an orchid, a chameleon or a scorpion, Beethoven or Rembrandt are concrete, distinctive phenomena in the world, each of which must be seen in its own particular and unique relationship to the world. Therefore, if we want to advance to a concrete grasp of the world, not one which gets lost in generalities, we must learn to recognize the various beings in their earthly manifestation as concrete spiritual entities: a rose, for instance, becomes, already in its external appearance, the expression of a formative force which is characteristically different from a lily.

The anthroposophical science of nature has come a long way, following in Goethe's footsteps, in the direction we have indicated here. It is able to move in comprehensible stages from the outer manifestation to the perception of spiritual entities. In this way, it forms the basis for the perception and understanding of the world and the universe developed by Rudolf Steiner, to which we have already referred. By this means, the spirituality which permeates the world can be grasped quite concretely in its very varied forms of expression, not merely in general terms, that is, pantheistically.

Levels of earthly and spiritual reality

One last fundamental question remains to be addressed. Frequently, the too general, undifferentiated, pantheistic world-view is accompanied by a lack of ability to distinguish between different levels of reality. The 'presence' of the divine can be of very different degrees of reality, of intensity. As we have already seen, this presence and 'effectiveness' can be completely obscured — as, say, in certain areas of material, atomic existence. It can even permit the presence of the opposite of itself, as we discovered, in certain human conduct, in sadism, pleasure in destruction, etc. On the other hand, there are things in earth-existence which can lead us directly to an experience of higher things in the world: a mountain landscape, a sunset, the experience of great art, a sincere and genuine meeting with a fellow human being, religious worship, true prayer and meditation ...

However, such experiences cannot be held fast; if in one moment we can raise ourselves to them, the next we find ourselves once more on a lower level of our human nature; and how low a human being can sink can barely be imagined in advance. We see, then, that within ourselves we also have the experience of different levels at which we move and at which we can be our true selves to a greater or lesser degree — or even become completely alienated from ourselves.

Such stages are to be found at all levels of being, for example also in the realm of the angelic beings; its nine stages have already been mentioned: they do not only indicate differences between these beings, but also higher or lower degrees of spiritual 'might.' The highest angelic beings, the Seraphim who are nearest the Godhead, tower above Man in this spiritual might; they are also high above the angels, for instance, who are nearest Man and who have the task of guarding and providing new impulses for his destiny.

In this context, we remind the reader of our description of the 'descent' of Christ through the nine angel spheres, which at the same time meant his leaving divine power and authority behind him by degrees; each stage brought him closer to the human dimension, at every stage he offered up something of his divine nature. As Man he was God, but 'in secret' — and only at the

35

'ascension' did he gradually gather together his divine powers again. On the other hand, from this point of view we can grasp the nature of Christ's 'return' even more clearly: it means that his already actual presence is increased, attains a higher spiritual might within the earthly sphere.

For our existence on the earth, it is of vital and fundamental significance that there are these levels of spiritual reality: on earth we live far from God; nothing compels us to be aware of God, let alone to accept his existence. Even if we take no notice of anything to do with God, we will not be struck by a divine thunderbolt. That precisely is the basis for human freedom.

But another, higher freedom has also been made possible: as human beings we can freely call the divine into the God-forsaken world again, and this, too, with the most varied degrees of reality; something of an experience of the divine can work into our thoughts (for example in a meditation and in the feelings that accompany it), in experiences of nature and art, in deeds of love — to a lesser or greater degree. And is not the whole point of all true divine worship to make 'the presence of God' possible, and, what is more, in a community of human beings, not only in the individual?

Here again there will be various levels of experience, of spiritual activity; even a festive shared meal can have something of the character of a Service; in fact, in earlier times, a meal — especially in the presence of a guest — was always felt to be something special. But the deepest reality of 'the meal' is only attained when the 'transubstantiation' takes place within the Christian Service, when the substances of bread and wine are 'transformed' into the 'body' and 'blood' of Christ. What is meant by this? In the context we have outlined here we can now express the secret that is hinted at with the word transubstantiation in this way: in the God-forsaken world of earth, the full presence of Christ can reveal itself not only in the soul and spirit, not only in the feelings and thoughts of the human beings who are taking part, but right into physical substance. Creation, which has fallen into the state of being plain matter, is raised one initial but decisive stage higher in the sacrament at the altar; it is brought close to its own origin, and thereby to the future of the earth.[21] And that means a different, deeper presence of the cosmic

Christ than in even the most intense experience in the feelings or thoughts. It is necessary to look at such degrees of spiritual reality with an eye for distinctions; otherwise one can get no further than diffuse experiences of spiritual beings and their working.

So far we have opened up five aspects which can serve as a basis as we now again take up the thread of our main subject. The next step will be to turn to the statements of the Bible about the cosmic Christ.

3. The cosmic Christ in the
New Testament

The cosmic dimension of Christ shines throughout the New Testament — in the Gospels, the Epistles and the Revelation to John. In this chapter we shall pay special attention to significant passages which illustrate this. (So as not to overload with quotations, I have relegated supplementary references to the notes.)

Apart from significant passages in the Gospels, it is especially in the letters of St Paul that we find much which throws light on the cosmic background of the Christ-event; evidently, this background was more apparent to Paul than to others, thanks to his 'initiation.'[1] Even so, something of it is revealed in the other Epistles, too.

In order to be able to keep an overview, we shall arrange the relevant passages by theme. Out of this arrangement, an overall picture will emerge — similar to what we presented in our first chapter.

The very Beginning

'I am the Alpha and the Omega, the very Beginning of the world and its ultimate purpose' — thus Christ expresses his own being in the Revelation to John (1:8, 21:6, and 22:13 with the addition of 'the first and the last'). Teilhard de Chardin takes this up when he speaks of the beginning of all evolution as 'the Alpha point' and of its aim as 'the Omega point' and thereby makes the whole of evolution spring from Christ and culminate in him. And it is a fact: contemplating the nature of Christ, we are led back to the 'ground' of all being, before all creation, before any kind of existence. In him we behold the very Beginning of all being, creation 'arises' with him and through him. He is the 'Alpha' — and that must mean the beginning of something which is to have a continuation. Or, conversely: nature, earth, Man and cosmos would have no existence but for the Christ. Nor would I — I have to tell myself — have any being, any existence, but for him. This is also contained in the words with which the Gospel of John begins so impressively:

> In the very Beginning was the Word
> and the Word was with God
> and the Word was a God;
> All things came into being through it,
> and nothing of what has come into being
> was made without it.
> (From the translation by Rudolf Steiner.)

Here, too, we are led back to the 'very Beginning.' Then, the 'Word' (the 'Logos,' that is, the cosmic Christ) was 'with God'; he was himself a divine being. Here we are afforded a glimpse of the original relationship between the divine 'persons,' as they have been called in Christianity: between the Father God and the Son God as it was in the Beginning; for, in verse 14 of the Prologue, this God of the Beginning is specifically called 'Father.' The 'Word' — says the text — is the 'only Son of the Father'; and at the end of the Prologue, even more clearly: 'the only Son who was in the bosom of the Father ...' (verse 18).

We find, then, two expressions in the Prologue for this original relationship between the Father God and the cosmic Christ: in one place, Christ is described as 'the Word,' in the other as 'the Son.' Both terms are derived from human circumstances, and are therefore also inadequate for characterizing the relationships between divine beings, that is to say: they are appropriate as comparisons. That is why the Creed of The Christian Community says of Christ that he is to the divine being of the Father 'as the Son, born in eternity.'

Nevertheless, both these characterizations can give us an inkling of the relationship of being between Christ and the Father God, the 'Ground of all being,'* if we keep in mind that they are a simile (the question of the 'third person' of the Godhead, the 'Holy Spirit,' we shall have to leave out of account for the present†).

---

* Phrase from the Christmas Service of The Christian Community.

† See H.-W. Schroeder, *Dreieinigkeit und Dreifaltigkeit*.

But now let us add two more descriptions of the Son God to the ones from the Prologue; first, from the letter of Paul to the Colossians:

'He is the visible image of the invisible God, the first-born of (before) all created beings' (Col.1:15).

And from the letter to the Hebrews:

'... because he is the visible reflection of his (that is, the Father's) glory and the image of his being ...' (Heb.1:3).

We see here that, as well as the expression 'Son of God' for the cosmic Christ, frequently used in the Epistles (Letters), others appear also: 'image' and 'reflection' of the Father God, and the 'first-born' of creation.

So, from the New Testament we gain a spectrum of terms for the origin of the cosmic Christ in the being of the Godhead, namely:

— the Word of God[2]
— the Son of God*
— the image of the invisible God
— the first-born of (before) all creation
— the reflection of the glory of God
— the Alpha (and the Omega)
— the very Beginning (and the aim)
— the first (and the last)

Let us look at these expressions in detail.

The Word is an extraordinarily eloquent term for the 'Son of God'; for what otherwise would be hidden in the depths of the Godhead, 'speaks' through Christ; it 'comes to ex-pression,' that is, the inner being of God opens outwards in the 'Word,' becomes a 'communication' of God.

At the same time, the term 'Word of God' also indicates this: a word is not meant to sound into a void, it is intended to be heard, it is directed towards other beings who can receive it; through the 'ex-pression' of the being of God in Christ, the Godhead becomes 'social,' as it were, does not remain in isolation, becomes 'communicative.' And still more: a word seeks a response, a 're-action' — from other beings. A 'conversation'

---

* This term can be found everywhere in the New Testament, for instance Matt. 16:16, John 6:69, Rev.2:18 and so on.

between beings and worlds is initiated through Christ's proceeding from the innermost heart of the Godhead.

A new element appears when we add the characterization of Christ as the Son of God, as the first-born of all creation. Although the 'Son' proceeds from the working of the Father, yet he is independent over against him; for the Father, he is the first 'antithesis.' And he represents progress, the 'younger generation,' the future. We should allow both aspects of this view of the cosmic Christ-being to live in us: that the Godhead desires through him to bring about an independent 'antithesis' of other beings also, and that a rejuvenating power, striving towards cosmic 'progress,' becomes active in Christ.

Yet another motif emerges when the cosmic Christ is called the 'image of the invisible God.' The invisible, that is, also unimaginable, not sense-perceptible being of God which, as it were, reposes in darkness, comes forth out of his dark seclusion and becomes visible and perceptible — in the same way as the 'Word of God' 'proceeds' out of the silence of God and therefore can become 'manifest.' The Greek word which Paul uses for image in the Letter to the Colossians is *eikon* — it is the same derivation as 'icon'; and according to the ideas of the ancient icon-painters, an icon is more than a mere copy: it is a 'likeness' which has about it the 'radiance' of the archetypal image.[3]

Therefore, in John's Gospel, Christ is able to say, 'Whoever sees me, sees the Father,' (John 14:9) for 'I and the Father are one.' (14:10 and 10:30) Christ is, so to speak, the true 'icon' of God. In the same way as reverential contemplation of an icon can kindle an intimation of the archetypal image, a reverent turning to Christ in inner contemplation can inspire in Man the intimation that 'there is more': an inconceivable depth, width, greatness and fullness, which nevertheless desires gradually to make itself known to mankind in Christ. Paul speaks of the 'world of light of divine revelation which streams towards us from the countenance of Christ.' (2Cor.4:6) And because the invisible Godhead appears in the image of Christ, Paul has 'painted' this image 'before the eyes' of the Galatians (Gal.3:1).

Yet another nuance of the 'image' comes to the fore in the Greek text of the Letter to the Hebrews; for there the image is not called *eikon,* but *charakter* — which actually means 'imprint,' as in the case of a coin which has an image stamped or imprinted on it. In this word, the will-aspect comes into the foreground: through Christ, it becomes possible to experience the world-moulding will of the otherwise invisible God.

Finally, in the Letter to the Hebrews we also have the phrase: Christ is the reflection of the glory of God; the Greek word *aplaugasma* which the writer uses here, would probably be better translated as 'radiation' or 'outflow,' as in the way in which light and warmth radiate and flow out from the body of the sun. In truth, we come here to an inner perception of the sun and its radiation of light, in which the being of the cosmic Christ is revealed. We shall return later to the last three characterizations 'Alpha,' 'very Beginning' and 'the first.'

When we look at the original relationship of the Father God to the cosmic Christ, we have a wonderful 'spectrum' before us, a multiplicity of inner perceptions which complement and intensify each other mutually, and which open out in three directions:
— towards experiences which are to be gained through light and image (reflection, image, imprint);
— towards experiences which can be made through hearing and speaking (word);
— and finally: towards everything that can be experienced when a new being appears (birth).

In the very beginning, Christ is:
— the image *(eikon)*
— the imprint *(charakter)*
— the shining forth of the otherwise invisible, hidden divine.
— the Word of God, the Alpha and the Omega which 'expresses' the hidden inner being of God.
— the Son of God, the first-born of (before) all creation, the Very Beginning itself.

We notice that these characterizations make it possible to formulate God's manifestation in Christ in complementary ways. It is precisely through forming an overall picture of the multiple differences that the images and comparisons complement one another — they would otherwise remain one-sided. The being and the substance of the Father God do not linger in age-long darkness, in profound silence, in divine isolation; they move on to becoming — overflowing, as it were, from the fullness of being. In Christ they appear as image and shining light out of the darkness of God, as Word out of the silence of God, as Son out of the innermost being of God.

All three characterizations have in common that they indicate that which strives towards revelation, becoming and creation. In the very Beginning, the creation of the world proceeds out of the Father God through Christ. The Father lets the Son 'be born' out of himself, and gives him the task, so to speak, of creating the world. In Christ, this creation already begins. He himself is its very beginning and the driving force of its evolution. This leads us to the subject matter of the next section.

Creation of the world and of Man

From the previous descriptions it has already become clear that we actually have to regard the cosmic Christ, the Son, as the creator of the world. On the one hand, this is a contradiction of the words of the old Christian Creed of which the very first article of faith states: 'I believe in God the Father Almighty, Creator of heaven and earth'; on the other hand it is in accord with the statements of John's Gospel and St Paul. We have already quoted the relevant words from the Prologue to John's Gospel: 'In the very Beginning was the Word ... all things came into being through him, and without him was not anything made that was made.'

When we look for the corresponding statement in Paul, we again come across the place in the Letter to the Colossians which we also have already cited:

He is the visible image of the invisible God, the first-born before all creation. Through him everything was created that is in heaven and on earth, the visible and the invisible, be they Thrones or World Guides, World Powers or Revealers.[4] Everything was created through him and for him. He was there before all else, and everything coheres in him. (Col.1:15–17).

And it is stated even more concisely in Paul's First Letter to the Corinthians: 'We have only one God, the Father, from whom all things are, and one Lord Jesus Christ through whom all things are, and we through him.' (8:6).

These last two quotations from the letters of Paul are significant: like the author of John's Gospel, Paul also regards Christ as the creator of the world. In the last quotation from the first Letter to the Corinthians, there is a concise differentiation between the creation which is from the Father (God, from whom all things are) and the creation which has come about through Christ (Jesus Christ, through whom all things are, and we through him).

So the creation of the world and of Man are accorded to the Son, the cosmic Christ, through whose working all things have been 'called' to life (through the 'word' which 'called' them). But the origin, the substance, the being exists from the Father, the Son 'takes hold' of the substance and being of the Father and forms it creatively, shapes it, leads it over from the sphere of tranquillity of the Ground of the world into a creative becoming.

The Letter to the Hebrews also refers to the Son 'through whom he [the Father God] made the world' (Heb.1:2).

We can therefore be certain that we are on absolutely safe New Testament ground when we regard the Son, the cosmic Christ, as the creator of the world. And, what is more, this world-creating does not only refer to the earthly and cosmic environment of Man, outer nature and the outer cosmos, but also to the invisible worlds which are concealed from us for the time being, the realms of hierarchical beings, some of whom are expressly named in the Letter to the Colossians; and indeed to everything which is called the beings of the spiritual world. In Colossians, Paul says expressly that 'the visible and the invisible' has been created through Christ.

So, when we consider any realm of the world, any being of the visible or invisible world, we can say: everything owes its continued existence to the working of Christ, nothing would have any existence without him. And we must also include ourselves and our own existence in this fact. This becomes clear in passages where the creation of Man is emphasized within a general description of creation, for instance already in 1Cor.8:6: '... through whom all things are, and we through him.'

At the beginning of the letter to the Ephesians, Paul again turns to this fact:

In him (Christ) He chose us all even before the world
was created, so that we can stand, hallowed and without

blemish before His countenance, in the stream of His
love. He formed us inwardly so that we can, according to
His will and pleasure, be of His sonship in (the power of)
Jesus Christ. (Eph.1:4f).

It is the case, therefore, that every human being bears a
'predestination' within himself: through his organization and
constitution he has the ability, in principle, to turn to the spiritual
world.[5] From the very Beginning, this has been what is distinctive about Man's being. This potential has been innate in every
human being since creation — through Christ. This means: a
profound relationship to Christ has been 'built into' Man's nature
from the beginning, from his creation.

And even more: the quotation from Ephesians says expressly
that since the Godhead has a Son and ensures the continuation of
the world through him, the Son has become a 'model,' as it were,
for Man, who also is to mature towards becoming a 'son' of
God. Here we are afforded a glimpse of the depths of the being
of Man; Paul says expressly: 'God has so formed us inwardly
that we can be of His sonship through the power of Christ.'
(Eph.1:5)*

Therefore, when Paul says in the Letter to the Colossians, as
we have quoted, 'Everything was created through him and for
him ...', then this 'for him' applies in a very particular sense to
Man himself. This is also in accord with a deeper understanding
of the Creation Story of the Old Testament, in which, at the
creation of Man, there is specific mention of Man being 'the
image of God.' When there is heard the call: 'Let us make
human beings, an image like unto ourselves' (at the end of
Genesis, Chapter 1), then, once again, behind these words stands
the cosmic Christ, in the sense of everything that we have just
described.[6] We can speak of Man being the image of God, not
merely in a general sense; now we can say more precisely: the
being of Man has been created through Christ and towards him.

The last book of the Bible says the same thing, where, in the
first chapter of the Revelation to John, Christ appears in the
image of Man. At the beginning of the Bible, in Genesis, Man is
created to become the image of Christ, the 'image of God' — at

---

* Paul also speaks of Man becoming a 'son' in Rom.8:15,23, Rom.9:4, Gal.4:5.

the end of the Bible, in the Revelation to John, God appears in the image of Man; Christ reveals himself as 'the Son of Man.' As regards the creation of Man and the original relationship of Man to the being of the cosmic Christ, an unbroken 'golden thread' runs through the Old and the New Testaments.

Life and light

Let us return once more to the words of the Prologue and continue the quotation a little further:

In the very Beginning was the Word ...
all things came into being through it,
and nothing of all that has come into being was made
except through it (or: him).
In him was life;
and the life was the light of human beings;
and the light shines in the darkness;
and the darkness has not comprehended it
(or: grasped, accepted it).

Here the concept and understanding of the creation of the world is expanded and made concrete in two directions: the creation through the cosmic Christ does not merely set the becoming of the world in motion in a general sense; rather, from his being, life and light shine out upon the beings and forms of the world. The life which works through the world comes from his life. Interesting is the fact that it is in Athens, where Paul encounters a particularly developed, philosophical awareness among the people, that he emphasizes this aspect of Christ's working. In the address on the Areopagus in Athens he says:

The divine Being who created the Cosmos and all beings who are within it, the Lord of heaven and earth, does not live in temples built with hands ...

He gives life and breath and all existence to all men ... He is not far from each one of us, for in Him we live and weave and have our being. That has also been expressed by some of your poets: 'We are his offspring.' (Acts 17:24–28).

Let us review the overall picture once more: it is not only the existence of all beings that has to do with the creating deeds of the cosmic Christ, but so, too, does the continued life which permeates all beings. At this point we can mention that in the wording of the renewed rituals of The Christian Community, a corresponding viewpoint is expressed; in the opening prayers of the Act of Consecration of Man it is said that our life is the creating of Christ himself. This conforms with Paul's words in Athens. It means: it is not that this life was just called into being some time, long ages ago, and now runs on, automatically, as it were; rather, his creating is also united with our life and existence now; he is also present and active in our life now — indeed, this life actually streams forth from his continued creating. The quotation continues: 'The life was the light of human beings.' The life of Christ also contains the 'light' for the creatures which emerge through this working. This 'light' is not an outer light-manifestation which fills an external space; what is meant is that the world is spiritually 'enlightened,' that it is an inner continuum filled with clarity and light — above all, that it has meaning.

The Greek word *logos* which is used in the Prologue, and which we translate as 'word,' also contains the component 'meaning': for *logos* does not only mean 'word' in the sense of 'wording,' it also means 'reason,' 'sense.'[7] The character of words is that they are endowed with a light-filled thought-content which speaks to the 'light' of our insight. When the Prologue speaks of the world-creating *logos* as the light-giver, then we are made aware that the world not only has existence, being and life, but is also based on a light-filled, meaningful thought, that is, an aim, a purpose.[8] We also find this in the formula which we meet in the Revelation to John: 'I am the Alpha and the Omega, the very Beginning and the aim.' (Rev.21:6).

In speaking in this way about the creation of the world and of Man, we come into conflict with current conceptions of the origins of the universe and Man. As far as is possible within the framework of this book, we shall be dealing with this question later.

The Fall and the descent of Christ to earth

In our first chapter we indicated the basic questions concerning the Fall. Here we are mostly concerned with that aspect of the Fall which relates to the being and working of the cosmic Christ, and not so much with what the Fall and its effects mean for mankind and the earth.

Again, the cosmic aspect of the Fall comes most clearly to expression in the Prologue to John's Gospel; and from a particular angle it becomes clear how the working of Christ is influenced by this fact and subsequently becomes involved in its further effects. First, let us quote the relevant wording from the Prologue of John's Gospel:

> And the light shines in the darkness;
> and the darkness has not grasped it (or: accepted it).
> There came a man,
> sent from God,
> his name was John.
> He came to bear witness,
> to witness to the light
> and so to awaken faith in all hearts.
> He himself was not the light,
> he was to be a witness to the light.
> The true light that enlightens all human beings
> was to come into the world.
> It was in the world,
> for the world came into being through it,
> yet the world did not recognize it.
> It came to men of individual spirit,
> but those very individuals did not accept it.
> (John 1:5–11).

Two things are shown here: we see how the divine light shines into the darkness, but also that the darkness, the world of earth and Man, cannot or will not accept this light. The Prologue does not say what must have taken place at some time in the evolution of the world; clearly, a rift of some kind has occurred; the working of the darkness is now a part of the whole, a tragedy in world evolution which we recognize from the Old Testament as the Fall.

The Prologue now goes on to describe the 'deeds and sufferings'* of the divine light. John the Baptist appears as the messenger and witness of the light in a world permeated with darkness. Verses 9 and 10 show clearly the tragic nature of the working of light versus dark in the history of mankind: 'The true light which enlightens all human beings was to come into the world. It was in the world, for the world was made through it, but the world did not recognize it.'

At first glance, there appears to be a contradiction within the words; for in verse 10 it says: 'The light was in the world,' although immediately before that we read: 'It was [still] to come into the world.' We have here one of the typical Johannine 'contradictions,' where an 'either/or' cannot do justice to the truth. With a 'both/and' we hit the mark: The working of the cosmic Christ created the world and gave it meaning and purpose, but human consciousness, human knowledge does not see this, and the human way of living life goes on as if this were not a reality. In this sense, the light has still to come into the world, that is, it must light up and be taken up in human consciousness and gradually permeate the lives of human beings.

That this meets the meaning of the words can be seen in the second part of verse 10 and in verse 11: 'It came to the individual human egos, but these egos did not accept it.'[9]

But then something can be added in the 12th verse of the Prologue; a view to the future opens up:

To all, however, who did accept it,
it gave the free power to become children of God.
They are the ones who trustingly
take its power into themselves.
They receive their life, not out of blood,
nor out of the will of the flesh,
and not out of human willing;
for they are born of God (John 1:12).

The Prologue, then, begins by speaking without reservation about the tragedy which lies behind the working of the *logos* as a result of the Fall: the light was in the world, indeed the world came into being through it, but the world did not recognize it!

---

* Goethe, *Theory of Colour.*

Here we see confirmed by the New Testament what we have described elsewhere: that the divine creates and sustains the world,
yet in certain areas gives space to other beings, indeed even
permits evil and makes it possible for it to be active — and itself
initially remains hidden, suffering, enduring, sustaining. The
entire Gospel of John is, then, a witness to the struggle between
the light and the darkness for the light nevertheless to be received
by human beings and bring about a new birth in them — to enable them to become children of God. This striving can be sensed
again and again in the many words about 'light' which are to be
found in this Gospel; they all attain their special significance
from the light-darkness words of the Prologue. Always, something of the cosmic background shines through. These words
reach a culmination when Christ says of himself: 'I am the light
of the world.'

The Fall of mankind into earthly-material circumstances makes
Christ's descent from cosmic heights into the world of earth and
Man necessary. We have already quoted the famous passage from
Paul's Letter to the Philippians which concerns the descent of
Christ from the heights of divine being, and the sacrifice of his
cosmic might:

> Be imbued with the same state of mind which also filled
> Christ Jesus himself. For although he was of divine
> nature and form, he chose not to lay claim for himself to
> be equal to God. Rather, he emptied himself in offering
> and took on the form of a servant. In human form he
> took on body, and he showed himself in the form of a
> man throughout his whole life. Humbly and selflessly he
> submitted to the laws of earth-existence, even to the
> experience of death, the death on the cross. (Phil.2:5–8).

With a few impressive words Paul here indicates that this
descent to earth by Christ into the realm of mankind meant a
profound sacrifice, a renunciation of the divine fullness of his
being.*

The reality that the Son incarnates in an earthly body which is
subject to sin represents an immeasurable sacrifice. The cosmic
Christ offers himself into the realm in which there are at work

---

*   Further hints can be found in Rom.8:3,32, Gal.4:4.

the powers of the adversaries, of aberrations and denials of the divine. It is not really possible for us to grasp what it meant for Christ not only to appear in the human world but also to allow its darkest aspects to come near him, indeed to take them upon himself and unite with them to the extent of going through bodily pain and the experience of death.

In the Letter to the Hebrews, too, an intimation of this can be found. Here a word from the Psalms is taken up and applied to the 'degradation' of the cosmic Christ: 'For a little while you have given him a lower rank than the angels' (Heb.2:7).

And in John's Gospel we find: 'The Father God showed His love for the world through this, that He offered up His only Son.' (John 3:16)*

It is not immediately possible to gain further insights from the New Testament into the way of Christ in his descent from cosmic heights to the earth. What we said about this in the first chapter — especially about his progression through the nine spheres of the angels — will only arise from a different context which we will present later.

Star and Sun: the cosmic background to the Christ

The four gospels describe for us the earthly work of Christ. In the main, they concentrate on the three years during which the Christ walked on earth. The interesting question now arises whether anything shines through in the gospel accounts themselves of the cosmic element which, if our considerations are correct, there must be about this man who wanders through the Holy Land. Does the cosmic dimension disappear completely on the earthly paths of Christ, or are there moments in the gospels when something of it comes to the fore?

Already in the childhood stories passed down to us by Matthew and Luke we find some indications. In both accounts, cosmic elements shine out. In Matthew it is the star which appears over the child and leads the kings of the East on their journey to worship the child. This star shows in a picture that with the birth of the Jesus-child on earth a worldwide being has

---

*   See also 1John 4:9f.

appeared, that a cosmic dimension lights up over the earthly being of the little child.

And another special motif is contained in this account by Matthew: the kings come from the Orient and worship the child, so that the significance of Jesus for mankind is emphasized from the moment of his birth. The one who is being born there is of importance not only for the Jews but also for the foreign, non-Jewish peoples. The most high-ranking representatives of mankind show this through their adoration of him. In this child lives something comprehensive and all-embracing.

In the Gospel of Luke it is the hosts of angels who tell the shepherds in the fields of a heavenly element which is to bring peace to the earth:

Revelation of God in the heights,
peace on earth to human beings
who are of good will (Luke 2:14).[10]

Here again we are shown the cosmic background to the appearance of Jesus on earth. And here, too, the angel proclaims expressly that the joy of this event is to become the portion of all peoples on earth: 'See, I proclaim to you a great joy which is to be for all peoples!' — again, an all-embracing element for all mankind.

A further event which brings to the fore the cosmic background of the appearance on earth of the Christ-Jesus is the Baptism of Jesus (Matt.3, Mark 1, Luke 3). The heavens open, the Spirit descends upon Jesus as he steps out of the river Jordan, and a voice is heard from the higher world:

You are my beloved Son.
In you I have revealed myself.

We see that the Gospel itself shows the cosmic background quite plainly. The same happens a little later at the Transfiguration on the mountain (Matt.17, Mark 9, Luke 9). Jesus leads his three most intimate disciples, Peter, John and James, up the mountain, and they experience how his appearance changes: 'His face and his garment became shining white, as if radiating lightning.' In Matthew it even says: 'His face shone like the sun.' And, as at the Baptism, a voice sounds from the spiritual world: 'This is my chosen Son, hear his word!' (Luke 9:35).

Star and sun are two different images for the cosmic Christ.

The star in Matthew's account of the birth expresses the relationship to the universe which extends past the planets to the widths
of the realm of the fixed stars. Yet at the same time, in the star
approaching the earth we also have the reality before us that the
cosmic being of Christ becomes knowable for human beings,
that, in approaching Man, it does not overwhelm him, as the sun
would do with its overpowering strength.

In contrast to this, the image of the sun radiating from the
countenance of Christ shows how the almighty cosmic power
which is present in him, controlled, contracted and concealed, can
nevertheless burst through his human appearance for a few
moments — although it then overwhelms those human beings
who are present: Peter and the two others fall to the ground,
unconscious.

There are, then, three moments in the gospel accounts which
confirm the cosmic dimension of the event:

Birth: The cosmic element lights up over the child as a star
and as the angelic host.

Baptism: The cosmic spheres (the Heavens) open, and the
world-Spirit descends into the thirty-year old Jesus.[11]

Transfiguration: The cosmic powers of light and sun ray forth
from the form of the Christ-Jesus.

Here we can see quite clearly the three stages of the increasingly profound union of the cosmic element with the human,
earthly appearance. Until the thirtieth year, the divine forces of
the Christ weave around the growing boy. With the Baptism,
Christ enters into Jesus of Nazareth. At the Transfiguration, the
human being is permeated to the degree that something of the
cosmic power of Christ can radiate out from the human form.*

And finally, at Christ's death images of the cosmic background
also arise; this time not in the human appearance but in sun and
earth:

And the earth shook, and the rocks were torn apart, and
the graves opened. (Matt.27:52).

And after the sixth hour [noon] there was darkness
over the whole earth until the ninth hour. (Mark 15:33).

---

* The stages of incarnation of Christ into Jesus are described by Emil Bock, *The
Three Years.*

> And it was about the sixth hour, and there was
> darkness over the whole earth until about the ninth hour,
> and the sun lost its light. (Luke 23:44f).

The sun and the earth react to the Jesus' death on the cross; this illustrates that the significance of the events of this death reaches beyond the human level. Similarly for the Resurrection: 'There was a great earthquake.' (Matt.28:2).

The stone which closed the burial chamber in the rock was rolled aside by this earthquake; because of that, the grave is open, as all four gospels report. In addition, Mark notes that the sun is rising just as the women arrive at the grave on Easter morning and find the stone rolled away: once again we have the sun motif — this time not in a human being but in the cosmos. This is hardly likely to be a mere external 'stage direction' in the Gospel of Mark, in view of the special relationship that this gospel has with the cosmic background.

Lastly, with our subject in mind, let us look at the endings of the three gospels, which point to a transition to a new level of the working of Christ, the re-establishment of his cosmic power; they do this in quite different ways:

> To me has been given all power in heaven and on
> earth ... See, I am with you all the days until the end of
> earthly time. (Matt.28:18).

> Go out into all the world and proclaim the Gospel to
> all created beings [or: all creation]. (Mark 16:15).

A particular cosmic feature stands out, again with Mark: the emphasis is on the significance of Christ for all creation, whereas Matthew speaks in more general terms of the power in heaven and on earth which has been given to Christ.

In Luke it is again different:

> He led them out towards Bethany [on the Mount of
> Olives] and raised his hands in blessing over them. And
> as he blessed them he vanished [for their awareness] and
> ascended into the heavenly spheres (Luke 24:50f).

At this point, then, there is already reference to the Ascension. Remarkably, it takes place precisely in immediate association with the blessing which Christ bestows on mankind and the earth. This is surely no coincidence, either.[12]

The cosmic background of the working of Christ can be

characterized, as we said earlier, through the images of star and sun: Christ is the spiritual sun of the cosmos, or, as John records, 'the light of the world'; but this sun has a relationship to the forces of the starry universe from whence it actually originates.

The cosmic significance of the earthly life of Christ is shown from yet another side, in the Letters of the New Testament. We shall restrict ourselves to just a few indications, not least because we shall return repeatedly to this significance of Christ's earthly life in the next parts of the book.

In the Letter to the Romans, Paul says that the appearing of the Son of the Father God 'halted the might of sin in earthly existence.' (Rom.8:3).

With this word of Paul we suddenly look into a deeper, cosmic dimension within earthly existence; for the Fall has permeated all spheres of earthly and human existence. If the appearing of the Christ on earth halts the effect of sin, then this shows the far-reaching significance of the Christ-event.

We find something similar in the Letter to the Colossians:

You, too, were once alienated and hostile ... but now he [Christ] has permeated you with the power of trans-formation, as members of his body: through the death which he suffered in his earthly body. (Col.1:21f).

A power of transformation rays out to all human beings from the Christ-death. In the same letter, this theme is developed further: ·

With him you have also been laid in the grave: through baptism. But with him you have also risen again ... He has extinguished and suspended the commandments and the violations which are written into the book of the world ... he has nailed them to the cross ... (Col.2:12–14).

In the gospels, the cosmic dimension of the working of Christ on earth is shown mostly in images; Paul grasps the deeper significance of this dimension for mankind and the earth, and translates it into knowledge and insight.

The Ascension of Christ

Instead of using the expression 'the Ascension of Christ,' we shall here speak of him being 'exalted.' We take the expression from the second chapter of the Letter to the Philippians, in which it says: 'Therefore the Father God has exalted him to the highest heights.' In the Gospel we only find a definite description of the Ascension in Luke, in the place which we have already quoted (p.54). In Matthew there is instead a reference to the 'authority' of Christ, which now extends to all realms of the cosmos: 'To me has been given all power, in heaven and on earth.' (Matt.28:18).

In Luke's 'Acts of the Apostles,' the cloud appears as an image for that which mediates between earth and cosmos, for the passing of Christ into the cosmos.* The text has been rendered in English as follows:

> And as he said this he was lifted up before their eyes, a cloud received him and they saw him no longer. And while they still directed their gaze upwards after him into heaven, see, suddenly two men in white garments stood by them and said, 'You men from Galilee, why do you stand there looking up to heaven? This Jesus, who has been taken up before you into heaven, will come again, revealed in the same kind of way as you have now seen him pass into the heavenly sphere.' (Acts 1:9–11).†

If we now again look to the Letters of Paul, we see once more that that which the Gospels mostly describe in images can be grasped in its full meaning by Paul, and can be passed on by him in concepts. Let us again take up the famous passage in the Letter to the Philippians (see p.50). Having referred to the cosmic sacrifice of Christ and how he 'emptied' himself, the Letter concludes: 'Humbly and selflessly he submitted to the laws of earth-existence, even to the experience of death, the death on the cross.'

But now Paul develops the description further:

> Therefore God has also exalted him to the highest heights and given him he name which is above every other name.

---

* See H.-W. Schroeder, *Von der Wiederkunft Christi heute.*

† The New Testament (A rendering by Jon Madsen), Floris Books, 1994.

> In the name of Jesus the knees of all beings should bow,
> in the heavens, on the earth and in the depths of
> existence. And so that the Father, the Ground of all
> existence shall be revealed, every tongue should declare
> the confession: JESUS CHRIST, THE LORD! (Phil.2:8–11).

Here we see something which at first we could only assume in regard to the descent of Christ to earth, namely that the ascent through the different spheres of the hierarchies also has an effect on the relevant hierarchical beings. This becomes even more clear in another passage, in Paul's Letter to the Ephesians:

> Through our faith we gain access to the mighty working
> of the power of His sunlike strength which He made
> active in Christ when He raised him from the dead and
> gave him the place on His right in the highest heavenly
> spheres; above all Spirits of Might and all Creating
> Spirits, above all World-Powers, even the World Guides,
> above every name that can be named, not only in the
> present age, but also in the aeon to come. He has placed
> everything under his feet and has made him the head of
> all things in the great community which is his body, the
> divine fullness of him who fulfils all in all. (Eph.1:19-23;
> rendering by Jon Madsen).

What Paul describes, then, is how the fact of Christ's descent to earth and his union with the human world now creates a particular effect in the spiritual world through his ascent.

We can make this clear to ourselves in the following way: For the forces of the Godhead, the creation and evolution of the world also means that they are 'unfolded' into a multiplicity; it is because of this that the wealth and diversity of beings can appear. Through this, there is a tendency throughout the entire cosmos for these powers to strain asunder. In becoming Man, Christ imparts to the cosmos the power which can gather it together again in a higher sense. Paul says this in the Letter to the Ephesians (1:10), namely a few verses from our previous quotation: 'All that is in the heavens and on the earth shall be renewed and united into one being in Christ.'

Man has within him the potential to be a microcosm over against the macrocosm, that is to say, a combination of beings and worlds. In a mysterious way, this combining, this centring of the universe into an inner unity, is a capacity present as potential within Man's existence, as we have already indicated (p.14) and will develop further at a later stage. Christ in his work on earth begins to free human beings from the powers of darkness — and thereby the hope dawns for the cosmos that the cosmic forces need not only not fall asunder but can be woven together in a higher unity; through that work, Christ carries this hope for the future back into the spiritual world.

Something of this becomes apparent in Paul's words to the Ephesians, for clearly it is not only a question of the powers of the spiritual world becoming subject to Christ again, but that he now becomes their 'head' in a way which evidently is different to what was possible previously; that he becomes the head in a great community which is his 'body,' that the fullness of being of the divine becomes woven together into an inner unity which 'fulfils all in all.'[13]

There is still one more place in the New Testament which describes the event of Christ's Ascension, his 'being exalted,' not simply as happening in one sudden moment, but as a gradual process:

> Since, then, we have a great High Priest who has passed
> through all the heavens, sphere by sphere, Jesus, the Son
> of God, let us hold to our confession with all our strength
> (Heb.4:14).

In the description of Christ's descent to earth we look in vain for some kind of indication of his descent by stages through the realms of the Spheres and Hierarchies; in the Letter to the Hebrews, however, this is expressed in connection with the ascension of Christ. The outcome of this ascent is described by the Letter to the Hebrews as follows:

> For Christ did not enter into a sanctuary built by human
> hands ... rather, he entered into heaven itself, there to
> appear for our salvation before the countenance of God.
> (Heb.9:24)*

---

* See also Heb.1:1–14; 1Pet.3:29.

The cosmic Christ's continued working with mankind

How does the working of Christ for mankind continue? When we recall the words from Matthew: 'See, I am in your midst all the days until the completion of earthly time,' (Matt.28:20) then we must also look in the New Testament for traces of this continuing working of Christ. A starting point for this can again be found in the Acts of the Apostles, for example in the Whitsun events:

> Then suddenly a sound came from the spiritual heights
> like the rushing of a mighty wind, and it filled the whole
> house in which they were gathered. And to their seeing
> there appeared tongues of fire, like flames which came to
> rest on each one of them. And they were all filled by the
> Holy Spirit. (Acts 2:2–4).

The 'rushing wind from heaven,' the 'tongues of fire,' 'being filled with the Holy Spirit' — all these are images and signs to show that the permeation of mankind by the cosmic Christ has begun. The purpose towards which this beginning strives is spelt out in the address given by Peter a little later in Acts, on the occasion of the healing of the paralysed man: '... when all existence is led back to its origins.' (Acts 3:21).

More of this further working becomes visible in the story of Paul's life. We have already indicated that it was granted Paul to attain a special insight into the significance of the Christ-event. In his letters he leaves no doubt that he experienced the presence of Christ in many ways, that every day he lived in this presence and could reap living insight from it. The starting point for this special closeness of Christ in Paul's life is his Damascus-experience. He is on the way to Damascus to persecute the Christians there. Then, so runs the account:

> suddenly a light from heaven shone around him. He fell
> to the ground and heard a voice saying to him, 'Saul,
> Saul, why do you persecute me?' He said, 'Who are you,
> Lord?' And he received the answer, 'I am Jesus, whom
> you are persecuting.' (Acts 9:3–5).

This event bears clear witness to the supersensible presence of him who 'is sheltered in the sphere of the heavens' (3:21) and to his further sharing in the fate of mankind. This participation makes itself known in concrete inspirations and measures, in this instance in the selection of the raging persecutor of the Christians to become the 'Apostle to the other nations.' Paul is to be the one who will carry the Gospel beyond the boundaries of Judaism to the other peoples. When the Christians living in Damascus, not surprisingly, are reluctant to accept Paul, it says specifically: 'He is my chosen instrument. He is to carry my name before the peoples ...' (Acts 9:15).

The 'cosmopolitan' character, embracing all mankind, of the mission which proceeds from Christ is stated anew. We will content ourselves with these few quotations from the Acts of the Apostles; others could be found, for example in Paul's speeches.[14]

We will turn directly to Paul's statements in his letters. Here, however, we come up against a difficulty if we want to single out individual quotations for our subject from the letters; for it is, after all, the purpose of the Epistles as a whole, not just the Letters of Paul, to show listeners and readers the continued working of Christ in their lives, in their faith, love and hope, in their knowing and their doing, in their suffering, striving and overcoming — and to give them new courage to take hold of the Christ-power: 'Let the intense strength of his might flow through those who want to serve the Lord.' (Eph.6:10).

The continued working of Christ in mankind, which is so impressive in Paul's own destiny, is tirelessly brought to expression by him and the other authors of the Epistles: 'Through the Law my higher self died to the Law, in order to live for the realm of God. I am crucified with Christ. So it is not I who live, but Christ lives in me.' (Gal.2:19f).

Again, a profound dimension of the Christ-mankind relationship is stated in the Letter to the Colossians:

If, then, you have risen with Christ, direct your striving
and your longing upwards to where Christ wields at the
right hand of God. Let the higher being fill your
thoughts, not the earthly. For you have died, and your
true life and being is united with Christ and hidden in the
spiritual world. But when Christ becomes apparent, who
bears our true being, then also your true being shall be
revealed with him in the light of the Spirit.' (Col.3:1–4).[15]

Here, there is reference without disguise to a deep relationship of human beings to Christ, including their earthly destiny. So we must ask further: what consequences should be drawn from the continued presence of Christ:

— for the moral and ethical demeanour of human beings
— for social ordering
— for bearing one's destiny
— for worship and prayer
— for the hope for the 'second coming' of Christ
— for the renewal of the whole human being: the new creation?

From the wealth of possible quotations I shall only select a few which deal with the last two themes.

The return of Christ

In the early stages of Christianity, there was a lively expectation that Christ would 'come again,' that is to say that he would not only be invisibly and supersensibly united with mankind, but that his supersensible presence would be revealed anew to mankind in the future. Not only certain individuals would experience this presence, as had often been the case in the Christian past; rather, this experience would in future become available to everyone. In the first chapter of this book I pointed out that we in the present time are standing at the beginning of these events of the return of Christ. I have developed this subject more thoroughly in a book about the 'Second Coming.'

In the descriptions which the gospels give of the events of the return of Christ, the cosmic background to these events is clearly perceptible. For that reason we will turn once more to the Gospel. The relevant passage in Luke can also represent Matthew and Mark who say something similar:

And signs will appear in sun, moon and stars ... the
forces of the heavens will be shaken. Then the Son of
Man will appear to seeing souls in the clouds ... with
(cosmic) world power, and radiant with the glory of
revelation ... the heavens and the earth will pass away,
but my words will not pass away. (Luke 21:25–27,33).

It would hardly be possible to express more clearly than with these words and images the cosmic claim that is here made for the working of Christ. The image of the 'cloud' alone, in which the returning Christ becomes visible, speaks a language which is 'cosmic' in character (see p.56). But the other motifs, too, are of this nature: the 'signs' appearing in the stars, the movement of the forces of the heavens, the heralding of the passing away of heaven(!) and earth and the creative future of Christ's word — this last theme already points to the Prologue of John's Gospel, and in a certain sense to the Apocalypse with the description of the creative 'Word' or *Logos*.

In the Letters there are also many places which relate to the renewed presence of Christ. Above all, here it becomes clear how the hope for the return of Christ can already now work into the earthly existence of human beings as a power and an attitude of mind.

> For: 'Only a little, quite short while, and he will come who is to come; and he will not tarry. Whoever would do justice to me must learn to live out of trust and faith. But my power of soul cannot be revealed in anyone who, cowardly, shrinks back.' Let us not be among those who draw back and fall victim to the decline. We stride forward on the path of faith, so that we can make that soul-power completely our own. (Heb.10:37–39).

These words express the expectation — as do also other texts in the New Testament and of early Christianity — that the return of Christ would take place soon. We must bear in mind that in the early days of Christianity, as an after-effect of the Christ-event on earth, the supersensible presence of Christ was still felt very powerfully, as if at any time he could move from being invisible to becoming visible in his full form.

At that time it had not yet entered people's consciousness that mankind still has great distances to travel, seeking, finding and becoming mature, in order to be equal to this future event of the return of Christ, that is to say: the full presence of the divine on the earth. Only now, in our time, do we find the beginnings of this happening. On the other hand, it is all the more clear from the evidence of early Christianity — nourished as it was by this 'early expectation' — that the presence of Christ will also be an event which will transform the whole existence of Man. I remind the reader of the classic passage from Paul's Letter to the Philippians:

Rejoice in the Lord at all times! And I say it again:
rejoice! Let your kindliness of soul be evident to all
human beings. The Lord is near! Let no anxiety take root
in your hearts, but let your concerns in all things be
known to God by sending your thankful thoughts
upwards in supplication and prayer. And the peace of
God which transcends anything that the intellect can
grasp will keep safe your hearts and thoughts in the
Being of Christ. (Phil.4:4–7).

The sense of the nearness of Christ and his transforming power
leads to a renewal of the whole human being. Paul speaks of this
with great insistence: through Christ, Man is placed into a new
creation.

Future — the new creation

The 'new creation' begins with the resurrection of Jesus Christ,
in which death and sin have already been overcome. In the Risen
One the new life is present in the universe and the earth, but it
has still to overflow into mankind. The next step through which
the new creation unfolds is that the Christ-life is passed on to
human beings. Paul's letters refer to this in many ways.* Here I
shall only quote two short extracts:

We are laid in the grave, since our baptism connected us
with his death. The meaning of this is that as Christ was
awakened from death by the light-glory of the Father, so
we, too, walk on our further ways with renewed powers
of life. As we have been united so closely with him that
we bear an image of his death in us, so we also grow
towards an image of his resurrection ... whoever has died
to its might, for him the way to the true being has been
cleared. If we have died with Christ, then our faith lets us
share in his life.' (Rom.6:4–8).

And Paul writes even more clearly to the Corinthians: 'Whoever
is in Christ, in him begins the new creation.' (2Cor.5:17).

But it is not sufficient that the transforming and enlivening
power of the Christ takes hold of human beings and mankind.

* See, for instance, Rom.5:16–22, 6:23.

Paul was aware that this transforming-power must also engage with the earthly kingdoms of nature. With clear and vivid words he speaks of this in the Letter to the Romans, and because of the importance of this passage we quote it in full:

> I consider that all difficulties and sufferings of the
> present age are trivial compared with the light-power
> of the world of spirit which will reveal itself. All
> around us creation waits with great longing that the
> sons of God shall begin to shine forth in mankind.
> Creation has become transitory, not through its own
> doing, but because of him who, becoming transitory
> himself, dragged it down with him, and therefore every-
> thing in it is full of longing for the future. For the
> breath of freedom will also waft through the kingdoms
> of creation; the tyranny of transitory existence will
> cease. When the sphere of the Spirit grows bright,
> unfreedom will be replaced by the freedom which is
> intended for all God's offspring. We know that the whole
> of creation suffers and sighs in the pangs of a new birth
> until the present day. And not creation alone; although we
> have received the first fruits of the new Spirit, we, too,
> are painfully waiting for the secret of sonship which is to
> bring redemption right into our bodily nature. The
> salvation which is given us works in us as a germ for
> the future and counts on our hope remaining alive.
> (Rom.8:18–24).

Not only Man, not only the kingdoms of nature — the entire cosmos is to be led through a transformation. We have already come across this theme in a saying of Christ: 'Heaven and earth will pass away, but my words will not pass away,' (Luke 21:33) and from there we can look towards the creation of a new earth and a new heaven, as it is described at the end of the Revelation to John. But in fact this motif can already be found in the Second Letter of Peter. The description in this letter is far more pictorial than what we are accustomed to from Paul's writings. It contains descriptions in mighty cosmic imaginations:

> With an enormous uproar the spheres of the heavens will
> enter into a new form of existence. The realm of the
> elements will be dissolved in fire. Then the face of the

earth is fully revealed, and all deeds that have been done on earth are written upon its face.

Since the dissolution of all being takes place in this way, how powerful must be your striving to prepare a place for what is holy by the whole of your lives and all your devotion! You must wait for the dawning of the Day of God with never-resting longing, when the spheres of the heavens will dissolve in fire and the realm of the elements will melt in it. Within us we bear the expectation of new heavens and a new earth, according to the divine promise in which righteousness dwells. (2Pet.3:10–13).[16]

The vision of a future new heaven and new earth now leads us to the last book of the New Testament: from its first verse to the last, the Revelation to John interprets the working of Christ in a cosmic sense.

The Revelation to John (the Apocalypse)

In the very first chapter of the Revelation to John, Christ appears with the attributes of cosmic power: in his right hand the seven stars, his countenance shining like the sun; his feet, reaching down into the mineral-forces of earth, appear to the seer as if dipped in glowing bronze. From this figure issue the words: 'I was dead, and see, I am alive through cycles of time, and I have the keys to death and the realm of death.'

All further descriptions in the Revelation arise out of this vision. They all bear the signature of the cosmic Christ and therefore the signature of the overcoming of death and the sphere of death. Here, we shall only single out a few particularly clear motifs.

After the tremendous 'throne-vision' in the fourth chapter, which shows the Father God in his almighty cosmic power, the fifth chapter depicts the 'Lamb' in the midst of the Godhead on the throne; this image definitely indicates the cosmic Christ:

And I saw: in the midst of the throne and the four living Beings and in the midst of the elders stood a Lamb as though it had already been slain. It had seven horns and seven eyes. They are the seven divine creator-spirits who

65

have been given the whole earthly realm as their place of working. The Lamb came and took the book from the right hand of Him who was seated on the throne ... and I heard all created Beings in heaven and on the earth and under the earth and on the sea, and all Beings who work in them. They said:

'To Him who sits upon the throne and to the Lamb belong all strength of blessing, dignity of soul, light of the spirit and creating power in all cycles of time to come.'

And the four living Beings said: 'Amen!' And the elders fell down and worshipped. (Rev.5:6ff).

Difficult as these images seem at first,[17] they nevertheless clearly speak the cosmic language: before the throne appear the 'seven creating spirits' who rule over the earth; there, too, are heard 'all beings in the heavens, on the earth and the sea and under the earth,' and so on.*

The renewal of the life of the universe proceeds from the centre-point of the events, from Christ. Towards the end of the Apocalypse, the destruction which comes over the earthly world reaches a climax, but it also becomes clear that this destruction does not lead merely into an abyss; rather, a new creation arises out of it: the new heaven and the new earth, the New Jerusalem appear.

And I saw a new heaven and a new earth. The former heaven and the former earth had passed away, and the sea was no more. And I also saw the holy city, the New Jerusalem ... And he who sat upon the throne said, 'See, I make all things new!' And he said, 'Write this! These are words of faith and knowledge.' And he said to me, 'It is done. I am the Alpha and the Omega, both the very beginning and the ultimate purpose of the world.' (Rev.21:1-6).

The creative might of the *Logos,* of the cosmic Christ, now appears with the power to bring into being a new, spiritualized cosmos.[18]

---

* This book has been opened to modern consciousness by Emil Bock, *The Apocalypse of St John.*

At this point we end our passage through the New Testament, having looked for various signs of the cosmic activity of Christ. It will have become apparent that there is a wealth of such signs. Despite this abundance, depth and significance for the cosmic aspect of Christ in the New Testament, this aspect has been lost to theological understanding for more than 1500 years.

Brief glance at the Old Testament

It would now be very appealing to look just as thoroughly at the Old Testament as we did at the New. However, we will only indicate three motifs here.

At the beginning of the Old Testament, in Genesis, the creation of the world and Man is described. Creation, it becomes apparent, proceeds from the speaking of God: 'And God said ...' We see that this agrees with the Prologue of John's Gospel: it is the *Logos,* the creative word of God, which creates the world. We shall not go astray if we surmise that the working of the cosmic Christ is also behind the images of the Creation Story in the Old Testament. The last thing to come about as a result of this creating activity of the cosmic Christ is the creation of Man: 'Let us make Man.' We have already mentioned that the profound nearness of Man to Christ is founded in the creation of Man (see Note 3.8).

The creator remains united with his creation. The Psalms describe this in a beautiful way, perhaps particularly so in Psalm 104 (1–5):

Bless the Lord, O my soul.
O Lord my God, thou art very great!
thou art clothed with honour and majesty,
Who coverest thyself with light as with a garment,
who hast stretched out the heavens like a tent,
who hast laid the beams of thy chambers on the waters,
who makest the clouds thy chariot,
who ridest on the wings of the wind,
who makest the winds thy messengers,
fire and flame thy ministers.
Thou didst set the earth on its foundations,
so that it should never be shaken.

Here the cosmic Christ is not confused in a one-sided way with the creation, as present-day theological works suggest; the light is not Christ; quite specifically, light is referred to as his 'garment.'[19] Later, in the same Psalm:

> These all look to thee, to give them their food in due
>   season.
> When thou givest to them, they gather it up;
> when thou openest thy hand,
> they are filled with good things.
> When thou hidest thy face, they are dismayed;
> when thou takest away their breath,
> they die and return to their dust.
> When thou sendest forth thy spirit (or: breath),
> they are created;
> and thou renewest the face of the ground. (27–30).

From these Psalm texts, something becomes clear which we have already deduced from Paul's words, namely that the working of Christ did not only play a role when the world was created. He is also present to this day in that creation with his own life.

This presence of Christ within creation is now formulated even more concretely, for instance in Exodus, where it is described how Moses receives his call 'from the burning bush.' The being of the Godhead reveals itself to him in the element of fire, and the Godhead even 'expresses' itself by its own name: 'I am the I-Am.' (Exod.3:14).

But this is the name which Christ claims for himself in the New Testament: in the seven 'I Am' sayings in John's Gospel. In the Old Testament the divine voice is heard in fire, an element of nature; in the New Testament, it is heard from an earthly human being. From this detail, too, we can see how the Old and the New Testament are related — and that behind the Elohim-Yahweh revelation of the Old Testament the being of the cosmic Christ is actually to be found, as we have already shown (see Note 3.6).

A further instance of this elemental working of the Godhead occurs later, when Moses climbs Mount Sinai to receive the Ten Commandments. The Godhead hovers over this mountain as fire and thunder — here, too, the earthly elemental processes are allied to the appearing of the divine. For Elijah, several centuries after Moses, the voice of the divine is no longer to be found in storm or thunder, but as a 'still, small voice,' that is, rather more as an inner experience (1Kings 19:12).*

The cosmic experience of the divine, which originally was reflected in phenomena of nature, contracts, as it were, and gradually becomes inward.

To demonstrate that the cosmic Christ is mentioned in the Old Testament, some theologians nowadays like to draw attention to passages which are about the wisdom *(sophia)* of God, for example the famous part from the eighth chapter of Proverbs, in which 'wisdom' says about itself:

> The Lord created me at the beginning of his way,
> the first of his acts of old.
> Ages ago I was set up, at the first,
> before the beginning of the earth.
> When there were no depths, I was brought forth;
> when there were no springs abounding with water.
> Before the mountains had been shaped,
> before the hills, I was brought forth;
> before he had made the earth with its fields,
> or the first of the dust of the world.
> When he established the heavens, I was there,
> when he set a compass upon the face of the depth,
> When he made firm the clouds above,
> when he established the fountains of the deep,
> when he assigned to the sea its limit, that the waters
> might not transgress his command,
> when he marked out the foundations of the earth:
> Then I was beside him, like a master workman;
> and I was daily his delight,
> rejoicing before him always,
> Rejoicing in the habitable part of his earth;
> and delighting in the sons of men. (Prov.8:22–31).

From these and other places[20] where similar things are said about the 'wisdom of God,' it is deduced that this 'wisdom' is

---

* How Judaism becomes predisposed for an inner experience of the divine will be discussed in more detail in the next chapter.

identical to the *logos,* that is, the cosmic Christ. In my view, this is an error. Rather, such descriptions indicate the third side of the divine being, the working of the Spirit, which is by no means the same as that of the actual *logos* itself.

We have already had occasion to refer to this fact: in the Prologue to John's Gospel it is said that not only life but also light proceeds from the working of the *logos.* From this we tried to make clear to ourselves that, in a sense, there are two basic elements to every word we speak: on the one hand the direct effect of the word in the sphere of life; on the other hand there is meaning and concept — in fact, one could say: light. Every word is a bearer of a spiritual idea and therefore has a light-aspect.

Firstly, then, every word has a shaping, formative power; this comes to expression, for instance, in the fact that the air comes into movement and the atmosphere around us begins to vibrate minutely when we speak, so that we thereby constantly shape our surroundings in a very delicate way, even quite externally.

This life-aspect, that is, the shaping, formative power of the word, becomes even more evident when we make clear to ourselves that we very often affect the lives of other human beings through our words, in either a positive or a negative way. This becomes quite obvious when we think of the calming effect that a mother's words can have on her child, irrespective of the meaning of any particular word — purely through the tone of voice and because of the living power which is in the word.

Secondly, though, we must consider the meaning, the 'light' and idea in the word. Now, it is possible to feel the life and the light aspects of the word to be an inner unity, and also to see the *Logos*-Christ activity as an inner unity with the working which proceeds from the Holy Spirit. For this reason, the divine 'persons' have always been spoken of as a unity. However, it is equally justifiable to differentiate between the two activities of the word, the life and the light aspects, as is indeed the case in the Prologue. Then one can observe that that which lives in the word as concept, meaning, as spiritual potency — we can also call it the power of wisdom in the word — is something existentially different from the life aspect. It is possible to differentiate between the working of Christ and the working of the Holy Spirit. (compare p.46; see also Notes 3.7, 3.8 and 3.20).

That is the reason why the sentences we have just quoted from the Old Testament sound very similar to the ones in John's Gospel about the *Logos,* the Word itself. And yet it is just not the cosmic Christ that is being referred to, but the working of the Holy Spirit, the third person of the Godhead, whose wisdom is to be found in the structures of the world. In our discussion of the Prologue we showed this: the world does not only present us with a wealth of structures and forms; deep wisdom is also contained in these forms and structures — and what is more, right down to the smallest detail. The activity which streams into the creating power of the *logos* from the Spirit-aspect can be seen in the active, wisdom-filled order of the created world.

Incidentally, this Spirit-aspect of the divine working is already hinted at in the wording of the Creation Story in the Old Testament. There it says specifically: 'The Spirit of God *[ruach elohim]* hovered [or: brooded] over the primeval waters.' So a distinction is made between this working of the Spirit and the *logos*-working, the divine speaking ('and God said').

As the last motif from the Old Testament we would mention something which is relevant to the subject 'New Creation.' We have pointed out that this subject culminates at the end of the New Testament in the Revelation to John, Chapter 21, and that there it is shown in the image of the new heaven and the new earth. Now, this motif already appears in the Old Testament, namely in the famous Chapter 65 of the Book of Isaiah. 'For, behold, I create new heavens and a new earth; and the former things shall not be remembered or come into mind.' (Isa.65:17).

These words of Isaiah correspond to words which follow only a few verses later: 'Thus says the Lord: "Heaven is my throne and the earth is my footstool; what is the house which you would build for me, and what is the place of my rest?"' (Isa.66:1).

Here there is a reference back to the creative power of the *logos* which is at the Beginning of creation. Through the cosmic Christ, everything which has come into being is re-cast as a new creation.

Summary and overview

This concludes our excursion through the New Testament, on the look-out for signs of the cosmic working of Christ. It has become clear that a wealth of such signs exists. Let us try once more to form an overall view of the insights we have gained in this third chapter. First, it will be appropriate to make a remark about our method and aim: we are not concerned here with establishing an exhaustive exegesis and scientific investigation of the references to the cosmic dimension of Christ in the New Testament. A thorough exploration would require much more space and attention to detail. In this respect, a few points do remain to be examined more closely in the following chapters. Here we have had to content ourselves with opening up a few vistas, from the conviction that it is possible to develop an insight into the cosmic being and working of Christ directly from the New Testament. To this end, we have become aware of the following:

The Very Beginning: For the relationship of the Father God to the Son God, that is, to the creative *Logos*, the cosmic Christ, a whole spectrum of expressions can be found in the New Testament, each one of which underlines a particular aspect of the Son God. In summary we could say: in the very Beginning, the creation of the world proceeds in Christ out of the divine Father-Being. The Father causes the Son to be 'born' out of His own Being, and gives him the task, so to speak, of creating the world.

Creation of the world and of Man: As understood by the New Testament, Christ is the creator of the world who calls creation into being, into existence, out of the being and substance of the Father. This also applies particularly to the creation of Man. We have seen that, from his creation, Man has the attribute of being particularly close to the Son God, to Christ. But it is not only existence as such that is closely united with the creative power of Christ; the life of the world and of Man are, too, and, what is more, not only at the Beginning but continuously, maintaining and enlivening.

A further fundamental element of the created world is its

overall 'meaningfulness,' which has to do with that aspect of the working of Christ which is called 'the light' in the Prologue of John, and which is a facet of the being of the Holy Spirit and its share in creation.

The Fall and the descent of Christ to earth: It is the fact of the Fall, the effect of the working of darkness into the evolution of the world, which makes Christ's descent to earth necessary. This fact is reflected in many ways in the New Testament; it requires an infinite sacrifice by the being of Christ.

The cosmic background to the earthly work of Christ — star and sun: In the Gospel, the cosmic background becomes particularly clear at certain places in the life of Christ. This is so in the case of the Birth, the Baptism, the Temptation and the Transfiguration, and then also the events associated with death and resurrection. 'Star' and 'sun' appear as images which sum all this up.

In addition, the Epistles (Letters) bring especially to our awareness that the earthly working of Christ involves a power which can transform everything and wipe out sin for mankind.

Ascension of Christ: In the New Testament, there are many and varied references not only to the Ascension of Christ, that is, his return to his cosmic power and authority, but also to his ascent through the spheres of the hierarchies into the highest heights of the realm of the Father. Because of this exalted status of Christ, a uniting, combining power streams forth towards all creation; thereby the restoration of all being at the end of the era will be possible through the working of the cosmic Christ. This restoration of all things will ultimately extend to the powers of the adversaries also.

Christ's continued working with mankind: This continued working begins with the Whitsun event. The 'exalted' Christ remains deeply united with mankind. Especially in the Epistles, it is made clear that the continued presence of

Christ has decisive consequences for the conduct of anyone who unites himself with Christ: morally, socially, in the capacity to bear one's destiny, in hopes for the future and in the renewal of one's whole nature, in the experience of worship and prayer. We looked particularly at two motifs: the Second Coming of Christ and the renewal of Man's whole being.

The return of Christ: In our time, the supersensible presence of Christ is beginning to condense into a new awareness of his being present; this completely alters human existence. From his present working for and with mankind a new human epoch will develop in future. The renewal of Man and the new creation also arise through this: the entire now present creation, including humanity, nature and the cosmos surrounding the earth, are included in the renewing activity of the Christ — leading to what is pictured in the Revelation to John as the new heaven, new earth, new Jerusalem.

4. The cosmic Christ in evolving human consciousness

If the working of the cosmic Christ represents a reality in the world, then it must be possible to find traces of that reality in the spiritual history of mankind, also outside the Old and the New Testament; for example in the religious experience and the myths of early mankind, including the environs of the Old Testament, in the spiritual streams surrounding the beginnings of Christianity, and, finally, in post-Christian spiritual history. We shall try to form at least the beginnings of an overview of this very wide field under these three main headings.

The cosmic consciousness of early mankind

If we wish to enter in thought into the conditions of early mankind, we must take account of something which is of fundamental importance in Rudolf Steiner's researches: the way in which we experience the world in our time — as a world of things, as strongly related to our ego, as thought-orientated — all this is the fruit of a relatively recent development within mankind.[1] The further back we go in human evolution, the less we encounter strongly defined personality-relationships as we know them today; and the more each human being experienced himself as being part of group and blood-relationships, within the family, the nation, the race; and the more his consciousness was permeated by dreamlike elements which passed over into clairvoyant states that made it possible to see a spiritual world in nature, mankind and the universe. The myths which we know from the traditions of early mankind are telling evidence of this.

Basing his work on the evolution of the initiation rites of kings in antiquity, Andrew Welburn points out this fundamental fact:

Each man did not feel himself to have a centre of being within him, an ego; rather he felt to be part of his people, could not even conceive of his existing at all except in terms of his place in the tribe or nation. In so far as he possessed anything like a centre of identity, an ego, it lay in the central figure of society — the king. It was only later that man became more individualized and demanded a spiritual autonomy, establishing his own personal relationship to the divine. In early times it was enough that the king was initiated into the divine secrets, for he was the identity of everyman. All this is clear when we grasp the different consciousness of those days ...

It is important to realize that this meant a totally different experience of the outer cosmos: a mythological living-together with the deep rhythms of the natural world and its indwelling powers. Awareness was more at the level of vivid dream, rather than sharp awakening, but correspondingly in touch with the hidden depths of the soul. *(The Beginnings of Christianity,* p.35.)

Against this background it becomes comprehensible that the myths of all peoples are permeated by cosmic elements. If we accept the view promulgated by Rudolf Steiner as regards the evolution of the consciousness of mankind, then we no longer need to relegate these mythological images and descriptions to the realm of invention and fairy-tale; we can take them as having evolved out of spiritual seeing, out of clairvoyant experience.[2]

At the same time, however, one has to understand that this seeing into spiritual-cosmic reality at that time was not oriented towards thought; rather, it called up pictorial perceptions (imaginations); this could lead to greatly varied images, since such spiritual realities are imbued with a great deal of 'vitality,' and also vary and evolve in the way in which they reveal themselves to mankind.

Therefore we should not be surprised that we encounter the most varied creator gods in the old myths; gods who have a decisive role to play in the creation and structuring of the world, but who, we can assume, represent an aspect of the cosmic Christ and his creating work.[3] As an example, I shall take the figure Vishvakarman from Indian mythology:

Tvashtri or Vishvakarman, the divine power who formed the world, is the carpenter who shapes the parts to fit, and

joins them together; the builder of the world who casts
the forms, who creates and gives all things their form,
who gave the heavens and the earth and all things their
great variety of form.[4]

The name Vishvakarman, that is, 'he who makes all things'
is also given to other divine beings, for example Brahma,
Shiva, Indra etc. The Power that creates the world appears in
different guises in order to work. But he himself is described
further:

Being the great builder of the universe, he is equipped
with eyes, faces, arms and feet on all sides; he gives the
gods their names, sacrifices all worlds in total offering
(sarvamedha) and ultimately sacrifices himself ...
Vishvakarman, who has given order to all things, who
sees all and, above all, decides upon the foundations and
the distinctions ...

Here, interestingly, the sacrifice motif appears which, in the
previous chapter, we already saw in connection with the creation
of the world. It agrees with the view that the cosmic Christ pours
out his life into all existence, in order continuously to maintain
the life of the world. Many myths from the most varied peoples
speak of the world being created by certain divine beings, behind
whom we may assume a knowledge of the cosmic creating power
of the Christ.

Now I would just like expressly to draw attention to an
Egyptian text which calls to mind an Old Testament image when
it refers to the 'God of the potter's wheel.' In the second chapter
of Genesis we find a mention of the working of Yahweh, who —
as the Hebrew text expressly puts it — shaped the human form
'out of clay,' and behind whom also is hidden an aspect of the
cosmic Christ:

You are the Lord of Esne, the God of the Potter's Wheel,
who formed the gods, who shaped human beings and also
the animals ... you are the venerable God whose form is
not known ... you are he who bears the heavens ... the
one and only who created all that is, who created Shuh
with his two eyes which enlighten both lands ...[5]

The echoes of motifs in the Prologue to John's Gospel are un-
mistakable.

But it is not only in the creator gods of the old myths that we encounter beliefs which point to an ancient level of the cosmic working of Christ, to the creation of the world. We reach a subsequent, second level when we turn our attention to the mythical images of the sun and the divinities which are associated with it. Here we are helped by a concept which we developed earlier: on his way to the earth, the cosmic Christ descended through the spheres of the planets and became the 'sun-being' for a while. To the Persian initiates of old he appeared there as the 'Ahura Mazda,' the sun-god who is opposed by the earthly powers of darkness and who fights against them.

In our prayer we revere the sun-ether-aura — mighty,
royal and promise-laden, god-created — which will be
passed on to the most victorious of saviours and to the
others, his apostles, and which brings the world forward,
which enables it to overcome ageing and death, decay
and corruption; which sets it on the way to eternal life, to
eternal health, to free will: when the dead are raised
again, when the living conqueror of death comes and the
world is advanced through the will. (Yasht 19:89).

In this connection, we can also recall Greek mythology (Apollo) and Egyptian ideas (Osiris), to mention but two. In this way, something of the cosmic sun-activity of the Christ shines through in many places in pre-Christian mythology (see also p.109).

But there is yet a third layer of the working of Christ in mythological-religious beliefs of antiquity: a premonition and prophecy of the divine saviour, such as we have just met in our example from the Persian tradition. So we can say that in pre-Christian times the notion of the working of the cosmic-divine appears in many different ways, in the most varied kinds of myth and among the most diverse peoples. The 'vision' of the cosmic working of Christ in the Old and the New Testaments, therefore, is an integral part of a mighty spiritual-historical panorama. What is special about the Christian vision, though, is the awareness that the cosmic being of Christ has already taken on flesh in a human being, in Jesus of Nazareth, or — as the Prologue to John's Gospel puts it — that 'the *Logos* became flesh and dwelt among us': the myth of pre-Christian times has become earthly fact.

This raises the question: what does the spiritual-historical panorama look like at the time when Christianity came into being? Do other, new perspectives arise, over against the picture we have drawn of the old mythological ideas?

The horizon of early Christianity

In *The Beginnings of Christianity,* mentioned above, Andrew Welburn deals in detail with much of the subject matter which belongs in this chapter. As regards the essential outline, we shall here refer to his picture of the various spiritual streams which form the background to the beginnings of Christianity.

As well as the direct evidence of the Old and the New Testaments, other texts belong to this broad picture: the so-called apocryphal writings of the Old and New Testaments, the Essene writings from Qumran (discovered in 1947) and the various writings of the Gnostics. Welburn also includes the world of the ancient Mysteries, together with initiation rites, in so far as they are known to us from the rituals of the mystery cultures of the time. At the end of his introduction he says:

> We have, then, three streams of religious wisdom around the time of the origins of Christianity: Christianity itself, as we know it from the New Testament with its hints of esoteric teaching; Judaism as it was being developed by the Rabbis; the frankly esoteric world of the pagan mysteries and the Gnostics (p.11).

Welburn's descriptions will prove fruitful for us because it will be possible to show that the hints of the cosmic background which we have found in the gospels, the Epistles and the Apocalypse in the New Testament must be considered within the framework of the spiritual history of mankind. Within the picture that emerges, the 'Christian vision' forms the core, the centre, which, however, radiates outwards, as it were, and can be recognized again in the variations, refractions and even the distortions of the spiritual life of the time.

THE UNIQUE EVOLUTION OF THE JEWS

The Jewish people occupies a special position within this overall picture. Welburn shows how the particular destiny of the Israelite-Jewish people leads them to separate themselves off from the general cosmic consciousness and to strive towards an evolution of the Ego. It is because of this that the particular 'mission' of the Jewish nation begins to take effect. We have already indicated this in the previous chapter in connection with the Elijah-inspiration. Step by step the Jews develop a growing consciousness of themselves as individualities.

And the experience of the cosmos is also influenced by this. Now:

> God reveals himself in the inner dimension rather than in
> cosmic-mythological patterns ... the type of experience
> common to the older Mysteries, in which man was raised
> above himself and felt part of the cosmic totality, is
> gradually replaced by an inner apprehension of the
> presence of the divine. Hence in the older sections of the
> Old Testament, Yahweh manifests himself in the power
> of storm and huge natural forces, which to the seers of an
> earlier form of consciousness were immediate revelations
> of spiritual energies. But in the later parts he no longer
> shows himself in this way, but as a 'still small voice'
> within. (Welburn p.36).

It is therefore not to be wondered at that the cosmic background only shines through faintly in the Bible, in comparison to the mighty cosmological images of the ancient mythologies; after all, the incarnation of the cosmic Godhead into Man was to be prepared for through this Jewish evolution. For that to be possible, it was necessary to retreat from the wide-ranging cosmic consciousness which did not lead to a personal experience of the Ego in human beings, and to turn towards inwardness of soul-experience. For it was from within a human being that the voice of the divine was to sound, it was from a human mouth that the presence of the divine was to be perceived. It follows quite consistently, therefore, that the 'education' of the Jewish people is directed towards the *'Logos* becoming flesh,' it is orientated towards making it possible for the cosmic God 'to dwell among us' (Prologue to John's Gospel).

In order not to endanger this necessary process of individuation, everything pertaining to cosmic relationships is placed into the background, also in the New Testament. Nevertheless, the references are there, as we have seen. Welburn shows that these hints in the New Testament of the cosmic perspectives become comprehensible on a deeper level if we turn to other accounts from the time of the beginning of Christianity — accounts which, however, were not included in the New Testament. In part, they are regarded as 'apocryphal literature'; what is meant is that they are writings which originally remained hidden and were not taken into the official canon. They are writings with very mixed contents, of varying standard and meaningfulness. Some of this apocryphal literature shows that there was 'esoteric knowledge' in early Christianity, knowledge which led more deeply into the secrets of Christianity and the cosmic background to the Christ-event, and which was accessible to small groups within the Christian congregations.

ESOTERIC CHRISTIANITY

Welburn approaches this area of interest by first making reference to passages from the gospels which are known to us:

And when he was alone with them, those who were about him as well as the twelve asked him about the meaning of the parables. And he said to them, 'To you the mystery of the Kingdom of God has been given; but those who are outside receive it in the form of parables ... they see with their eyes and yet do not see; hear with their ears and yet do not understand.' (Mark 4:10–12).

Welburn comments:

We can discover something of the character of the esotericism in the Gospel of Mark if we connect Jesus' difficult saying with the many instances in Mark where Jesus enjoins secrecy. Frequently when a healing has been performed, or some mystery revealed, Jesus imposes a solemn charge of silence, whether it be on his disciples, on the sick who have been healed, or on the demons who have been exorcized. Perhaps the supreme instance is that of Peter's confession, where he acknowledges Jesus as the Christ: Jesus' immediate response is to charge the disciples that they tell no-one of him. Mark has been termed a Gospel of 'secret epiphanies.' (Welburn p.3).

Something similar can be found in Paul:

What we proclaim is the wisdom which lives in the circle of those who have been consecrated. It is not the wisdom which belongs to the present aeon, nor that belonging to the leaders of this aeon, who are already becoming powerless. What we speak comes out of the divine wisdom of the mysteries which has lived in secret after having been preformed through the divine Ground of the World already before all cycles of time, in order to be revealed to us. None of the leaders of the present cycle of time recognized this wisdom. (1Cor.2:6–8).

In Welburn's words:

Paul still appears to be saying that Christianity does have its 'initiates,' does have a cosmic knowledge, a 'wisdom of God' that can stand in its own right against the wisdom of the pagans or the pagan-Christian mixture in Corinth, but which is yet not of the same exclusive, 'closed' kind. We shall understand more of his distinction after our further studies — the idea of a mystery that is shouted from the rooftops, a secret available to all. (Welburn p.6).

And further:

I know a man, living in Christ; fourteen years ago — whether in the body or in a condition freed of the body, I do not know; God knows it — he was transported into the third heavenly sphere, and about this same man I know — whether he was in the body, or in a condition freed of the body, I do not know, God knows it — he was transported into Paradise and perceived unspoken words which may never be spoken by human mouth. (2Cor.12:2–4).

There are a number of such indications of 'esoteric' knowledge in the New Testament.[6]

ESOTERIC WISDOM IN JUDAISM — THE ESSENES

When one asks oneself where esoteric knowledge was to be found in the environs of early Christianity, then one first of all encounters the Jewish sect, the Essenes. As early as the beginning of this century Rudolf Steiner pointed out the significance of this group — at a time when the few clues we have about the Essenes from antiquity were still being regarded with great suspicion by the scientific establishment.[7] Among other things, the Essenes were obviously in possession of extensive cosmic knowledge. Welburn demonstrates that the Essenes had absorbed a great deal from the mysteries of the Near East, especially from the Iranian mysteries. All the same, this knowledge had undergone a transformation among the Essenes; they had combined it with the inwardness which was being striven for in Judaism. On this point, Welburn writes:

> No change could be more significant ... the Essene
> initiate was no longer simply lifted out of himself in
> ecstasy and translated into the world of cosmic realities.
> He had to balance the forces of darkness by means of the
> light awakened in himself. He was an active moral agent,
> given by God the responsibility of 'governing' the earth.
> He was participating in an historical struggle, in
> accordance with 'the mysteries of God' until 'the time of
> his visitation,' that is, the advent of the Messiahs ... We
> can see in Essenism the advance-guard of a highly
> significant transformation of religious consciousness: a
> Mystery fused with the sense of self that had evolved in
> Judaism; a kind of initiation that could be combined with
> a feeling for history as the revelation of 'the mysteries of
> God,' and a responsibility for the earth. (p.50f).

And yet there was an important step to be taken from the Essenes to Christianity. The closeness of many Essene motifs and writings to the words of the gospels should not mislead us; Christianity nevertheless had something essentially new to bring.

The Essenes lived towards the appearance of the promised Messiah, they expected his coming and, in a certain sense, pre-pared for it through their spirituality. But, in that this event became reality through the appearance of Christ, it was not a 'mystery' which took place among the circle of the Essenes, or which was only available to outstanding initiates; it was to be for all mankind. And, above all:

the step from Essenism to Christianity was no small one, even if it was the Mystery-knowledge of the Essenes which provided much of the thought-life and social organization of the early Jewish Christians. The Essenes had lived by strict rules of purity — a spiritualized inter-pretation of the Torah. The Christian lives out of his experience and conviction of the Christ within.
(Welburn p.55f).

Let us take up at least two themes through which the close re-lationship of the gospel descriptions to the world of the Essenes can become a little clearer. To begin with, there are the birth stories. In the previous chapter we already stressed their cosmic background. About the descriptions given in Matthew it can be said:

They point to the world of the Essenes, linked mys-teriously to the visionary universe of Zoroastrianism and the Magi; or to the expectations of a divine 'wonder-child' like those of oriental mythology.
(Welburn p.137).

But not only Matthew's birth story, his whole Gospel shows a close relationship to the world of the Essenes. Rudolf Steiner had already established a link between the Gospel of Matthew and the Essenes; according to Rudolf Steiner, the very name Matthew indicates an association with Matthai (a disciple of Jeshu ben Pandira), the founder of the Essene movement. Matthew is a pupil of Matthai.

This comes to particularly clear expression in the interest which Matthew shows in the physical descent of Jesus of Nazareth at the beginning of his Gospel. When Matthew traces back the ancestors of Jesus of Nazareth through three times fourteen generations, via David to Abraham, he is thereby taking up one of the most vital concerns of the Essenes: 'the prediction of the birth and physical characteristics of the expected Messiah.' (Welburn p.75).

That this concern with the physical descent and the predicted physical appearance of the Messiah was Essene has been proved by the physiognomical and astrological fragments at Qumran.' (Welburn, *ibid.)*

We thus see an important concern of the Essenes reaching directly into the Gospel; or, in other words: the Gospel is the fulfilment of what the Essenes have been preparing for.

In Matthew we also find a great number of echoes of Essene writings, such as have been found in Qumran; so much so, that many researchers go so far as to speak of the Gospel of Matthew as the 'Gospel of the Essenes.' Of the many pieces of evidence which could be brought forward here, we shall only cite one fact: the place at which John the Baptist was active is not far from where the Jordan flows into the Dead Sea, in close proximity to the Essene monastery in Qumran. There, installations for ritual baths and purification have also been found, which were for maintaining the ritual purity of the members, and maybe also played a role as 'baptizing baths' for those who joined the order.

Just as did the Essenes, John the Baptist expected the arrival of the Messiah in the immediate future, and — like the Essenes — he prepared in his own way for this arrival through 'ritual baths.' Again the difference from the Essenes is that he did this in public, not within a closed order, and that his activity had become widely known among the Jews at that time; so that we see something of the Essene background also appearing, transformed, in the gospels, when they describe the Baptism — and this time not only in the Gospel of Matthew, but also in Mark, Luke and John.

But in contrast to the Essenes, the Gospel can say that the Messiah-expectation is fulfilled in John's working. It does not remain an expectation and a promise, as was the case with the Essenes; rather, in the sphere of the gospels it becomes a present fact.

We realize that the traces of cosmic consciousness which light up in the birth and baptism stories in the Gospel are only like a brief flashing-in of a reality which, however, was current as extensive knowledge among the Essenes, that is to say, in the environs of the emergence of our gospels.

ESOTERIC WISDOM OUTSIDE JUDAISM — THE GNOSIS

The word Gnosis embraces a very varied and multi-layered spiritual stream whose sources lie far back in pre-Christian times; it is fully alive in the environs of the emerging Christianity and plays into its beginnings. In the first Christian centuries parts of it even develop a 'Christian Gnosis' version. With the discovery in 1945 of an entire 'gnostic library' in Nag Hammadi, quite new perspectives have opened up within Gnosis research, in some instances overtaking earlier research results. The scientific evaluation of these new discoveries is still going on. Andrew Welburn, who has been involved in this evaluation and has published several reports on the subject, includes these new aspects of gnosis-research in his book.[8]

In this way, he succeeds in characterizing the particular quality of the gnostic stream; and on the other hand, the relationships to the emergence of Christianity can now be worked out more clearly. Welburn has discovered an interesting point of view for the development of the different gnostic systems. Let us recall once more his characterization of the Essene movement; he understands it as having emerged out of a meeting between Judaism and the ancient wisdom of the orient which was heathen/cosmic in its orientation.

To a degree, the Essenes were able to integrate this ancient cosmic consciousness into the consciousness of Self developed in Judaism. This was not the case in Gnosticism; on the contrary, in the gnosis there is 'the shocked reiteration of the archaic-oriental point of view.' (Welburn p.57).

This gnostic dualism sees the physical world, the world of matter, but is no longer able to see its relevance to the mystery-contents of the ancient world, deriving as they do from visionary conceptions. The two world-elements, physical-earthly world and the spiritual world which includes the cosmic consciousness are, so to speak, in opposition; this goes so far that, as a consequence, the Creator experiences this material universe as a fallen god.[9]

Rudolf Steiner characterized the gnostics as:
> 'the successors of the old initiates,' who preserved into
> later times the archaic attitude of the Mysteries. As such
> they are to be distinguished, he said, from the forward-

looking synthesis represented by the Essenes and their successors. (Welburn p. 59).

It is immediately obvious that those who concerned themselves with the esoteric truths of Christianity developed a special relationship to the gnostic world-systems. This explains the closeness of many a New Testament wording to the world of the gnosis.

Naturally, we cannot here quote all the interesting details from this wide-ranging field of research. Let it suffice that we can widen the spiritual-historical horizon of early Christianity towards the gnosis; and we shall now bring a few examples which show that against this horizon a deeper dimension of a whole series of New Testament passages becomes perceptible.

For instance, an interesting new light falls upon the expression 'Son of Man' which Christ uses as a description of himself in the New Testament.

We can establish that the title 'Son of Man' was indeed being actively employed among the Gnostics ... the Gnostics have preserved a part of the background to Jesus' teaching and world of ideas ... which has otherwise disappeared from Christian tradition. (Welburn p. 147).

Of course, that does not mean that Jesus himself was a gnostic. Yet in this way we gain a new view of the spiritual-historical background, against which the expression Son of Man appears in a quite different dimension, namely with its original cosmic meaning:

It was the Gnostics who especially preserved from older Mysteries the vision of the cosmic Man ... their description of the cosmological process whereby individual men are 'imprinted' below as children of the Man, the macrocosmic original, is modelled after older Mysteries, and some version of it might certainly have been current among the esoteric baptizers of Gnostic leaning in Palestine at the time of Christ. (Welburn p.148).

From another point of view, Rudolf Steiner emphasizes the situation indicated here when he says that 'we have to see the universality of the cosmos through the body of Jesus after the Baptism in the Jordan.' There may well have been an awareness of this fact in some circles in early Christianity, arising from the gnostic periphery.

We can find further examples in Paul. In earlier chapters we have already said that it fell to Paul to permeate Christianity with the clear light of thinking. Welburn is able to show how Paul in a certain sense holds the balance between the two streams which accompany Christianity: the Essenes and the Gnostics.

One instance which shows this is Paul's concept of the 'head' and the 'members,' as we find for example in the Letter to the Ephesians. Paul visualizes Christ as the head of a supersensible body, whose members are the different Christian congregations on earth. This concept of a 'cosmic human being' in Paul's thinking has been attributed to oriental and gnostic sources. On the other hand, this very concept can show clearly that with Paul it has evolved in a direction away from the gnostic idea. For in contrast to the gnosis, in Christianity it is not a matter of turning one's back on the world in order to merge into a higher cosmic pattern. Nor do the Christians form élite-communities which separate themselves off in a one-sided way from other human beings. Entering upon Christianity, therefore,

> far from taking them out of the world ... intensifies their
> sense at once of their earthly role and of its mythic
> overshadowing by the vaster issues of the cosmic
> struggle ... yet the individual self has an active role in the
> linking of earthly and spiritual ... [the Letter to the
> Ephesians] concludes with the imagery of a soldier being
> equipped for battle — spiritual warfare, certainly, but
> definitely not a retreat from the world: 'Stand fast, girded
> about the loins with truth' (Eph.6:14) ... it is as if the
> 'holy war' anticipated in the future by the Essenes had
> been transferred to the struggle of the individual now in
> the Christian's life on earth. (Welburn p.209).

We gain a further point of view when we turn to Paul's relationship to the question of the Resurrection. In this connection, the fifteenth chapter of the First Letter to the Corinthians is particularly striking; we have already referred to it in our previous chapter. At first glance it might appear that Paul tends very strongly towards gnostic ideas. In the world-view of the gnostics, the earthly, bodily nature was seen as very problematic. Living in a body was experienced as the chaining of the immortal spark of light to a 'dying animal.' By contrast, how are Paul's descriptions to be evaluated?

> When he characterizes the 'resurrection body' of Christ, or the bodies in which redeemed mankind will live, Paul evokes something more elusive, hinting at it by means of strong contrasts which are highly poetic but do little to define its corporeality: corruption/incorruption, shame/honour, weakness/strength. It prompts images of celestial radiance, like that of sun, moon or stars. It is a pneumatic or spiritual body, essentially different from everything that is 'of the earth, earthy.' No wonder that the Gnostics found so much in Paul that seemed to buttress their spiritualistic interpretation, and that they could refer to him as the Apostle! (Welburn p.219).

On closer inspection, though, it becomes clear that it is precisely the transformation of the bodily-earthly existence that is important for Paul — in the spirit of the resurrection-idea which takes hold of the earthly and leads it into a higher dimension:

> Christ's resurrection is therefore not the rejection of bodily existence, but the raising of it to a new level, not the avoidance but the overcoming of death ... Paul's thought on the subject of resurrection, then, is charged by the new consciousness. Christ's death is the central mystery: without it, 'resurrection' would simply be a return to the ancient Mysteries. (Welburn p.220).[10]

We can say, then, that an ingredient in the spiritual-historical environs of the gospels is the esoteric doctrine of the Essenes and the gnosis, in which a cosmic world-view plays a very particular role. The number of examples which might be cited to show this in detail could easily be multiplied significantly. However, we shall now turn to a third sphere which has been more thoroughly researched and which is therefore also much easier to survey as regards its relationship to the Gospel.

GREEK WISDOM — THE TEACHING ABOUT THE LOGOS

Here again, our glance falls on the Gospel of John, and in particular the Prologue. In the previous chapter we discussed how, through its *logos*-motif, the Prologue describes and clarifies the connection between the Son and the Father, the Son's proceeding from the Father, and his relationship to the creation of the world and to the creation of Man. If we now go on from there to consider the spiritual-historic horizon of early Christianity, we come across a widespread *logos*-doctrine; if we include that in our considerations as we did the Essenes and the gnostics, yet another dimension opens up.*

An outstanding representative of the pre-Christian *logos*-doctrine is Heraclitus of Ephesus *(c.*550–480 BC), who is inseparable from the mystery-background centred in the Artemis Temple in Ephesus. The Ephesian mysteries were *logos* mysteries. It is no coincidence that it was in Ephesus that the aged John wrote his gospel, overshadowed and inspired by the *logos* wisdom that had long lived there. Rudolf Steiner assigned an important role in spiritual history to the mysteries in Ephesus:

> In Ephesus, those who attained initiation could definitely discover something of the gigantic, majestic truths of the ancient orient. They were still touched by an inner sense and feeling for the connection between Man and the macrocosm and the divine-spiritual beings of the macrocosm. The mystery of Ephesus was, so to speak, the last mystery of the Greeks in the East, in which the ancient gigantic truths still came towards human beings; for in the East, the mysteries had otherwise fallen into decadence. (R. Steiner GA 216, December 28, 1922).

But Steiner also describes the fundamental difference between this path of initiation and that of the ancient oriental mysteries. Here we encounter a similar motif and a comparable development to the one we have already discussed in connection with the transition of ancient mystery-knowledge to the Essene life and practice. Wilhelm Kelber writes:

> Whereas in these latter [in the ancient oriental mysteries] the outcome of supersensible experiences depended upon the Seasons, particular places and upon periods and constellations of the stars, in Ephesus the pupils became emancipated from these factors of nature and the cosmos.

---

* See: Wilhelm Kelber, *Die Logoslehre von Heraklit bis Origines;* also Reinhard Wagner, *Die Gnosis von Alexandria.*

The aims of the initiation could now be reached at any
time and independently of the character of the locality.
Now, however, they became dependent upon the diligence
with which the pupil practised his exercises and upon the
degree of his personal maturity. *(Die Logoslehre,* p.17).

Despite this, it was possible to transmit an experience of
cosmic existence to the pupils in the Ephesian mysteries: 'It was
not the earthly substantiality that they experienced inside their
skin, it was their cosmic being.' (GA 216, December 26, 1922).
In other words, they discovered the link to the realm of cosmic
forces of becoming and so arrived at the twofold content of the
Ephesian initiation:

On the one hand to a perception of 'how things outside Man
have come into being on the earth, how everything on earth outside him has gradually been formed out of an original substantiality.' *(ibid.)*

But over and above that, the pupil was also led to an understanding of:

what human language actually is. And by the experience
of human speech — that is to say, the human image of
the *logos*, the *logos* as it is to be found in a human guise
— as compared with the world-*logos*, the cosmic *logos*,
the pupil was brought to realize how the world-word
surges and weaves creatively through the world. (GA 216,
December 27, 1923).

Kelber, in summary, writes: 'The *logos* which creates the
world, and the *logos* which reveals itself within Man as thought
and which comes to expression in speech — these were the two
sides of the Ephesian initiation.'

Heraclitus, too, was a follower of this ancient *logos*-wisdom
from the mysteries. Kelber says:

The primary thing is that the *logos* is regarded as eternal;
indeed, this characteristic serves as the axiomatic point of
departure for the train of thought. This property is also
the premise for the second statement, that everything (or:
the universe) has come into being in accordance with the
logos; since the *logos* must have existed before all else.
(p.25).

Two fundamental insights light up for Heraclitus: the character of the Beginning, the Very Beginning of the world, has to do with the *logos*, with the divine creator-word, which is endowed with reason. And this *logos* works in the creation of the world. The *logos* is the basis for everything that has been created. Here we see the correspondence between Heraclitus and John's Prologue. Heraclitus also knows about Man's fundamental closeness to the *logos* when he says: 'The *logos* is a feature of the soul, which grows of itself.' (Fragment 115).

But the tragic aspect which we have come to know from the Prologue to John's Gospel also sounds in Heraclitus:

> Although they are so intimately and permanently united with the *logos*, the Guide of the Universe, human beings turn away from him, and alien seem to them the things which they encounter every day. (Fragment 72).

The doctrine of the *logos* undergoes a significant development in the Stoa. The Stoics take up the *logos*-idea again and develop it further, beginning with the founder of the school Zeno (350–264 BC) up to the last great Stoic, the Emperor Marcus Aurelius (AD 121–180). Here I shall only indicate with a few quotations the wide range that the *logos*-idea now attains. The fundamental thought of Heraclitus permeates everything and is also formulated by Marcus Aurelius: 'Everything comes into being in accord with the *logos* and is guided by it [him].'*

In Zeno we find the following:

> If an olive tree were to produce harmoniously sounding flutes, would you doubt that it had some knowledge of flute playing? Or if rhythmically sounding lutes grew on the planets, you would of course also judge that the planets are musical. Why then should the universe not be regarded as alive and filled with the *logos*, since it brings forth living and *logos*-endowed beings?

Somewhat later, Poseidonius (AD 135–151) states: 'The entire cosmos is a living being, ensouled and permeated by the *logos*.'†

An important concept in Stoicism is that of the *logos spermatikos,* the seedlike *logos* within Man. We have already seen in Heraclitus that he credits the human soul with a *logos* which

---

* *Meditations* VI,1.
† Diogenes Laertius VII, 138.

grows 'of itself,' that is, has the character of a seed. This thought is developed further in Stoicism. According to the Stoa, there is indeed such a *logos spermatikos* within Man, but it has split off from the original spiritual cosmos from which it is descended. Within Man there live separate *logos*-monads whose development towards consciousness of self is not inevitable, just because this is not attended to by the cosmos. (See Kelber).

Something of this notion can be found again in the First Letter of Peter:

> You are souls reborn, who have your lives not from perishable but from imperishable seed: from the life-giving Word *[Logos]* of the Godhead who bears all present and future life in Himself. For all physical existence is like grass. The grass withers and the flower drops off, but the word [logos] which the Lord speaks outlasts the cycle of time. (1Pet.1:23–25).

Again, we shall limit ourselves to these indications. Kelber pursues the traces of the *logos*-doctrine as far as Jewish wisdom and to the form in which it was cast by the early Church Fathers. Presently we shall include some of this in our considerations. My intention here was to show that there does exist a spiritual-historical background in the environs of Christianity for the important *logos*-motif of John's Gospel and also, as we have seen, for other parts of the New Testament.

Nevertheless, it must be said again: within Christianity there is, over and above this, the conception that that which has to do with the creative-cosmic nature of the *logos* has not only scattered its 'seeds' in mankind, but has appeared on earth 'in person' in a human being, Jesus of Nazareth.

Post-Christian evolution

The first two thousand years of post-Christian evolution are initially marked by an almost total loss of awareness of the cosmic dimension of Man — not only within Judaism and Christianity, but also within the rest of mankind. The ability to know and experience is reduced, until it extends only to what is earthly-material. Only in some areas beyond Europe, especially in the nature-religions, for instance among the American Indians and in shamanism, have some remnants of the old cosmic experience been preserved into our time. Perhaps some of the old cosmic experiences still extend in a few places into the spiritual-religious life of Asia.

The evolution which we described in connection with Judaism in the previous section — the withdrawal from cosmic consciousness and cosmic experience in favour of earthly experience of the Ego and personality-development — this continued within Christianity, and from there took hold of all European spiritual life, and all spiritual life which was dependent upon Europe.

In the first instance, this development must be evaluated altogether positively, for it gives Man the possibility to unfold his spirituality out of himself, out of his experience of his own Ego; and not to remain dependent upon the superior might of the cosmic powers to whom he owes his existence. From that point of view, this development is in accordance with God's will, and one which is necessary for the future of mankind.

We see, then, that at the time when Christ appears on earth, remnants of an understanding of his cosmic dimension are still to be found, so that small groups of people, at least, can recognize him for who he is: the '*logos*' incarnated in a human being, the 'Son of God.' But within Christianity this awareness later becomes something which is merely propagated as dogma: the dogma of the Son of God who became man. This dogma ossifies more and more into an empty formula without a concrete content, and therefore not only can no longer be understood, but ultimately loses any significance. At best, what remains is the outstanding person Jesus of Nazareth; a cosmic dimension is no longer mentioned.

This development was furthered outside Christianity, in that the spiritual horizon also grew dim there. Insofar as the mysteries had not already become decadent in pre-Christian times, they now lost their power; the mystery-cults died out. The Essenes and their wisdom vanished — indeed so completely that hardly anyone attached any significance to the scanty reports that existed about them until the finds in Qumran in 1947. The gnosis, too, was lost or completely extirpated by the growing strength of Christianity. Certainly, the gnostic wisdom remained alive for centuries, but:

the need to centre the Christian vision on the conscious
I AM, instead of including the cosmic vision in its new
configuration, soon led many churchmen to exclude the
cosmic vision altogether, for fear that in the hands of
radical Gnostics it would itself exclude the earthly and
historical aspect of the self ... early Christianity included some Gnostic elements, broadly definable in
the sense that man could 'ascend' to knowledge of
the spirit through inner growth and development.
The 'orthodox' church threw out Gnosticism.
(Welburn p.298).

We find a similar, if perhaps not quite so dramatic, development
in the case of the *logos*-philosophy in early Christianity. Let us
follow this development, at least through some of its phases.

THE CONCEPT OF THE LOGOS IN EARLY CHRISTIANITY

We find a wonderful confirmation that the *logos*-idea, and thereby also an understanding of the cosmic dimension of Christ, lived
on within early Christianity, in the *Letter to Diognetus,* which
probably dates from the second century. It contains a hymn of
praise to the cosmic *logos:*

He sent the *logos,* that he might appear in the world. He
was maltreated by his people, proclaimed by the Apostles
and received with faith by the heathen. He it is who was
from the Beginning. He appeared as someone New, and
proved to be Ancient. He is born ever new in the hearts
of the saints. He is the Eternal One, of whom it is
proclaimed that 'today he is the Son.' Through him the
congregation is made rich ...

A further witness to the continued working of the understanding of the cosmic Christ is Justin Martyr (also from the second
century); about him, Wilhelm Kelber — using a saying of Justin
himself — writes: 'Justin's real subject is the *logos* in which the
whole human race has a share!' In Justin we find the words:
'Christ, the Son of God, is the eternal law for the entire cosmos.'
(Dialogue with Trypho 43) Another formulation is: 'The *logos*
was begotten by God as *Archae* (power of the Beginning) before
all created things.' *(Dialogue* 62) Or: 'Before all creation, the

logos was in Him, the Father, and he was begotten when He (God) created and ordered everything through him. He is called Christ.' *(Apologia* II,6).

In general, however, it is soon possible to notice:
a neglect of a significant facet of the *logos*-wisdom, beginning already with Philo. Certainly, the *logos*-idea still refers to the cosmic aspect of the being of Christ; but the activity of the *logos* as the pre-existent Christ now basically only interests the Christian teachers as regards the historical side, that is, the already past revelation to mankind. Over against that, the working of the *logos* in nature is barely mentioned. (Kelber, p.146).

For a third witness to our theme, let us turn to Clement of Alexandria *(c.*150–216) Kelber writes about him as follows: 'The *logos* is the absolutely dominant element in the teaching of Clement. In his surviving works there is barely a thought which does not have a direct or indirect relationship to the *logos*-concept.' Yet also in the case of Clement, as already with Justin, the cosmic aspect of the logosophy retreats into the background. The *logos* has become man and teacher, above all; Man now has the task of taking hold of the *logos*-power within him and thereby become like the *logos* itself.

Yet there are also elements in Clement which point to the cosmic background of the *logos*. The following passage, for example, characterizes the activity of the *logos* as the harmonizing power which permeates Man and the world:

He [the *logos* as 'pure song'] also gave the universe its harmonious order and tuned the discord of the elements into concordant melody, so that the whole world might become harmony for him. He left the sea unfettered, but forbade it to flood the earth; and the earth, which floated free, he anchored firmly and made it a strong boundary for the sea; and indeed, he even softened the impetuosity of the fire by means of the air, by, as it were, blending the Doric and the Lydian melody. The divine *logos* ... spurned the lyre and the harp, those lifeless instruments; through the holy spirit he filled this world — and also the microcosm Man and his soul and his body — with harmony, and he praises God with this instrument of

many voices and sings to this instrument: Man.
(*Protreptikos* I,5).

We are reminded here of the ancient knowledge of the 'harmony of the spheres' which derives from the sounding forth of the world-word, the *logos*.[11]

Here is a second place in Clement which points to the cosmic dimension of the *logos:*

[The Son of God] is not divided, not separated, does not change from one place to another, but is present everywhere at all times and knows no boundary; fully spirit, fully light of the Father, all eye, seeing all, hearing all, knowing all, penetrating the powers with power. The entire host of angels and gods is subject to him, since, as the *logos* of the Father, he is the holy ruler of the world 'by reason of him who hath subjected the same' [Rom.8:20 AV]; therefore all human beings belong to him; some, however, through insight, others not yet; some as friends, others as faithful servants, and yet others simply as labourers. He is the teacher who educates the gnostic through the mysteries, the faithful through hope, the hardhearted through improving discipline and through what can be learned via the senses. (*Stromateis* VII.5.4f; 6.1).

And a final quotation from the writings of Clement:

In the same way as the sun does not only light up the whole sky and the whole world by shining over earth and sea, but also sends its rays through windows and small openings into the inmost chambers of the houses: in this way the *logos* is poured out over everything and sees the smallest deeds that are done in life. (*Stromateis* VII.21.7).

These few examples prove that the cosmic aspect of Christ's being was by no means unknown to the early Christians — in fact, this idea is one of the 'bedrocks' of Christianity. Indeed, one can go further:

It was the conception of the *logos*-being in Christ which raised Christianity to the stature of absolute religion. Through this cosmic dignity, Christ was distinct from the class of inspired human founders of religion. And as the

logos, he was the Son of God. Without this conception,
the notion of 'sons of God' was bound later to lose more
and more of its concrete content. (Kelber, p.200f).

This development has been necessary, spiritually, and it is not
until our time that we see first signs appearing that the reduction
of the conception of Christ to the historical figure of Jesus of
Nazareth, the denial of the pre-existence of Christ, and indeed his
cosmic dimension, can be overcome. But first the development
went in the direction we have indicated, not least through the
extraordinary influence of Augustine, who highlighted the
significance for Man's innermost soul of redemption through
Jesus Christ. This view also became a determinant for Luther,
and it has played a significant role in shaping Protestant religious
life. We have already pointed out the evolutionary steps in this
connection. (See beginning of Chapter 2, p.24.).

THE DEVELOPMENT IN TWO CHRISTIAN MILLENNIA

Although cosmic vision disappears almost completely from
Christian consciousness, there are still single sparks of light to be
found in the growing darkness: for example, Cyril of Alexandria
(died 444), Maximus the Confessor (580–662), John of Damascus
(675–749) and later Nicholas of Cusa (1401–64).

Let us linger for a moment over Dante, who, in his Divine
Comedy, displays an enormous world-panorama: down to the
deepest depths, the realms of the Adversaries — and reaching
into the highest heights of the spheres of the hierarchies and the
planets. The centre of this panorama lies in the Being of divine
love, as the end of the *Paradiso* expressly says:

The exalted flight of vision broke; yet already
every wish and will of mine was seized
by the almighty power of love, which,
silently and alone,
guides the circling of the sun and stars.

Here Dante characterizes the divine love as all-permeating and
all-moving, not only of the sun and the stars, but also the soul-
powers of the poet. An inkling of the cosmic activity of Christ
comes to expression in poetic form (although, in view of the
eternal punishments in hell which he sets out in the first part of

the Divine Comedy, we feel bound to ask how this accords with
the closing theme of the poem).

We find a tremendous breakthrough to cosmic consciousness
in the Christian Middle Ages, a century before Dante, in the great
visions of Hildegard von Bingen (1098–1179):

Without God's word no creature has come into being.
For through God's word all things were made, whether
visible or not, every kind of creature which exists in this
Being, namely in the living Spirit, be it in power of
'greening,' be it in power of 'working.' [Translator's
note: German *Grünkraft* and *Wirkkraft* — possibly
referring to the world of plants and the world of ensouled
creatures.]

Now when the word of God sounded, this word
appeared in all created things, and this sound was in
every creature.

Like unto God was this word which is with God, like
Him a divine being, because the word exists inseparable
from God in God, since it is of like being with Him *(Welt
und Mensch,* p.171f).

Or she has God, the creator, the Ancient of Days (an expression from the Old Testament) say:

Being the Ancient of Days, I say: I am day out of my
own being, a day which does not shine forth from the
sun, but rather, which ignites the sun ... In order to
behold my countenance I have created mirrors in which I
contemplate all the wonders of my nature which never
cease. I have created these reflecting beings so that they,
too, may sound in the song of praise, for I have a voice
like the sound of thunder, with which I keep the entire
universe moving by the living sounding of all creation. I
have done this. I, the Ancient of Days.

The intimate closeness of Man to the Creator God comes to
expression, too: 'He, Man, is the image and the fullness of all
creation. In the deepest, innermost part of his soul he asks for the
kiss of his God.'* The earth is holy and may not be injured, for
even 'the elements take their complaints before their creator.'

* *Der Mensch in der Verantwortung.*

This profound knowledge of Hildegard von Bingen is not rooted in theological or philosophical speculations about the nature of creation and the creating Godhead; rather, it burst through in visions to which she then also gives pictorial form. One of these visions shows the divine creating-power, with the universe and cosmic Man in the arms of God. In the centre of the picture is seen a human form with arms spread out, embracing the entire cosmos and the elements, irradiated by the forces of the cosmos, which in turn is enveloped by the macrocosmic human being; behind and above the head of this human being appears the countenance of God Himself (see illustration opposite).

THE MODERN ERA AND THE BEGINNING OF THE TWENTIETH CENTURY

A few more sparks shine in the darkness along the path of the spiritual history of mankind. We could, for example, look at the Romantics who sense something of the all-embracing being of the divine in the world and in nature, albeit in a manner which often strikes us as sentimental. We have already spoken of new departures in renewed cosmic consciousness and experience. In this context, the name Teilhard de Chardin deserves a special mention. More profound and comprehensive, and, above all, based on cognition, was the way in which Rudolf Steiner spoke in the early part of this century about the cosmic dimension of Christ and his working in the universe and in mankind. We shall consider his descriptions in more detail in the next chapter.

From Hildegard of Bingen, Liber divinorum operum simplicis hominis. *Lucca, c. 1230.*

5. The cosmic Christ in Anthroposophy

A meaningful spirit is brought into the earthly evolution
of mankind and its laws when one learns to join this
earth-evolution of mankind to the cosmos through the
Mystery of Golgotha, by becoming able to look up to the
cosmic being of Christ. One learns to recognize how
Heaven has continued to care about the evolution of the
earth, how the cosmos has continued to be concerned
about the affairs of mankind; and this widens that
character of cosmology which I have already characterized here, the character of a spiritual cosmology, into a
Christian cosmology.*

It was not questions of a religious or theological nature that
were the starting point for Rudolf Steiner. Coming from a background of scientific and philosophical research (especially in the
field of epistemology), he found ways into the realms of 'higher'
knowledge, which then also made it possible for him to have a
spiritual conception of the being of Christ. Indeed, Christology is
at the very heart of anthroposophical knowledge. Rudolf Steiner
stressed the importance of distinguishing his insights from the
uncontrolled paths into the spiritual world which are propagated
in a large number of writings nowadays. Anthroposophy sets itself the strict standards of a scientific method of perception.†

In our presentation we shall have to gather together much that
is scattered among Steiner's lectures and books. We do this here,
not to introduce anthroposophy as a new dogma, but in order to
include in our considerations the descriptions and statements of
a man whose life's work is freely accessible to all and who
achieved an extraordinary amount in the most varied spheres of

* R. Steiner, *Philosophy, Cosmology and Religion in Anthroposophy.* (GA 215,
September 12, 1922).

† See Note 5.7.

life. We believe that his voice on our subject deserves to be heard, even though we by no means expect the reader to agree at once with his often unusual statements. Nevertheless, it will prove worthwhile to take note of his words on our subject.

It would seem that Rudolf Steiner was the first person in our century to take up the subject of the cosmic Christ, earlier than Teilhard de Chardin and in a much more comprehensive and profound way. It permeates his entire life's work. Our task, therefore, is to illuminate the three great chapters of Christology of which we have spoken, through anthroposophy. Quotations will be given verbatim or supplemented through notes.

The cosmic Christ in his pre-existence

In many of his lectures, Rudolf Steiner takes up the *logos*-motif from the Prologue to John's Gospel. For him, the *logos* is the cosmic Christ, the 'second person' of the triune Godhead, the Son of God of Christian tradition. He says, for example:

Behind all living things is a divine being ... It is the same spirit which also works in our speech. For this reason the Christian religion calls him the Word. Something quite precise and real is meant by this ... This spirit which is behind all living things also works in our speech now, in every one of our words, and is therefore quite properly called 'the Word.' Another name is the Son, or Christ. He is the spirit which lives in everything. (GA 93a, October 12, 1905).

And elsewhere:

Words sound through the air, otherwise we would not hear them. The forms of the words which we speak are now 'contained' in the air. If it were possible suddenly to 'freeze' the air while I speak, then the waves buzzing around in the air would fall to the ground as solid, rigid bodies. Everything around us is the condensed Word of God. In that way, said the mystery-teacher, the world around us is a frozen word of God, a frozen *logos*. 'In the Beginning was the Word, and the Word was with God.' It was still within His being, it was itself a god. Then it permeated space, and solidified. This *logos* is now present everywhere. Everywhere around us we have the 'crystals of the *logos.*' ... One has to live into this fully, in order to penetrate so deeply into the world that one becomes aware: the *logos* is alive in the world. (GA 97, February 12, 1906).

This was known in the ancient mystery-centres. The working of the *logos* in the world was brought vividly to the awareness of the pupils by the mystery-initiates. When their attention was directed to various phenomena in the world, in nature, in the cosmos, they could be told straight out: 'In them are embodied individual words of the universal *logos.*' (GA 220, January 13, 1923).

A cycle of lectures by Rudolf Steiner from the year 1923 bears the title: *Man as Symphony of the Creative Word.* Here, Steiner gives an insight into the world of nature and its beings, that is, the elemental beings who are active in nature, creating, structuring and forming it. He shows that these various beings, who permeate and enliven the air, the water, the realms of earth and of warmth, are themselves parts of the great, all-embracing world-word, individual letters or syllables, as it were, partial aspects of the all-creating power of the *logos.*

The ancient conception, which arose from instinctive clairvoyance, that the world is formed through the Word, is definitely a deep truth. But the world-word is not just a random combination of a few syllables; rather, the world-word is that which sounds in a 'symphony' from countless, countless beings. Countless and countless beings have something to say in the totality of the universe, and the world-word sounds forth from these countless beings together. The generalized, abstract truth that the world is born of the Word cannot give us the fullness of the truth which we arrive at when we gradually and concretely grasp that the world-word in its various nuances is a combination of the voices of separate beings, that is, that these different nuances resound and speak in the great world-harmony and the mighty world-melody as it creates. (GA 230, November 4, 1923).

In earlier stages of human evolution, this working, forming and shaping in nature by the world-word could still be experienced by human beings:

For these early human beings, trees were not such prosaic objects as they are for us now: there was something in every tree, in every shrub, in every cloud, in every spring which made itself known as a soul-spiritual, cosmic entity ... The forest did not rustle in an inarticulate way; in the rustle of the forest, they perceived the language of the eternal world-word ... modern people can only have a faint idea of the intense vividness with which human beings experienced the world in those bygone days.

Something similar is said (in the same lecture) about the view of the stars:

Look upwards to the eternal world-word which, for one who is receptive to it, expresses itself in the movements or positions of the stars; then the reality reveals itself within the *maya*. If one wanted to know and understand something which was important and significant for one's life, then one tried to search it out from the stars and their language. (GA 209, December 24, 1921).[1]

LOGOS AND MAN

We take a further step in our conception of the *logos* when we do not only consider the *logos* as it forms, shapes and creates in the world, but now turn directly to Man. Here Rudolf Steiner says:

The fact that you have this form, that this human body has its present form, is because the Word was the basis for the whole plan of our created world. The entire body of Man is formed 'towards' the Word, and from the Beginning it has been so prepared that, ultimately, the Word should sound forth from him. So when an esoteric Christian looks at this physical body of Man and asks: what is its original archetype, and what is its image? then he says to himself: This physical body of Man has its archetype from the Word or the *logos;* the *logos* or the Word worked from the Beginning in the physical body of Man. And the *logos* still works now: when the physical body of Man lies in bed and is deserted by the Ego, then the divine *logos* works in the members of Man's being which have been deserted by him. If we ask after the first origins of the physical body, we must answer: first came the *logos* or the Word. (GA 103, May 19, 1908)*

Other descriptions by Rudolf Steiner also indicate that the world-word is at work in Man not merely in a general way, but that Man himself becomes a bearer of this Word, although in a muted sense, and lacking the creative powers of the world-word. But if we consider the whole being of Man, it does not appear, as do the other phenomena of nature and the world, as single 'letters' or 'syllables' of the world-word, but as a combination, in fact, a 'sounding together,' a 'symphony' of everything which otherwise is spread out through the world, having been 'called' into being through the Word. Within Man, the multiplicity of all the forming and shaping forces which are spread out and unfolded in nature is gathered together into a new central point. Thereby he becomes the bearer of forces which themselves are *logos spermatikos,* as it was formulated in the ancient Stoic doctrine (see p.92); that is to say, of forces which themselves can become the starting point for a new-born world. We shall be returning to this theme later.

DESCENT TO EARTH

Christ's transition from his cosmic status to his incarnation as man is characterized very clearly in anthroposophy. At first sight, we encounter a difficulty for our thinking here: how can the world-word, which, according to the previous descriptions, brought forth the entire universe and still permeates it — how can he become Man, 'dwell' in a human being, as John's Prologue expressly puts it: 'The Word [the logos] became flesh, and dwelt among us ...' (John 1:14)? Did the *logos* then leave the rest of the world when he became Man?

Certainly not! But — we might think of it like this — the centre of his being shifted, as it were, out of the world and into his appearing as a man. Just as we can 'con-centrate' on someone we love, and indeed, at least with our feelings, 'get inside' that

---

* More on this subject in GA 231, November 13 and 14, 1923; GA 222, March 23, 1923.

person — without this leading to the cessation of the other human functions: heartbeat, breathing, and so on — the *logos* became concentrated in Jesus, without giving up its cosmic functions.

Two ideas can help us further with this thought: in the first place, this concentration of the *logos* from out of the cosmos into Man occurs in stages through a long development which we have characterized as the 'descent' of Christ through the planetary spheres. Secondly, Man is no stranger to the *logos,* as we have seen: 'The entire body of Man is formed "towards" the Word ...' So there is an intimate relationship between Man as microcosm and the *logos* which is the foundation of the macrocosm.

Let us again take up the description of the experience of early mankind, which we have just been considering: the nature of the world-word could be known through the starry heavens. In connection with this, Rudolf Steiner says:

> In the very Beginning, the Word spoke out of the procession and the position of the stars. From out of the cosmos it sounded, this Word ... the writer of the Gospel of John dared to say: and the Word became flesh and dwelt among us — that is to say: that which lives out there in the stars lived in the body which hung on the cross. That which previously was sought for in the widths of the world was to become visible in a human being. Man's whole approach to life was guided from a world-wide cosmology to an awareness of that central human being who was permeated by what shone down from the stars, who was permeated by the living world-word.
>
> And this is the meaning that is to be revealed to mankind through the mystery of Golgotha: that it is also possible to look to the origins of the world by looking into the inner human nature of Jesus and establish an intimate relationship between one's own innermost soul and this innermost human aspect of Jesus — just as in earlier times such a relationship was established between human beings living on earth and the eternal world-word which speaks from out of the stars. (GA 209, December 24, 1921).

But Christ's appearing on earth, his descent from cosmic

widths and the heights of the Godhead through the various spheres of the hierarchical beings — all this meant an enormous sacrifice for him:

> Christ left the heavens to exchange that home of his for the earth. I ask you to see this in the right light and to experience with inner sensibility and feeling what it was that happened through the mystery of Golgotha, what happened through the person of Christ, what the actual sacrifice of Christ was — namely, to leave the spheres of the spirit, in order to live with the earth and human beings on earth, and to guide human beings and the evolution on earth onwards through this impulse. (GA 148, October 3, 1913).

Somewhat later, the following is added:

> Christ's earth-existence grew out of the most profound suffering, a suffering which exceeds all human notions of suffering ... [Or even more pointedly:] There can hardly be an experience to compare with the suffering involved in the union of the Christ-being with the bodily nature of Jesus of Nazareth; one becomes aware what a divine being had to suffer in order that an ageing humanity might experience rejuvenation, so that Man should become able to take full possession of his Ego. (GA 148, November 18, 1913).

In our description we have already mentioned several times that in anthroposophy the cosmos out of which Christ descends is seen as having other levels than is postulated in contemporary astronomy. The present-day view is an external picture of the cosmos, the planets, the sun and the fixed stars. If we wish, in the sense of anthroposophy, to grasp the reality of the cosmic spheres, we must add an inner perception to this picture.

Just as we are only aware of one layer of a human being when we merely consider him according to his earthly-material body and disregard what is in him as life and soul and Ego-being, so it is also with the cosmos as regards its outer form. Our system of planets including the sun, and the realms of the fixed stars, are, in their outer appearance, indicators of the living, ensouled and spiritual forces which are united with them.

Therefore anthroposophy can say that the *logos,* the cosmic

Christ, descends from beyond the sphere of the fixed stars, by stages through the spheres of the planets and on to the earth, and at the respective levels unites with the hierarchical angel-beings who share in the forming and further evolution of the created world and Man.*

For our understanding, the most important stage in this cosmic descent of Christ would seem to be his tarrying on the sun, in the sphere of the sun. As Rudolf Steiner says:

> The Christ who is now seen as the being who went through the mystery of Golgotha at the beginning of our era ... had descended from even greater heights to the sun. That is where Zarathustra saw him. Then his power passed over into the rays of the sun; now he was seen by the Egyptian initiates. Then his power lived in the periphery of the earth, and the Greek initiates saw him. (GA 211, February 24, 1922).

If — asks Steiner — the cosmic spirit had had to describe himself in ancient times, what would he have had to say about himself? The sun-spirit whom, for example, Zarathustra saw, who worked as spirit in the light, would have had to say: I am the light of the world.

> That which sounded towards the earth from the cosmic heights as innermost self-characterization of the leading cosmic spirit: we hear it sounding again from out of a human being, since that being now lived within a man. We hear it sound from Jesus of Nazareth, and rightfully so, since the Christ is within him: I am the light of the world (John 8). (GA 112, June 27, 1909).

In summary, Steiner says:

> Together with the externally shining sun, people in earlier times experienced the Christ from beyond this world. When he has come to the right conception of the mystery of Golgotha, Man will be able, through Christ, to see the sun within this earth-existence. It shines out there in the world — it shines through history; outside physically; in history spiritually: sun here, sun there. (GA 207, October 16, 1921).[2]

---

* Compare p.27, 109 and Note 2.7.

The earthly work of Christ

Rudolf Steiner also made a great number of statements about the second chapter of Christology, the earthly work of Christ, in which he takes account of the fact that it was not only a human personality that was incarnated in the earthly man Jesus, but an exalted divine being. This fact has consequences for how we view the earthly life of Christ, and for the interpretation of the gospels.

The very first question is: what was the intention of the writers of the gospels as they wrote? We must bear in mind that the gospel writers were by no means only dependent upon external tradition, for, clairvoyantly, they had their own direct access to the events of the mystery of Golgotha. The gospels arose out of immediate spiritual experience.[3]

This gives one a feeling of cosmic greatness, for instance in the case of John's Gospel:

> It is as if the human being is standing there below,
> looking up to a pinnacle of world-existence, saying to
> himself, 'Small as you are as a human being, the Gospel
> of John nevertheless enables you to sense that something
> is entering your soul which relates to you and which
> comes over you as with a feeling of the eternal.'
> (GA 123, September 1, 1910).

What that is, is stated even more concretely: It is the 'inner side of the sun-spirit,' the cosmic dimension of Christ:

> He [the evangelist John] is not primarily concerned
> with the physical life; rather, he directs his gaze towards
> the most high, the sun-*logos* itself, and the physical
> Jesus is for him the means whereby he can follow how
> the sun-*logos* acts within mankind. (GA 123, September 12, 1910).

And, looking to the other gospels:

> Whereas the Gospel of John describes for us the
> wisdom of the Christ-Jesus in all its spiritual
> grandeur, the Gospel of Luke shows us the im-
> measurable power of sacrifice of this Being, and
> helps us to sense what has taken place within the
> whole evolution of the world and of Man because of

this loving sacrifice which pulses and weaves through
the world, a force among other forces ... (GA 123,
September 1, 1910).

In several series of lectures about the four gospels, Rudolf
Steiner described the points of view which we are only referring
to briefly here; he went into great detail, and drew certain
consequences for the interpretation of the gospels.[4] Through these
descriptions it has, for the first time, become possible to accompany in feeling Christ's life in the body of Jesus of Nazareth,
even what He felt and went through, and which stages of
development are relevant in this context. In what follows we shall
concentrate on a few points from the wealth of material available.

BAPTISM IN THE JORDAN

Anthroposophical research shows that another conception which
also lived among the early Christians is true:[5] the deeper union
of the Christ-being with the man Jesus of Nazareth was only
established in the thirtieth year of that human life, and it took
place through the event of the Baptism. Rudolf Steiner says this
about it:

During the discussion of John's Gospel there was already
an opportunity to point out that in those days baptism
was something quite different to what is has become later
— a mere symbol. And it was also carried out in a quite
different way by John the Baptist. Those who were
baptized were submerged under water with their whole
body. Even in everyday life, if, for example, a person
comes near to drowning and receives a shock, it happens
that his whole previous life stands before him as in a
great tableau. The reason for this is that for a brief
moment there occurs what normally happens only after
death: the ether body is lifted out of the physical body,
becomes free of the dominance of the physical body. This
happened to most of those who were baptized by John;
and it occurred particularly at the baptism of the 'Nathan'
Jesus; his ether body was drawn out. And during this
moment, that exalted Being whom we call the Christ
could enter in and take possession of the body of this

Jesus. So from that moment of the baptism by John, the 'Nathan' Jesus is permeated by the Christ-being. That is the meaning of the words which are to be found in certain early gospel documents: This is my beloved Son, today I have begotten him. (GA 114, September 21, 1909)*

Rudolf Steiner describes the background to this event like this:

The Christ descended out of that world, came down from the cosmos to the earth. And because the cosmos no longer was accessible to human beings in the way it had been in ancient times, because they would not have been able to find the Christ in the way they once could, because the kind of knowing and soul-condition had died through which they had once beheld the world in which Christ lived — for that reason Christ had to come down to human beings. And he did so. Therefore everything which had once been recognized and understood about the spiritual world by the enlightened spirits in ancient times in the pagan mystery cults, in pagan mystery science, now had to be summed up in Christ. It all had to be seen in Christ. One must know what kind of a being the Christ was, he who had come down to earth from the cosmos. (GA 181, August 6, 1918).

The consequence of this fact now was that a 'centre-point of cosmic forces' was present on earth in the Christ-Jesus:

The forces through which the Christ Jesus worked were forces which streamed down from the cosmos due to the power of attraction of his body, which radiated from his body and were poured out over his disciples. And now it came about for the disciples that because of their receptivity they could feel as an absolute certainty, 'This Christ Jesus who stands before us is a being through whom the forces of the

---

* Steiner speaks in a similar way about the event of the Baptism in almost all his gospel cycles (see Note 5.4); see also the relevant descriptions by E. Bock, *The Three Years* and *Das Evangelium,* and R. Frieling, *New Testament Studies.*

cosmos come to us like spiritual nourishment. They pour out over us through him.' (GA 123, September 10, 1910).

This fact is reflected in the gospels, for example in the feeding of the four thousand and the five thousand.*

BECOMING MAN

According to Rudolf Steiner's descriptions, however, the relationship between the cosmic Christ-being and the body of Jesus of Nazareth in which he was to become human changed fundamentally as time went on. The powerful working with cosmic forces which we have described, only happened in its full strength at the beginning of the three years. Rudolf Steiner describes this as follows:

At the beginning of the earthly life of Christ, what this Christ-being did worked as something from beyond the earth. But increasingly it made itself like the body of Jesus of Nazareth, squeezed and contracted itself more and more into earthly conditions, and had to experience that the divine power waned. All this the Christ-being endured as it became ever more like the body of Jesus of Nazareth ... Like someone who, with infinite pain, sees his own body fade away ever more, so the Christ-being saw its divine power decline, in that, as an etheric being, it became ever more like the earthly body of Jesus of Nazareth, until it had become so similar that it could feel fear like a human being ... his divine power to work wonders departed from him. So we see the stages of the Passion begin at that moment, soon after the Baptism in the Jordan, when the astonished people who had seen what Christ was able to do, said that no-one on earth had ever done such things ... (GA 148, October 3, 1913)†

---

* For further insights into these gospel accounts, see E. Bock, *Das Evangelium.*

† Christ's Passion is portrayed in these lectures on 'The Fifth Gospel' in a new and moving way.

TRANSFORMATION AND SPIRITUALIZATION OF
BODILY NATURE

But this suffering of Christ described by Rudolf Steiner was not merely something he had to endure, it was an active power which permeated and purified the bodily nature of Jesus of Nazareth. This fact, too, is described in the gospels. It appears, as we have mentioned earlier, in the image of the 'Transfiguration' on the mountain (Matt.17): here the bodily nature of Jesus lights up like a cosmic sun. We see in picture form: the bodily nature of Jesus of Nazareth is no longer surrounded by the cosmic powers of Christ; instead, something of the cosmic, sunlike being of Christ shines out from the body itself.

Perhaps one could also express it like this: whilst the divine being of Christ contracts itself from out of the cosmic periphery within the body of Jesus of Nazareth as if into a point, spiritual energy is, as it were, 'bunched up'; thereby a power arises which can not only purify and cleanse the bodily nature of Jesus of Nazareth of the consequences of the Fall, but can spiritualize it from within. This process ultimately leads to the most exquisite bodily pain in the Passion — through scourging, crowning with thorns and crucifixion. Through this bodily pain, the Christ-being becomes even more constricted within the body — all pain contracts and concentrates forces. Here, too, there is the reversal we have already indicated: what has been active in the cosmic periphery now appears transformed, inverted, as the power which spiritualizes the physical body of Jesus from within and transforms it into the Resurrection Body.

It would lead too far to describe in detail the individual steps which lead to this transformation of the bodily nature of an earthly human being. Literature dealing with this question is mentioned in the notes.[6] Our concern here is the cosmic aspect of the working of Christ.

THE 'MYSTERY OF GOLGOTHA'

Whilst the death on the cross and the resurrection of Christ take place, the process already described is again reversed. The concentration of the cosmic powers of Christ within the body of an earthly human being now becomes an expansion, ascent and a return to the original cosmic state. If we are not to meet the following descriptions with a complete lack of understanding, we must keep reminding ourselves that we are here looking at the working of the *logos* which is the original basis for all existence and life; this existence has become estranged from its own origins, but the working of the *logos* has the power to help it find itself and at the same time guide it towards a new world-aim.

According to Rudolf Steiner's descriptions, the death on the cross itself already has within it a power which extends beyond the local place Golgotha.

The cross on Golgotha is not only to be seen as though it merely expressed something earthly, but rather, the cross on Golgotha is significant for the whole cosmos: this is what was known in esoteric Christianity. (GA 211, April 2, 1922).

Elsewhere Steiner describes this event even more clearly, this time in connection with the blood of Christ which flowed from the cross into the earth.

In the same measure as the blood flowed from the wounds on Golgotha, something spiritual occurred. At that moment, for the first time rays went forth from the earth towards the cosmos in a way that had not happened before; we must imagine newly created rays streaming out towards the universe. The earth had become ever darker as time went on, until the event of Golgotha. Now the blood flows on Golgotha, and the earth begins to shine!

If, in pre-Christian times, some being or other equipped with clairvoyant abilities had been able to look down on the earth from a distant planet, it would have seen how the earth-aura gradually grew dim and became its darkest in the time before the event of Golgotha. But then it would have seen how the earth-aura lit up in new colours. The deed on Golgotha permeated the earth with an astral light which gradually will become an etheric and then a physical light ... At that moment, the earth began to shine, in the first instance with astral light, so only visible to someone clairvoyant. But in the future, the astral light will become physical light, and the earth will become a shining body, a sun-body. (GA 112, July 6, 1909).

And later he says:

And because at that time the earth was permeated by a new power, because the basis was laid for the earth to become a sun — this made it possible for that power also to shine into human beings. The first impetus was given to what I described yesterday: the shining of the power of Christ in the human ether body. And, by virtue of that which shone into it astrally at that point, this human ether body could begin to absorb new powers of life as they will be needed for the further future.

... When the cross was raised on Golgotha and the blood flowed from the wounds of Christ-Jesus, at that moment a new cosmic centre-point was created ... but this we must understand: when we behold the dying Christ, we are witnessing the beginnings of the formation of a new sun. (GA 112, July 6, 1909).

And in summary:

In that moment when Jesus of Nazareth died on the cross on Golgotha, something was born for the earth, something which previously had only been present in the cosmos. The death of Jesus of Nazareth was the birth of cosmic love in the sphere of earth. (GA 148, October 2, 1913).

Two details must still be mentioned here; they have to do with the spiritualization of the body of Jesus to which we have referred previously, and to which we must return later. Just now, mention was made of the spiritual power of the blood which flowed from the cross. From Steiner's description it further becomes clear that this blood:

should not be regarded merely as a chemical substance; rather, it is something very special, due to all that we have described about the nature of Jesus of Nazareth ... What happened to the blood in the following aeons? In the course of earth-evolution, the blood went through a process of etherization ... The ether body of the earth is permeated by what has

become of the blood which flowed on Golgotha.
(GA 130, October 1, 1911).

It is described further how human beings can develop an 'inner power of attraction' for this spiritual-etheric bloodstream of Christ, when they seek a relationship to Christ. Something similar applies to the resurrection body of Christ Jesus. It, too, continues to work spiritually; it did not simply vanish at the 'Ascension.' In his description of this fact, Rudolf Steiner takes up St Paul (1 Corinthians 15):

Just as the first, perishable body is descended from
Adam, so must the imperishable body be descended from
Christ, the second Adam. So that every Christian should
say to himself, 'Since I am descended from Adam I have
a perishable body, because Adam had one; and when I
form the right relationship to Christ, I receive an
imperishable body from Christ — the second Adam.'
This conception became obvious to Paul through the
event of Damascus. In other words: If we have a certain
number of people at a given time, Paul would trace their
descent back to the first Adam from whom they all have
sprung and who gave them their perishable body.
According to Paul, something else must also be possible.
Just as the natural lines of descent lead to Adam, so it
must be possible to draw lines which lead to the
imperishable body which, according to the Pauline
conception, we can have in us just as much through our
relationship to Christ as we have the perishable body
through Adam. (GA 131, October 10, 1911).[7]

As understood in this conception, the body and blood of Christ continue to work in a quite real way; we must attribute to the cosmic Christ a spiritual body which is connected with cosmic streams of life (blood).

And finally, a further motif belongs here, one which becomes easier to understand in view of what we have just presented; again Steiner takes up a Pauline formulation (1Cor.5:15, and also 1Tim.2:6):

Through the mystery of Golgotha, Christ actually placed
a cosmic event into the evolution of the earth ... Christ
came down from spiritual heights, united himself with

mankind in the man Jesus of Nazareth, went through the
mystery of Golgotha, united his own evolution with that
of the earth. It was a deed done for the whole of
mankind.

In this connection, Steiner indicates that this truth has quite
concrete consequences for each individual human being; that has
to do with the effects of the Fall which, already at the time of
Christ's appearance on earth, were causing human bodies to become ever more decadent and unsuitable for human incarnation.

... Christ's deed on Golgotha is an objective deed; its
significance does not depend on what human beings
believe about it.

An objective fact is an entity in itself, just as it is. If a
stove is hot, it does not become cold because a number of
people believe it to be cold. The mystery of Golgotha is
the salvation of mankind from the decline of the physical
body, quite irrespective of what people believe or do not
believe about it. Indeed, the mystery of Golgotha took
place for all human beings, including those who do not
believe in it ...

For this mystery of Golgotha happened in order to
provide new forces for the human physical body, that is
to say, to renew earthly mankind, as it were, to refresh
them, as far as it is necessary to rejuvenate them. This is
what happened. And thereby it has become possible for
human beings on earth to find bodies into which they will
be able to incarnate into a future which still has a long
way to go. (All quotations from GA 224, May 7, 1921;
see also Note 5.13.)

THE 'HARROWING OF HELL'

After the death on the cross, that event took place which in the
Christian Creed is called the descent of Christ into the 'underworld' or 'hell.' The significance of this event becomes clear
through further statements by Rudolf Steiner; he describes how
in pre-Christian times the consciousness of mankind had grown
ever darker as a result of the influence of the adversary powers
and as a consequence of the Fall; this led to an increasing sense

of oppression and anxiety after death; the life of human beings after death became ever more an 'underworld,' a 'hell.'

...in the moment when the Mystery of Golgotha was fulfilled, another faculty was instilled into mankind — the faculty whereby the influence of Ahriman can be turned to good. Out of his life on Earth man can henceforth take with him through the Gate of Death that which will free him from isolation in the spiritual world. Not only for the physical evolution of mankind is the Event of Palestine the centre and focal point; the same is true for the other worlds to which man belongs. When the Mystery of Golgotha had been accomplished, when the Death on the Cross had been suffered, then did the Christ appear in the world where the souls of men sojourn after death, and set limits to the power of Ahriman. And from this moment on, the region which the Greeks had called the realm of Shades was shot through by a spiritual lightning-flash announcing to its dwellers that Light was now returning to it again. What was achieved for the physical world through the Mystery of Golgotha shed its light also into the spiritual world...

All that was conferred upon human evolution through the coming of Christ has been working in it like a seed. Only by degrees can the seed ripen. Up to the present, no more than the minutest part of the depths of the new wisdom has found its way into physical existence. We are but at the beginning of Christian evolution. *(Occult Science,* Chapter IV, p.217).

Elsewhere, Steiner characterizes the same event in the following words, saying about Christ:

... because he went through death in a human body, he could, after death, do something which his former fellow-gods were not able to do. These former fellow-gods were opposed by something like a hostile world, which in earlier times was called Hell. But the power of these spiritual beings extended only as far as the gates of Hell; the divine-spiritual beings experienced it as a world in opposition to them. They saw it arise out of the earth, they experienced it as an extraordinarily formidable world; but of course they were only in contact with that world in an indirect way through Man, they could only look at it, so to speak. Because Christ had descended to earth and himself had become Man he was able to enter into the realm of ahrimanic powers and conquer them. (GA 223, April 1, 1923)*

The cosmic Christ since his earthly incarnation

Christ does not desert the earth at his so-called Ascension. Although his being expands again from a purely human to a cosmic dimension, this does not mean that he has been drawn away from conditions on earth. In a certain sense the earth now becomes the centre of his working, also within the cosmos. Therefore it can be said that the spiritual sphere of the earth 'is permeated, as if saturated, by the Christ-being since then.' The clairvoyant eye 'looks into the ether sphere of the earth and beholds the Christ-being.' (GA 129, August 21, 1911).

CHRIST AND THE EARTH

From our considerations so far it has already become clear that we must regard the Christ, the *logos* in the sense of the Gospel of John, as the creator, also of things earthly; the earthly substances and forces have been permeated by divine activity and life from the beginning. But this origin has become darkened, hardened, estranged from itself through the working of the adversary powers and the consequences of the Fall. As a result, the world now appears to exist without spirit and devoid of all divine beings.

In contrast to this, Rudolf Steiner describes how earth-existence, too, has been permeated anew by the cosmic working of Christ, as a significant effect of the deed of Christ:

When the mystery of Golgotha took place, what had been raying in from the cosmos passed over into the spiritual substance of the earth, and since that time it has been

---

* Regarding the 'descent into hell,' see also GA 155, July 15, 1914 and GA 161, April 2 and 3, 1915.

united with the spirit of the earth. When Paul became clairvoyant outside Damascus, he could perceive that what previously was in the cosmos had now passed over into the spirit of the earth. (GA 15, Lecture 3).

In this same connection, Rudolf Steiner goes a step further: The working of Christ does not only extend to the spirit of the earth (etheric and astral); it reaches as far as the physical substances, too. He says that, in times to come, leaders of mankind:

will be able to teach people that substance is permeated by the spirit of Christ, down to the smallest particle of the world. And, however strange it may seem, in the future there will be chemists and physicists who will teach chemistry and physics not as it is taught nowadays ... but who will teach: matter is constructed according to the way in which Christ has gradually ordered it! It will be possible to find the Christ even within the laws of chemistry and physics. Spiritual chemistry and spiritual physics — that is what will come in the future. *(ibid.)*[8]

In this sense one can say that Christ has become 'the spirit of the earth,' that is, the earth is 'his body.'

In the same way as your spirit and soul live in your body, so the soul and spirit of the earth live in the earth-body which consists of stones, plants and animals, and on which you walk; and this soul-spirit, this earth-spirit, that is the Christ. Christ is the spirit of the earth ... he can say [that he is] the spirit of the whole earth, and will become so ever more. (GA 103, May 26, 1908).

What we have just said about the continued working of Christ's resurrection body applies to the whole earth in a wider sense: the earth is, as it were, spiritually-potentially irradiated by the power of the Resurrection, and will ultimately have transformed and spiritualized its earthly-bodily aspect, just as the body of Jesus was transformed and spiritualized as a germ for everything that was to follow. What is 'potentially' present in everything earthly is to become ever more 'actual' and effective now.

This secret of Christ's union with the earth comes to expression in a central place in Christianity: in the concept of Communion. Within earth existence, the Christ urges onward the spiritualization of everything earthly. This becomes reality to the highest degree in the sacrament, when bread and wine are transformed into his 'body' and his 'blood.'

> In the sense of John's Gospel, we attain an infinitely deeper insight into the concept of Communion when we know about Christ, the spirit of the earth, and about bread which has been obtained from the body of the earth. Christ points to it and says: That is my body! We reach an infinitely deeper level of feeling for the Communion when we learn in this way to feel that the blood flowing from the wounds of the Saviour is significant not only for human beings but for the cosmos, in that it gives the earth the strength to continue its evolution. (GA 103, May 26, 1908).

In this central sacrament, then, we see something of the beginning spiritualization of the earth, which is to lead into the future. Something which, as we have said, is already potentially and spiritually present in all things earthly — the resurrection-reality of the cosmic Christ — becomes full, actual reality in the transubstantiation, the transformation of the bread and wine on the altar into the body and blood of Christ. Therefore Rudolf Steiner can say:

> Sacramentalism is not symbolism ... processes which are perceptible to the senses are performed, into which the spirit streams in the doing. Real spiritual phenomena occur within the ritual in a manner perceptible to the senses ... it is not so that in the Communion we eat merely the substance we are given; then it would not be a sacrament. (GA 318, September 8, 1924).

Outer earth-existence will in due course vanish, ultimately nothing of it will remain:

> but if one were then to look back at those events which have always taken place on this earth as Rituals of Offering, then their effects would be present; for, when it is carried out in the right way, the ritual is more real than nature. More real than nature; if this is acknowledged not only theoretically but in its full import, it means something tremendous — it adds even more weight to the saying, 'Heaven and earth will pass away, but my words will not pass away.' (GA 344, September 7, 1922).[9]

CHRIST AND MAN

We may therefore regard the permeation and gradual spiritualization of the earth by the cosmic creating-powers of Christ as a first significant effect of his Resurrection. A second effect, however, relates to mankind itself. We have already considered one aspect, under the motto: 'Christ died for all human beings.' About this, Rudolf Steiner says:

Christ left heaven in order to exchange this, his dwelling-place, for the earth ... since the event of Whitsun, the Christ-being is with human souls on earth; previously, it was not with human souls on earth[10] ... for what reason did the events of Palestine take place? It was in order that the divine-spiritual Being of Christ could assume the form which it needed so as to be able to be in community with human souls on earth. (GA 148, October 3, 1913).

The consequence of this is:

If a modern human being only delves deeply enough into himself, he will find the Christ. Because ... Christ has united himself with mankind on earth, human beings find Christ in the depths of their own being, if they probe deeply enough. (GA 221, February 10, 1923).

And with regard to Christ, a human being can say:

At one time I looked up to the constellations of the stars in order to fathom human destiny on earth. Now I look to Man, and learn to recognize how this human being lights up for the universe, after having attained humanity on earth, being permeated by the Christ-substance. *(ibid.)*

At the same time, this is a progressive, evolving process which is directed at a certain aim:

But now, we know that through this Christ-impulse something has come to earth, something has flowed into mankind, which is for the benefit of all mankind, in that it shines out into the culture of mankind; that which went through death is like a seed which multiplies and which can enter into the individual souls of human beings and flourish there ... what will be the outcome when the earth shall have come to its goal, its end? The Christ who drew near from regions far from the earth and united himself with the earth — he will be the reality of the earth at its end, he will be the spirit of the earth. Certainly, he is that already now, only: human souls will then be permeated by him, human beings will form a totality together with him. (GA 143, May 8, 1912).

Another statement by Rudolf Steiner describes the relationship between Man and Christ vividly:

Since the mystery of Golgotha, Christ is reachable for the human soul. And its relationship to him does not need to remain undefined and darkly emotional-mystical; it can become a connection which is completely concrete, humanly profound and of total clarity. Then, however, what the human soul must know about its own supersensible nature will stream into the soul from its life with Christ ... Within himself, in a cosmically justifiable way, Christ bears the future impulses for mankind. For the human soul, to unite with him means taking into itself its own germs for the future in a way which is cosmically justified. [Through such a relationship to Christ, Man experiences something which leads to a deeper acknowledgement of Christ] ... when the experience of life with Christ is duly attributed to grace: the flow of the spiritual into the human soul. (GA 26, November 2, 1924).[11]

THE EFFECT ON THE LIFE AFTER DEATH

A further important motif arises from Rudolf Steiner's descriptions of the effect which Man's relationship to Christ has on life after death. Let us recall the account of Christ's own experiences of death, the underworld and the realm of those who have died; linking on to that we can say: Christ's working for Man also extends to the life after death now. In many lectures by Rudolf Steiner he shows how the relationship to Christ which a human being forms during his lifetime continues to work on beyond the threshold of death, helping, awakening, enlightening, guiding.[12]

THE FUTURE OF EARTH AND MANKIND

With the death of Christ, a power for the future appeared for both earth and mankind, a power which is to become increasingly active in earthly being and within the evolution of mankind:

> What would have happened to the evolution of the earth after its decline, caused by Man [through the Fall], if the mystery of Golgotha had not given it a new impulse? Certain as it is that a plant cannot develop further if the fruit-bud is torn off, just as certain is it that the earth could not have continued its evolution if the mystery of Golgotha had not taken place! (GA 175, April 12, 1917).

But for this development to work in the right way, human consciousness, human understanding and the human will must be engaged in it and make a contribution in the right way. Steiner says:

> [Christ] gave the impulse for this. I might say that the inclined plane has continued still further downwards; and greater and greater power needs to be applied by the Christ-impulse to impart an upward movement to the earth. In a certain respect we have definitely been raised up a little since the mystery of Golgotha, but it has largely happened without Man's thinking consciousness. But human beings must also learn to assist the world-process in a conscious way. (GA 175, April 12, 1917).[13]

Elsewhere, Rudolf Steiner turns his attention to human guilt and straying which are bound up with our destiny on earth. He describes how only a part of these failings and this guilt can be made good by human beings themselves (in future incarnations on earth); a remnant is left which Man cannot deal with. This touches not least on the damage which Man does to the existence of the earth through his life here. All this cannot be made good by him. Especially here, it would be necessary to explain the whole context; however, we must content ourselves with extracting a core statement which relates to our subject:

This is what Rudolf Steiner says:

> Because he belongs to another realm, Christ is the one who is able to wipe out our guilt and our sins in the world, to take them upon himself ... It is as a result of the

deed of Christ that the whole earth continues to evolve with Man. All the guilt which would accumulate for the earth would expel the earth into darkness, and we would have no planet for further development. (GA 155, July 15, 1914).

And similarly, later:

Because we carry death within ourselves, the living Christ must permeate us, so that he may enliven what we leave behind as spiritual earth-being. The Christ, the living *logos,* permeates and enlivens that which separates off from us by way of objective sin, of objective guilt which we do not take further in our karma; and because he enlivens it, a living earth will develop into a living Jupiter. That is the result of the mystery of Golgotha. (GA 155, July 16, 1914).[14]

With the words about the future Jupiter, a motif has been raised which we now ought to look at in more detail. Rudolf Steiner dealt with it from the most varied points of view in many lectures; a fundamental description can be found in his book *Occult Science* at the end of Chapter VI, 'Present and future evolution of the earth and of mankind' (GA 13).* He describes how, to clairvoyant sight, a 'future form' of the earth becomes visible, which is contained within the present earth 'like a seed':

On closer inspection it becomes apparent that what, in a sense, is the outcome of what happens on earth continuously flows into this future form ... we could call this future structure the Jupiter condition.

Man is already now engaged in working on this future form of the earth;[15] the aim is that something which has never before existed in this form should be created in the evolution of the world, something which only Man can bring about in evolution. Man will evolve further; the core of his being, his 'Ego' will attain a high degree of creative independence.

This is the secret of all future evolution: that the knowledge, and also everything which Man achieves out of a true understanding of evolution, is like a field of

* See also *Cosmic Memory* (GA 11), Chapter 13, 'The earth and its future'; and GA 110, April 14, 1909.

grain which must ripen into love. And according to how
great the yield is of the power of love, that same
amount of creativity will be achieved for the future. The
most powerful forces will be in what will have become
of the love, and these will lead to the previously
described outcome: spiritualization of the earth. And in
proportion to the amount of spiritual knowledge which
flows into the evolution of mankind and earth, there
will be viable germs available for the future. Through
what it is, spiritual knowledge is transformed into
love ... (GA 13).

From the time of the earth-condition onwards, the
wisdom of the outer world becomes inner wisdom in
Man. And when it has become internalized in him, it
becomes the germ of love; wisdom is the precondition for
love. Love is the outcome of wisdom which has been
reborn in the 'Ego.'

In the same way as the earth — as the outcome of its previous
evolution — displays wisdom everywhere, the future Jupiter will
be characterized throughout by love; a 'cosmos of love' is to
arise: a future form of existence for the earth, which, in the
Revelation to John, is called 'the New Jerusalem.'

Now, all this is intimately bound up with the working of
Christ in Man; for how does Man achieve the ability to develop
love?

The Christ became the centre as regards the hallowing
and purification of the separate personalities of human
beings. Everything which a human being can carry over
as fruit from his single personality into his individuality
he achieves by having a connection to the Christ-being.
Our personality is purified and ennobled when we look to
the Christ-being and feel connected to him. (GA 102,
March 24, 1908).

THE NEW CREATION: A NEW COSMOS

It has probably become apparent from what has been presented
up to this point that Rudolf Steiner's descriptions of the future
evolution of mankind and earth surpass by far what it has been

possible to say about it before, and that applies to both the diversity and concreteness of his statements.

All the same, we must now take one last step further, for up to now it might seem as if this future evolution only concerns mankind and earth, inasmuch as they are both to go through a transformation and spiritualization in future stages of development. However, already in the New Testament the 'heavens' — that is, the entire 'cosmos' — is included in a process of decline and new creation, for instance Luke 21: 'Heaven and earth will pass away'; immediately before that, there is mention of 'signs' which will 'appear' in (or: on) 'sun, moon and stars'; or in the Revelation to John, 21: 'And I saw a new heaven and a new earth. The former heaven and the former earth had passed away'; the new creation appears as the 'New Jerusalem,' that is, no longer in the picture of Paradise, the garden, the divine creation as it was originally, but in the picture of a city; yet a city is man-made, or at least shaped by human beings. We have seen how concrete and varied the description can be of the participation of Man in the shaping of the 'future form of the earth,' the future Jupiter — with and through Christ. Can something similar now also be said as regards the whole cosmos?

There were already a few hints in the previous descriptions, for instance that 'the cross on Golgotha is not only to be seen as though it merely expressed something earthly, but rather, the cross on Golgotha is significant for the whole cosmos: this is what was known in esoteric Christianity' (see p.115); or: 'When the cross was raised on Golgotha and the blood flowed from the wounds of Christ-Jesus, at that moment a new cosmic centre-point was created ...' (see p.116).

In the section about the 'descent into hell' it became clear that the descent of Christ into Ahriman's 'realm of shadows' opened the access to this 'realm' anew to those spiritual beings to whom it had been barred. '... it was experienced as extraordinarily significant for the spiritual world that Christ descended into a human body and went through death' — for '... because he went through death in a human body, he could, after death, do something which his former fellow-gods* were not able to do'

---

* Rudolf Steiner uses the expression 'gods,' for spiritual (angel) beings.

(see p.119), namely: begin to guide the human and spiritual forces which had fallen prey to the death-forces of Ahriman into a forward direction of evolution once more.

This is an extraordinarily significant statement; it is not for nothing that the cross and the death of Christ occupy such central positions in Christianity; for, through Christ's 'victory over death,' access was achieved to the precious forces which, on the one hand, Ahriman had seized for himself, but which also had arisen within Man through his struggle with death and evil, and which were waiting to be redeemed and raised up; these words of Christ point to that fact: 'I was dead — and yet I bear the life of the world through all aeons. Mine is the key to the realm of death and of the shades.' (Rev.1:18) It cannot be a matter of indifference to the Godhead and the spiritual beings what happens to the realm and the forces of Ahriman — whether their return to ongoing evolution, and thereby also the redemption of evil, will succeed, so that the divine world may receive back what was lost to it through the Fall and the influence of evil: that that may be returned in a new form, matured by having passed through death, transformed, enhanced.[16]

These three motifs offer an insight into why the deed of Christ is significant for the spiritual world and its (angel) beings; and that means: for the cosmos. For, as we have mentioned several times already, the cosmos which surrounds us is by no means only a mass of material processes; rather, it is a manifestation of the spiritual world and its beings, who have created the planets and the world of the fixed stars as their external expression, their cosmic 'body.' It is into this realm of spiritual-cosmic beings behind the external cosmos that the deed of Christ works; the cross is relevant for the whole cosmos, insofar as that is permeated by the spirit; it forms 'a new cosmic centre-point'; Christ guides the underworld-forces of Ahriman — which, as such, also have a mighty, 'cosmic' dimension — back towards ongoing evolution: this is bound to lead to a change in all 'spiritual constellations'; whilst the spiritual world and its beings themselves undergo further development, are transformed, enlivened and ripened through the deed of Christ, new cosmic relationships and movements are created which can best be described as 'a new heaven.'[17] In the Revelation to John, this fact is shown in image as the disappearance of sun and moon, their light being replaced by the indwelling of the Godhead in the New Jerusalem (Rev.21:23).

After all this, we can safely assume that, in Christ and together with him, Man has a part to play in all these processes; that is also implicit in the image of the 'heavenly city,' as we have already mentioned. Let us therefore ask what anthroposophy has to say about this.

THE CO-OPERATION OF MAN: FREEDOM AND LOVE

It is here that we come to the most profound and probably also the most far-reaching description in this whole connection. It is an integral part of the image of Man in anthroposophy. As we have already seen from previous statements, Man is not the insignificant being in the universe which at first sight he may appear to be. Through his union with Christ, Man does not only find a future for himself; he also becomes the starting point for a new creation. This is not only an anthroposophical truth — it can be found already in Paul (Romans 8).

Rudolf Steiner says that we can become aware that:
the cosmic Christ descended from spiritual worlds,
because that world must be closed to human perception
from now on, and because Man must grasp what is lying
within him as a germ for the future ... the germ for the
future lies within Man. But this germ must be made
fertile through the Christ-Jesus. If it is not rendered
fertile, it takes on ahrimanic form, and the earth is lead
towards a chaotic goal. (GA 181, August 6, 1918).

Let us add a few details from Rudolf Steiner's description:
Just as we human beings have to use materials from the
kingdoms beneath us for constructing our machines —
that is, principally from the kingdoms of minerals and
plants, iron and wood — so the Angeloi, Archangeloi and
Archai also need materials to — well alright, let us say
'build,' even though the word is, of course, very crude —
to build what they have to build up. And what are their
materials? For much of what the Angeloi, Archangeloi
and Archai have to achieve, the material is precisely those

thoughts which human beings regard as their own property. It is really so: While we wander through the world
and harbour our thoughts, looking at our thought-life from
the inside, so to speak, and regard it as our property, the
Angeloi, Archangeloi and Archai work upon our thoughts
without us knowing it ... they carry out their exalted
activity with these materials through their wisdom which
transcends the human entity; but the materials must be provided by what lies within us. (GA 174b, March 15, 1916).

The description goes even further in other lectures: if we come
to an awareness of the far-reaching significance of the power of
human knowledge, this can lead us to work on enhancing our
potential for insight, so that 'higher spiritual beings can receive
a certain "nourishment" from the concepts we have made our
own.' (GA 170, August 7, 1916).

This motif of 'nourishment' also appears in another lecture,
where it is widened and also deepened:

[Man] introduces into this spiritual world what he has
experienced here on earth while waking and sleeping.
That is nourishment for the cosmos, that is what the
cosmos needs constantly in order to continue to exist.
What we human beings experience on earth in easy and
hard destinies, this we convey into the cosmos some time
after death; and therefore we feel our human nature
dissolve into the cosmos as nourishment. These are
mighty and exalted experiences which Man has between
death and a new birth ... what we go through here on
earth is shared out in the cosmos, so that it can become
nourishment for the cosmos, so that the cosmos can
continue to exist, so that the cosmos can gain new
impetus for its stars and their movements. (From GA 226,
May 16, 1923).

And lastly, the following motif takes us into even higher
realms, to the highest sphere of angelic beings, the Cherubim: for
the third and second hierarchy, Man's higher powers of knowledge is 'building material' and 'nourishment'; for the first hierarchy it becomes 'light.' 'What happens to this "spirit-light" ...?
The Cherubim come, gather this light and use it for the future
ordering of the world.' (GA 156, December 19, 1914).

It becomes clear that it is by no means only human powers of knowledge which are of significance for the continued existence and further development of the spiritual world; powers of morality, the capacity for love, reach even higher into that world:

> ... insofar as [human actions and deeds] are moral actions and deeds, these moral deeds are gathered by the Seraphim. These moral deeds are the 'source of warmth' for the entire structure of the world ... under the influence of moral deeds, the Seraphim attain those forces through which the order of the cosmos is maintained, in the same way as the physical world-order is maintained through physical warmth. *(ibid.)*

All these far-reaching thoughts are probably only more or less acceptable if we bear in mind that the image of God is 'invested' in Man — hidden, concealed by the consequences of the Fall, but not destroyed. And in the freedom of Man's knowledge and insight, in the love within human actions, these buried divine possibilities awaken and make themselves felt — initially quite tentatively, but growing towards ever greater sovereignty in the future. This 'investment' of divine possibilities in Man is the soil in which the future significance of Man grows.

But let us go a little further in unfolding these motifs:

> At this point, you begin to sense what the life which is poured out in the world actually is. Where are its sources? They are to be found in those impulses and ideas which stimulate moral ideals, which in turn arouse enthusiasm in human beings. We come to the point where we can say to ourselves that when we allow ourselves to be fired by moral ideals now, then these ray out life and tone and light and become world-creating. We become bearers of world-creativity, and the source of this creativity is morality. (GA 202, December 18, 1920).

In this sense, it is our moral will which 'represents the growth-forces in the universe.' (GA 202, December 25, 1920).[18]

We can now summarize all that we have considered so far, by once more relating it to the working of the cosmic Christ:

> When Christ shall have found a dwelling in human souls, then the Christ-power will again shine out from the earth-aura towards those worlds which the Christ left for the

salvation of human beings on earth, and the entire cosmos
will be permeated by Christ. (GA 152, June 1, 1914).

And further:

The power of Christ imprints the image of Man upon the
cosmos ... from the time since the Christ-impulse has
been living with the earth, Man, as a self-aware being,
is being given back to the cosmos. Once a being of
worlds, Man has become a being of earth; he has the
potential to become a being of worlds again, when first
he has become himself as a being of earth. (GA 26,
January 1925).

In Man, something completely new enters into the world; and
the spiritual beings are to gain a share of this new, future-
orientated achievement. Because of the importance of the next
quotation it will be given at length; once again, it is about
coming to terms with evil, with Lucifer* who gave Man the
impulse to assert himself, and thereby enabled him to take a first
step towards freedom:

A time will come when the luciferic powers — which
had to descend to a certain lower development during the
moon-evolution for the benefit of human freedom, and for
this reason did not themselves have the opportunity to
experience the Christ-power on earth — a time will come
when these powers will experience the Christ-power
through Man and be redeemed. Man will redeem Lucifer
if he takes the Christ-power into himself in the
appropriate way. And thereby Man also becomes stronger
than he would otherwise have become. For imagine that
Man had not received the luciferic forces; then the Christ-
power would shine forth, but it would not encounter the
resistance of the luciferic forces, and it would be
impossible for Man to advance as far in goodness, truth
and wisdom as he can when he has to conquer these
opposing forces ...

Only now do we understand the whole dignity and
significance of Man among the members of our

---

* For the distinction between Ahriman and Lucifer, see H.-W. Schroeder, *Der
Mensch und das Böse*.

hierarchies, and when we look up to the glory and
magnitude of the higher hierarchies, we say to ourselves:
Although they are so great, so wise, so good that they
never can stray from the true path, yet it is Man's great
mission to bring freedom into the world, and only
through freedom that which one can call love in the true
sense of the word. For without freedom, love is
impossible. Any being which is obliged to obey an urge
or impulse — well, it obeys it; but for a being who could
also act differently, there is only one power to make it
follow: love. Freedom and love are two polarities which
belong together. Therefore, if love was to enter into our
cosmos, it could only happen through freedom, that is to
say, through Lucifer and his conqueror, and at the same
time through Man's redeemer, through the Christ. That is
why the earth is the cosmos of love and freedom ... in
this way we have tried to fathom the meaning of Man
through the meaning of the cosmos. (GA 110, April 18,
1909).

So when Man, bearing within himself the fruit of a long and
thoroughgoing development, slowly grows into being the image
of God again in a new way and thereby reveals his origins in the
Godhead, then something of the being of the divine itself can
come to revelation, something which until then had been concealed. Not until shortly before his death did Rudolf Steiner
speak in this way about that most profound mystery:

[Man lives] as a God-permeated being in a world which
is not permeated by God. Into this world which has
become God-forsaken Man will bring what is within him,
what his being has become during this aeon.

It will be 'humanness' which will unfold itself into the
evolution of the world. The divine-spiritual world in
which Man had his origins will be able, in the form of an
expanding cosmic human entity, to illumine the cosmos
which, for now, is only present as an image of the divine-
spiritual world.

It will no longer be the same entity that once was the
cosmos which will light up through the agency of
mankind. In going through the stage of 'humanness,' the

divine-spiritual world will take on a nature which it has not revealed before. (GA 26, October 25, 1924).

Let us conclude this section with a text from Rudolf Steiner's fundamental book *How to Know Higher Worlds*. At the end of that book he discusses the question with which we have been concerned here:

[Man] sees that he himself belonged to a supersensible world before he arrived in this world of the senses for the first time. But this former supersensible world needed to pass through the sensory stage; without this passage, its further development would not have been possible. It will only be when certain beings within the realm of the senses shall have evolved appropriate capacities that the supersensible world will be able to go forward. And these individuals are the human beings. It follows that, as they live now, they are descended from an imperfect stage of spiritual existence, and that, even within this existence, they are led towards the degree of perfection which will make them fit to work further in the higher world. — And here the vista opens on the future. It reveals a higher stage of the supersensible world; within that world will be found the fruits which have been formed in the world of the senses. This latter world as such will be overcome; but its results, its products, will be incorporated into a higher world.

SUMMARY

In this chapter I have given an overview of Rudolf Steiner's statements about the being of the cosmic Christ. For any reader who is not familiar with anthroposophy, some of the quotations I have presented will have been rather challenging. However, it is my hope that the great and freely accessible life's work of Rudolf Steiner will make it possible for even a critical reader not to judge too quickly about subjects which actually demand a much more thorough presentation.

My aim, nevertheless, was to give at least an outline of the great, encompassing and finely detailed picture of the cosmic working of Christ which can arise through the statements of

Rudolf Steiner. Anyone who wishes to work through and fill out this picture for himself will find indications to this end in the relevant notes.

In conclusion, let us attempt a brief summary:

I. Pre-existence
— The *logos* — the second person of the Godhead — the cosmic Christ is the 'creator.'
— The world was created through the 'Word' — it is a 'solidified' word of God, every created being is, as it were, a letter in this word.
— In earlier times, Man experienced the 'echo' of the speaking word in earthly nature and in the world of the stars.
— As 'micro-*logos*,' Man is himself a creature of the divine Word — not as a 'letter,' however, but himself a complete 'word.'
— That is why he has been given the word in the form of language.
— The cosmic Christ descends by stages through realms of angelic beings to the earth. These realms are represented outwardly by the world of the fixed stars and the planetary spheres. During this descent, Christ becomes a 'sun being' for a while — he was revered in this form by Zarathustra, in Egypt, in Greece.

II. The earthly working
— At the Baptism by John in the Jordan, the cosmic Christ enters into the earthly body of Jesus of Nazareth.
— The Evangelists had clairvoyant access to the Christ event; the gospels show something of the cosmic dimension of Christ, each in its own way.
— For the Christ, becoming Man meant infinite suffering. From this suffering proceeded the power to transform and spiritualize the earthly body, and which led eventually to the Resurrection Body.
— This Body is, as is also the spiritualized blood of Christ, a reality which continues to work in mankind and the earth.

— They form the basis for the transubstantiation of bread and wine into the 'body and blood of Christ,' and also for the ongoing spiritualization of the earth.

— Christ died for all human beings: his victory over death brought about rejuvenation and enlivening for all human bodies — his descent into hell brought light into the realm of shadows of Ahriman for all souls who had died.

III. The continued working

— Christ continues to keep the earth as a new cosmic centre-point, even as he returns to the cosmos.

— he begins to permeate the earth ever more, right into the substances — the earth becomes his 'body.' This is full reality already now in the Eucharist (transubstantiation and communion).

— Mankind, too, is being increasingly permeated by the cosmic working of Christ — within the depths of his being, Man finds the Christ.

— The working of Christ also extends to the life after death.

— Christ makes it possible for Man to have a cosmic future: He takes upon himself the failings and sins which Man cannot make good himself; thereby he makes it possible for the earth and mankind to go forward in a living way towards the future Jupiter.

  He enables Man to play an independent part, and later to be creative himself, in this development: above all, it is out of the higher insights and knowledge and the moral deeds of Man that the future is built.

  For the spiritual beings these become light and warmth, nourishment and 'building materials' — the new cosmos is made out of them, even beyond the future Jupiter.

— Through Christ, the possibility of freedom and love arise in Man; they are to be imprinted upon the cosmos as new powers, brought in offering by Man.

— Thereby a revelation becomes possible for the Godhead also; a revelation which previously had to remain concealed.

137

6. The cosmic Christ within The Christian Community

Right from the beginning of its work, The Christian Community has always spoken of the cosmic dimension of Christ. Above all, knowing about the cosmic Christ proves to be fundamental to a deeper understanding of the Old and the New Testament. The Christian Community stands within the tradition of early Christianity in that it looks to the cosmic aspect of Christ and includes this in its religious life and worship.

Divine worship in The Christian Community, which unfolds in the renewed sacraments, brings the cosmic aspect of Christ to expression in manifold ways.

The Act of Consecration of Man

The Act of Consecration of Man, the Christian Mass in renewed form, constitutes the centre of the worship of the congregation. The 'transformation' (transubstantiation) of bread and wine takes place there: the cosmic life of Christ is imparted to the earthly bread and the earthly wine, takes hold of them and permeates them, thereby making them into nourishment of a 'higher' kind for Man. Bread and wine are accepted by Christ and taken up into his supersensible body, into his spiritualized blood. To the clairvoyant eye, this becomes perceptible: in the transubstantiation, both substances begin to shine, sunlike, in the spirit, because something of the cosmic life of Christ has joined itself to them.

We have mentioned earlier (see p.35f) that the reality of Christ can be actual at very different levels: at the level of the spirit, for instance, in concentration, meditation[1]; at the level of the soul in adoration, devotion, prayer; already at a deep level when it enters into the circumstances of our life and our conduct (etheric), but then even more deeply — right into the physical nature of the body and into earthly substance.

Furthermore, we were able to acquire a deeper understanding of transubstantiation from anthroposophy (see p.121f above). We had to say to ourselves: if it is true that all being and all existence has come about through the Word, the *logos,* that is, through the cosmic Christ (John 1), then it must also be within Christ's power fully to reclaim for himself, right into the depths of material substance, this existence and being which was partially torn from him through the Fall and the working of the adversaries. It is not for nothing that the Gospel of Matthew concludes with the Christ-word: 'Now all creative power in heaven and on earth has been given me.' (Matt.28:18). This power was at work in the Last Supper when Christ suffused bread and wine with his power of life, so making them into his 'body' and his 'blood.' This same power also becomes active now when the 'transubstantiation' is fulfilled at the altar.

In that sense, the centre of Christian worship in the 're-collection,' the 'calling to mind' of Christ's life, is itself a 'cosmic-earthly' mystery. At a tiny point within earthly events, on the altar, the meaning of all things earthly radiates forth like a sun — not as a pale symbol or ineffectual image, but as earthly-cosmic reality: a point of germination for further transformation in the future.

OFFERING

The presence of Christ is already called upon during the preparation for this event of transformation: May the spirit who permeates the widths of space and the depths of time come to us, invokes the offering prayer. The 'presence' of Christ, which ultimately permeates everything, is nevertheless 'real' in varying degrees; it will be more 'present' for us in a deed of love than in one of hate: in the former, helping in spirit, in the latter, sharing in the suffering. In prayer, Christ will be able to be more consciously and actually present for us than in moments of dull brooding; and his presence can be experienced more 'densely' and 'deeply' in a praying congregation than in the prayer of a single individual.

So when we speak of the cosmic spirit 'coming to us' in the Offering, this is no contradiction of the fact that he already 'is there'; after all, at the same time — and later, repeatedly — we hear 'Christ in us!'; and the call 'Christ in you' is heard throughout the entire Act of Consecration of Man. But this 'being there' can become ever deeper, denser and more encompassing, stage by stage.

It is entirely possible to find comparable experiences in our everyday, human life: a meeting with one person may be spiritually stimulating and brilliant for us, yet leave us 'cold' in our deeper feelings. With another person we are also touched and warmed in our feelings and will; and finally, we also know of human encounters which go even deeper, which perhaps resound for a long time in the depths of our humanity, and which can accompany us, enlivening and even healing us.

And, as well as interactions between human beings, there are also effects of human beings upon the world. This becomes particularly clear through negative examples: a place which was the scene of an evil deed will long retain its spooky atmosphere. But places of positive spiritual activity we can experience as 'consecrated,' without having to succumb to mere simple-minded fancy.

Against the background of such thoughts it can become clearer what can be meant by this 'coming-to-us' in the Offering: the presence of Christ which — expressed in general terms — is 'already there,' is to be strengthened. Christ is addressed as the Spirit who works in the widths of space and the depths of time; and, in another place, as the 'Spirit Word' who wields through the world. In other words, his cosmic power is being indicated, the power which now is to work in the congregation's offering. The word about 'coming-to-us' is therefore taken further through words which speak of the 'hallowing' of the offering by the 'holy being' of Christ. And surely, if the hallowing is to become concrete, it can only be through this: that the offering — bread and wine — is taken up by the power of Christ, permeated and transformed into becoming bearers of his body, his blood.

TRANSUBSTANTIATION

Let us now look at some other words of prayer which immediately precede the event of transformation. In them, the Father God is addressed: may He let live in this offering the body and the blood of His Son who has his being in love. Again we have the cosmic aspect before us here — just at the moment when the being of Christ is about to unite with the earthly substances of bread and wine: in them, something of the cosmic life of the Son is to be present.

These words contain extraordinary statements about the cosmic Christ: his 'being' is love — a very Johannine saying. In John's Prologue, the unfolding of the *logos* into life and light is depicted; in John's Gospel itself this unfolding forges ahead towards a third revelation. This revelation is love. 'A new task and aim I give you: Love one another!' (John 13:34)[2] Life — light — love: these are the three stages of revelation of the cosmic Christ, but his deepest being is love.

Now a third statement is made; for there is mention of the 'body' and the 'blood' of the Son, even before bread and wine have been 'transformed.' If we take these words seriously, this means neither more nor less than that even the cosmic Christ is not to be thought of as 'purely spiritual,' but that he has his being in a supersensible bodily nature and in a supersensible stream of life. Here we can cast our mind back to thoughts developed earlier where we spoke of the continued working of the resurrection body of Christ and of his spiritualized 'blood' which continues to circulate supersensibly within the life of the earth, in its 'aura.' It became clear to us that the 'body' and 'blood' of Christ are not to be thought of as being in one 'place,' in isolation — in the way in which our earthly body is bound to one particular place at any given moment and is separate from all other bodies. Rather, here the situation is — to use a not unrealistic comparison — as with the sun: it rays forth its being in the light which proceeds from it; this light is imbued with warmth as with a stream of life; sunlight and sun-warmth can penetrate into anything which exposes itself to its power.

In the 'transubstantiation' we, as it were, raise the bread and the wine towards the spiritual sun, the cosmic Christ: we expose the earthly substances to his sunlike influence. The cosmic Christ is, so to speak, surrounded by a supersensible 'body' of radiating spiritual forces, that is, by resurrection power and authority; and this in turn is imbued with a spiritual stream of life which bears within it healing, strengthening and harmonizing impulses of life. These radiating forces and this stream of life can also take hold of earthly substance and permeate it — in the sense of the Christ-word we have already quoted: 'All creative power in heaven and on the earth has been given me.' As this supersensible 'body' and this spiritualized 'blood' of the cosmic Christ stream out over bread and wine, surrounding them with a shining, sunlike aura and permeating them, the bread and the wine become bearers of this body, this blood of Christ; and thereby for us human beings they become his body and his blood.

COMMUNION

At the end of the transubstantiation, the cosmic aspect of Christ is again affirmed and emphasized even more. There it is said that the Father God works in the world through Christ, creating, healing and ensouling it, and, together with the Spirit God, 'fulfilling' the ordering of space and the further evolution of time. With these words the event of transformation is placed into the large (cosmic) context of world evolution.

This theme receives a final enhancement when the event of the Act of Consecration of Man progresses from the transubstantiation to the communion, that is, to the fourth and last part of the Act of Consecration. Three times a wording recurs there which emphasizes the cosmic dimension of the life of Christ in an unsurpassable way: Christ is described as the One who wields through the world, bearing and ordering its life, as he receives it from the Father and makes it whole through the Spirit into all future. The communion, which is among the most intimate experiences of our existence, is thereby also opened up to reveal that dimension of it which points beyond our everyday and personal lives — for the One with whose body and blood we unite in the communion is himself of cosmic nature; in a new way which is no longer subject to the Fall, he places the most intimate aspect of our personality into the evolution of the world;

as the text indeed also says, with him we can 'continue to live';
he takes the might of the adversary from us; he transforms bread
and wine for us into 'everlasting medicine'; through him, we may
'hope for the overcoming of the sickness of sin, for the continuance of Man's being and for the preservation of our life destined
for eternity' (Words from the Creed).

We have now shown the motifs in the Act of Consecration of
Man which are relevant to our subject. We have seen that without
the cosmic aspect, the depths of the Christian Service could not
be fathomed.

The 'Christ Year'

In the cycle of festive seasons, the being of Christ unfolds, step
by step, through the course of the year: it is as if rays stream
forth, ninefold, from the fundamental unity of his being and form
the inner substance and content of the nine festive seasons:

> *Advent:* — he is eternally present; but this eternal presence
> desires to reveal itself to us, to 'arrive' among us.
> *Christmas:* — he reaffirms his relationship to earth and human
> beings.
> *Epiphany:* — he walks with us in our destiny.
> *Passiontide:* — he suffers and dies among and with mankind.
> *Easter:* — his victory over death and evil.
> *Ascension:* — he is raised to the heavenly sphere.
> *Whitsun:* — he sends the Spirit into Man's innermost being.
> *St John's Tide:* — through his messenger John the Baptist, he
> urges us to turn to the sphere of the heavens and its cosmic
> sun-power.
> *Michaelmas:* — through the Archangel Michael he strengthens
> Man's innermost being in the fight with evil.

In this context, there are two things we must bear in mind: this
entire cycle, which to us human beings appears in the Christian
Festivals as a sequence, one after the other, is in Christ himself
a unity: in him, Christmas, Passiontide, Easter, Ascension, and so
on, are reality, all at the same time. That is to say, we will
always be able to find him (and not only at Easter time) as the

'Easter Christ,' as the conqueror over death, whether it is Spring, Summer, Autumn or Winter; and equally we will also be able to experience him in any season of the year as the 'Lord of the heavenly forces upon earth' (Ascension sentence from the Creed); he is eternally present in the fullness of all his powers, encompassing heaven and earth. Nevertheless, this unfolding of his fullness into the individual stages of the cycle of the year serves an important purpose, and that for two reasons: firstly, because we human beings can only begin to experience and grasp the fullness of Christ in this way; secondly, because something actual and real happens to earth and Man with each festival.

Every year as we wend our way through the cycle of Christian festivals step by step, we can unite fully with one particular aspect of the working of Christ: so, for example, at Easter we can permeate ourselves through and through for forty days with the death-conquering power of Christ and make it our own anew every year; at Ascension, his relationship to the universe and the Father God comes into the foreground for us — and so on. What would otherwise overwhelm us — the infinite fullness in unity of Christ's being — can thereby become concrete and fathomable for us.

The second aspect of the 'Christ Year' is less immediately comprehensible, but is all the more important for that. It is so, that in every festive season something goes forth from the fullness of the Christ-being which does not only recall the events of Christ's life two thousand years ago, but which renews them, makes them present. Let us look at this more closely for Passiontide and Easter:

The Passiontide and Holy Week of the year in which we are living now, is not merely a time of remembrance of what Christ experienced and suffered two thousand years ago; rather, in the Passiontide of this year he unites anew out of his eternal presence with contemporary suffering and death in mankind. The Passion of mankind becomes his Passion this year in the time before Easter — he shares it anew, and thereby renews that power in his being which does not leave us human beings alone in the abyss. A kind of new, topical 'Yes' to the suffering and death in humanity, valid for the current moment in mankind, proceeds from the fullness of his being; he takes them upon himself anew and renews the word which he spoke then: 'What you did for the least of my brothers, that you did for me.' (Matt.25:40).

Neither is Easter merely a festival of remembrance of the Resurrection of Christ. Just because he has permeated himself anew with death and suffering, the Christ can now also fulfil anew the victory over death and evil for mankind and the earth; here, too, the events of long ago become 'topical': into all death and suffering which has occurred in mankind since the last Easter Festival he can plant the germ of his resurrection at Easter, and so also the germ of victory. Thereby the aura of the earth — as the Easter Epistle says — can shine forth anew in the universe, as it lit up at the first Easter.[3] Similar thoughts apply with regard to the other festivals.

In this way the 'Christ Year' becomes a contemporary, present event for us, because the Christ out of his fullness allows ray after ray of his being to shine into the life of earth and mankind. The new 'Epistles' of the Act of Consecration of Man speak of this; each one of them uncovers an aspect of the cosmic working of Christ.[4]

THE CHRISTIAN FESTIVALS

The basic form of the Act of Consecration of Man remains unchanged through the year. And yet the Christian festivals appear, each in their own characteristic way, through the year in an impressive manner. A midnight Christmas Service, for example, is characteristically different from a Service at Easter; different colours, different seasonal prayers bring about this different 'feel,' which then communicates itself to the mood, the 'aura' of the Service. In the wording of these different 'seasonal prayers,' which we call 'Epistles,' unique pronouncements about the cosmic dimension of Christ are to be found.

There is, of course, a cosmic component in the very notion of the Christian festivals. It comes to clear and varied expression in the 'Epistles' that these festivals are intended to be placed into the contemporary life of the earth and the cosmos.

It would be possible to misunderstand this, to think that it is being proposed that the Christian festivals should again be made to relate in a 'pagan' way to the natural year: Easter as a Spring

Celebration, St John's as Midsummer Festival, Christmas as the celebration of the winter solstice and the 'victory of the sun' in nature — and so on. This would be a narrowing of the idea of the Christian festivals, if for no other reason than that the same festivals are related to the opposite seasons in the Southern Hemisphere.

In other words, it is not the phenomena in nature which are the reason for Christian events, but the other way around: from the present life of Christ there proceed events which strive to overflow into the life of the earth also; in different regions of the earth they encounter the most varied conditions of nature with which they unite in the most varied ways. In some instances, consonances arise (for instance Easter in the Northern Hemisphere with Spring in nature), but also dissonances (Passiontide and Spring; Easter and Autumn in the Southern Hemisphere).[5]

ADVENT — CHRISTMAS — EPIPHANY

Let us look at some wordings in the 'Epistles' which speak of the cosmic aspect of Christ. In the process, we will mention a wealth of detail which will only come together into an overall picture at the end.

In Advent, the 'Divine Strength of Worlds' is referred to, who gleams in the sun and shines in promise in the bow of colour; in the first instance, we are here looking at the 'World-Word' whose past working in sun and bow of colour continues 'in promise.' Over against that, does the divine Word work in the present? The Epistle points to Man; the World-Word, it says, now speaks directly within us human beings: it calls up forces for the future in us; it awakens a 'divining' in us of the 'picture of Man's becoming' within which the becoming of God is concealed.

With this, something extraordinary, indeed enormously daring, is stated right at the beginning of the 'Christ Year: The becoming of God continues in the becoming of Man. This statement links on to John's Prologue: the Word from the Very Beginning becomes Man. The working of the divine is to develop further in and through Man; God's becoming is 'veiled' within Man: the image of Mary arises, she who bears the becoming of God within herself. That is altogether the image of the human soul: Man becomes a Christ-bearer. The *logos spermatikos* of which we have spoken (see p.92) is found again in the Advent Epistle: The eternal Word which holds within it the future of universe and Man seeks dwelling-place in Man and desires to evolve further through human destinies. Advent is the time when, every year, the strength for new becoming streams forth from the being of Christ, and when we may sense and hope for something of his strength to create future.

Advent leads us on towards Christmas, when the motif of the continued working of the *logos* in Man is developed further, indeed condenses into the incarnation of the cosmic Christ-being as human being on earth. That is to say, Christ proves to be not only the bearer of a distant future, as in Advent — he himself is Man; he is humanly near to us. Therefore the Christmas Epistle speaks of the 'drawing near' of the Creator Word which comes to heal and bless us; the Creator Spirit of the Father, it says, has chosen the earthly body for dwelling place. And more: the divine love becomes visible to us in the human being Jesus, so that our love for the unseen may be kindled. And out of this love we may join in the song of praise, the *Sanctus* of the heavenly choirs, at Christmas — sensing that the germ for the working together of mankind and the angelic world has been planted through the Christmas event.[6]

At Epiphany, the festive season which follows on from Christmas, we have an image before us which we have already considered in the chapter about the New Testament (see p.51). The cosmic dimension comes to expression in the star; but the star does not remain remote from the earth, it comes down to us human beings from distant worlds, it unites with humanity as the 'star of grace.' May the Act of Consecration be fulfilled in its light — the light of this star (the prayer continues) is to be the guide on the way for us on earth.

Thus Epiphany takes the Christmas motif of the nearness and love of the divine a considerable step further: this divine love is to become light on our everyday paths on earth; it accompanies us, 'full of grace,' in our actual, concrete destinies, in our strivings and failings; it 'walks beside us,' comforting, admonishing, forgiving, uplifting and encouraging ... a 'star of grace' which is to show us the way.[7]

Advent — the dawning sense of a divine future in and through Man; Christmas — human nearness of the divine love; Epiphany — gracious accompanying of destiny.

Now there remains only one more step to be taken to Passiontide.

PASSIONTIDE — EASTER — ASCENSION

We have already spoken in some detail about Passiontide. Here Christ does not only accompany Man on his earthly paths, as in Epiphany — here he takes the cross of mankind fully upon himself. Carrying, com-passionately, he unites with our suffering, our guilt, with want and pain; he enters into the abyss of evil.

The Passiontide Epistle therefore speaks first of Man's condition: our Self is, as it were, thrown to the ground by our entanglement in evil; the sting of evil is there and takes effect. But for just that reason our prayer is directed to the Spirit who wields in worlds afar and in the nearness of earth: that he may help to carry this and raise our Self from its fall. We call upon the cosmic love of Christ to incline towards us, to help, to heal.

This, however, already leads us beyond Passiontide towards the Easter event. For at Easter — as we have already seen above — the whole development turns around, as it were. From Christmas via Epiphany to Passiontide we have a 'descending line': Christ takes on body, incarnates into earth and mankind. But at Easter we celebrate with him the overcoming of death and darkness. Initially, therefore, Christ's victory over death on earth is referred to in the Epistle. But then the cosmic aspect of the Easter event also shows itself clearly in the Easter prayers: through the Easter victory, the earth's aura begins to shine anew in the cosmos, as it once did on Golgotha.[8] With sunlike strength, the earth begins to shine, spiritually. Christ renews the sacrifice made for mankind; this sacrifice works out into the cosmos and there tells of the future significance of the earth in the universe.

At Ascension we experience a continuation of this line, which leads out of the earth-depths of the Passion, through the Easter victory and back to the cosmos. For Ascension is the raising of

Christ to his original cosmic might, without his thereby leaving the earth behind. In the Epistle, therefore, it is said, firstly, that he continues to live in earth-existence, that he transfigures earthly with heavenly being; and that we can behold him, elevated to the heavenly for the sake of earthly being. Finally — addressing the Father — it asks that Christ may 'abide' with us, in that he now also 'abides' with the Father (John 14:23). In a second part of the Epistle, this mediating work of the cosmic Christ is characterized still further: it is said there that the power of Christ reveals itself in the heights and that we can divine and sense him in the 'realm of the clouds,' bestowing blessing on earthly being.[9]

In this way, the mystery of the cosmic Christ is proclaimed in ever new formulations, particularly at Ascension. So we have: from Passiontide to Easter — the earth begins to shine in the cosmos — and until Ascension a mighty enhancement in this respect in the Epistles.

WHITSUN — ST JOHN — MICHAELMAS

Let us now look at the last three festive seasons of the Christian year.

At Whitsun, the festival of the Holy Spirit, the words of the Epistle are about the sending of this Spirit into our souls through the Christ. Christ, having been raised to the Father, is the mediator who enables the divine Spirit to enter into the innermost being of Man. This Spirit is called the 'world physician' who can heal the sickness of mankind and earthly existence — once again, a cosmic perspective.

The Epistle for the feast of St John represents a further high point. Let us linger over this for a moment, linking up with our earlier descriptions. For now, in addition to the star (Epiphany) as an image for the cosmic working of Christ, the sun appears again. We remember that, in the gospel, star and sun were the images for the cosmic dimension of Christ at the Birth and the Transfiguration (see p.51); and we have had occasion to draw particular attention to the sun as a stage in the descent of Christ from the cosmic sphere of the stars (see p.27, 109). So when now at St John's Tide, when the external sun reaches its highest point in the Northern Hemisphere, the image of the inner, spiritual sun is used for the cosmic Christ, this is easy to understand, bearing in mind the gospel and the cosmic evolution of Christ.

The St John's Epistle begins by looking to the all-wielding and all-blessing working of the Father God. This, however, is centred in the appearance of the cosmic Christ, it 'ripens' — as the wording says — in the midst of worlds into the 'Christ-Sun.' This formulation offers an opportunity to ponder how Christianity has most often interpreted the appearing of the Son through images of an eternal 'birth' of the Father or a proceeding of the 'Word' *(Logos)* from the Father.

Here another picture can be added to these two: in the innermost centre of the Father, the 'sun' of Christ 'ripens' as a precious fruit of the being of the Father; perhaps we may add: as the 'heart' of the Father, as the very middle of His being which, sunlike, gives light and warmth to the world, radiating love — a wonderfully telling image for the cosmic Christ and his going forth from the Father God.

At the end the Epistle asks that we take Christ into our soul, him, the creator and bestower of the light. That the Christ who desired to be humanly close to us at Christmas, Epiphany and Passiontide may now appear to us again in his cosmic greatness and fullness, and so lead us on beyond ourselves.

At Michaelmas, dedicated to the Archangel Michael and the last festival season of the year (end of September to the end of October), the cosmic dimension of Christ is not missing, either: the Father God graciously sent Christ from heights of spirit into the depths of earth; his 'deed of life and death' is to continue to create into the future, so that the heavenly light should not be extinguished, which is to lighten into all future.

This reference to Christ being sent from 'heights of heaven' and to his mission for the future forms the bridge to Advent and Christmas; we have now gone through the 'Christ Year.' A nine-fold revelation lives in it for us human beings, one which renews itself year by year and thereby can unite ever more deeply with our insight and experience.

Now, in addition to the nine festive seasons during the year, there are also times 'without festivals'; at those times the 'Trinity Epistle' is read in the Act of Consecration — that is to say, an Epistle which is concerned with the three realms of Father, Son and Spirit (Trinity). The second part of this Epistle looks to the Son. First, the relationship of Christ to the nature of our humanity is indicated. But then here, too, there is heard the Johannine motif of the *logos:* he wields through the world as 'spirit-word.' Our being and life are intimately bound up with his creating and his life, indeed, they are his creating life. And finally it is said — and here something of the great perspective of the Advent Epistle works into this text — that he creates in all our soul's creating.

We can see, therefore, that in the Epistle for the 'times between' during the year we return — like music to the 'home' key — to the fundamental and basic facts which are given by the cosmic dimension of Christ: his creative working in the world, his one-ness with us human beings from the very Beginning and his 'permeation' of all that in our soul represents creative strength for the future.

Priests' Ordination, Baptism, Marriage and Burial

At the very beginning of the Ordination of Priests the cosmic dimension of Christ is indicated in an impressive way, when he is described as the One who creates in all the world's becoming. Once again, we meet the Johannine thought of the world-creating power of the *Logos,* the cosmic Christ.

But this thought is deepened and taken further in the Ordination Service, for now the aim of the creating in the world lights up in a twofold way: to 'bear' the eternal being of the Father God in this creating, and to bring about eternal spirit-light in this becoming. The evolution of mankind and the world is not to descend into chaos, into the abyss — Christ, working creatively in all evolution, continues to bear the being of the Father God as the 'foundation' for all future development; at the same time he helps the striving for spirit-light in mankind. It is to this creating and working of Christ that the priest commits himself through his Ordination.

A further motif is joined to this; it shows us anew that in Christ we have a being before us to whom — to quote Matthew's Gospel once more — 'all creative power in heaven and on earth' has been given: the wording of the Ordination Service says that this being, 'mighty in spirit,' wields 'through all cycles of time.'

In him, the power and might of the Spirit meets us, creating and working into the future.

This vast horizon which opens up in such an impressive way, particularly in the Ordination Service, remains rather more concealed in the other sacraments; yet it is active in the background.

The Baptism speaks of the creating and working of the cosmic Christ in relation to the soul of the child which we baptize; this soul has been 'sent down' from the spiritual community of pre-natal existence to the community of earth, that is to say, it is not here by chance. But who, then, 'sent' it from the heavens to the earth?

An answer emerges when it is said that this soul has sprung from the working of the divine Word, the *Logos;* and it is also he who sends the soul. Here we can be helped by our earlier discussion of the Pauline ideas of Man's origin in Christ, his relationship to Christ (see p.45).[10] The resonance with the Trinity Epistle is evident; and John's Gospel also speaks of Man being sent by Christ: 'I have chosen you and appointed you that you should go and bear fruit ...' (John 15:16).

It is Christ in his cosmic dimension who is behind the fact that we human beings seek our ways from pre-natal existence, from the 'community of spirit,' to the 'community of earth' in which he desires to work. One aspect of the cosmic working of Christ is the sending of human souls.

Another aspect of this working is shown in the Marriage sacrament; this time it is the creating and working of Christ in and with human destinies on earth. Through his deed of offering he was able — the wording says — to transmute work of earth into 'work of spirit.' The sacrament of marriage stands under this sign: the striving for community within marriage is not to be regarded as only an earthly matter — through Christ and his commitment to us human beings it can take on a spiritual dimension. What begins as 'work of earth' can be taken up as strength, as substance born of love and suffering, and be transformed in the world of spirit.

That this is what is meant at the beginning of the sacrament of marriage, and that we are placing the marriage into the light of Christ's destiny-transforming power — this is confirmed at the end of the sacrament; for there the ceremony takes the marriage far beyond the boundaries of the personal and places it into the greater sphere of mankind; the marriage is — it states — to be not only for the 'life's happiness' of the couple, but for the good and happiness of all mankind. Such words spoken in a sacrament are not meant sentimentally, as 'beautiful words'; they indicate a reality that has become possible through Christ, they are to be taken concretely; although it is not referred to directly, behind these words we again sense the might of the cosmic Christ, working on a grand scale within the whole human race.

In the Burial, this significance of the working and creating of Christ, going beyond the purely earthly, becomes apparent from yet another side. Christ is also able to lead Man back across the threshold of death into the spiritual world, just as he first led him down to earth through birth. Through him, the soul can find its true 'home' again, because, through his death, he has overcome Man's death of soul and has the power to open the 'eye of the soul' for Man after death, so that he shall be able to behold the world of spirit, and work among the beings of the spiritual world. The Burial is imbued with the words of Christ: 'I am the resurrection and the life.' (John 11:25).

In The Christian Community there is one more event which takes place in addition to the funeral when a person has died: the congregation celebrates an Act of Consecration of Man in memory of the deceased; this Act of Consecration contains a special prayer which describes the Christ as leader of souls, as awakener of the dead; the prayer asks that at the threshold of death the Father may take this soul into His power, out of the hand of Christ. We see that birth and death have a very particular relationship to the cosmic working of Christ which mediates between the earthly and the spiritual world.

Summary: The Christian Creed

This chapter has probably been able to show some of the many ways in which the being of Christ strives to light up in the worship of The Christian Community; the fullness of the Christ-being is brought home to our insight and experience in ever new turns of expression. In his Prologue, John says: 'Of his fullness have we all received grace upon grace.' We can sense the reality of this when we now try to look back and form an overview of what we encountered throughout our study and particularly in this chapter: namely, 'fullness' and 'grace.'

In order to facilitate this, we now turn to the renewed wording of the Creed, the Christian confession of faith, as it lives in The Christian Community.[11]* The purpose of the Creed has, of course, always been to gather together the fundamental Christian truths into manageable sentences and to formulate them like a confession. The major part of the twelve sentences of the Creed concern the being of Christ — for, as we have seen again and again, there is nothing in the world which is not in some way related to the cosmic-earthly working of Christ. In everything, he proves to be the 'fullness.' This fullness of being becomes 'grace' for us human beings, for 'of his fullness have we all received grace upon grace.'

We shall now take, one at the time, the sentences which contain an indication of the cosmic working of Christ; we shall then relate themes from our previous descriptions to the statements from the Creed, and thereby complement, vary and deepen it. In this way we shall gain an ordered overview of the themes which appear scattered among the texts of the Services; a certain amount of repetition will possibly be welcomed by the reader as an aid to deeper penetration of the contents.

THE RELATIONSHIP OF THE SON TO THE FATHER

The second sentence of the Creed speaks of the relationship of the 'Son' to the Father God: 'Christ ... is to this divine being [the Father God] as the Son born in eternity.'

Here the Father-Son relationship within the Godhead is characterized in a familiar way, namely through the picture of 'birth in eternity'; other traditional pictures and expressions for this origin of the Son from the Father also exist — we have already dealt with this in detail (see p.39f). In the Epistle for the feast of St John, however, we came across a quite unusual image: there the origin of the Son from the 'all-wielding' and 'all-blessing'

* For the complete text of the Creed, see Note 6.11.

working of the Father is portrayed as a 'ripening' — in the 'midst' of the world, the being of the Son 'ripens' into a 'sun,' the 'Christ-sun.'

At first, one may be taken aback by the unfamiliarity of such an expression; we have already said something about the inevitable onesidedness of any image, any term used about the nature of the Godhead. If we apply that to this expression also, then the image of the 'ripening' of a 'sun' out of the all-wielding and all-blessing might of the Father will begin to speak to us: the best life-forces of a plant or other being are drawn together in the ripening seed or fruit; they concentrate in a point in such a way that this being may live on in it, that it may evolve anew in the future. The life of the Father 'ripens' like that into the Son; and in this process, the Son appears, spiritually, as 'sun.' We have already seen that this image does not imply that we are falling back on old, mythological notions of God — Apollo, Helios as sun-gods etc. — but that it is precisely in this image that something of the cosmic dimension of Christ also appears in the New Testament, for example at the Transfiguration on the Mountain (Matt.17), or with the appearance of Christ at the beginning of the Apocalypse.

At the same time, the sun is the expression of the centre of a whole world; it has the power to bestow light and life on an immeasurable number of other spheres of existence out of its vast, inexhaustible fullness — as John's Prologue says about the *logos*. And yet the outer sun of our planetary system is only an image, a reflection of the spiritual sun, the Christ. With this thought we touch upon a motif from the Advent Epistle, in which it is said that the divine strength of worlds gleams in the 'chariot of the sun' and shines in the 'bow of colour' (which itself is a revelation of the sun); but who 'guides' this 'chariot' of the sun across the heavens? According to the Advent Epistle, it is not Helios, the sun-god of Greek mythology; rather, it is the divine strength of worlds itself who gleams in the sun, as in an image which has become visible; who, as it were, makes the sun into its visible 'chariot.' The Psalms said something similar: '... [thou] coverest thyself with light as with a garment.' (Ps.104:2).[12]

It is therefore quite consistent when the end of the St John's

Tide Epistle speaks of Christ as the bestower and creator of light — this is in accord not only with John's Prologue, but also with the Old Testament, for instance with Psalm 8: 'When I look at thy heavens, the work of thy fingers, the moon and the stars which thou hast established ...,' or Psalm 19: 'The heavens are telling the glory of God; and the firmament proclaims his handiwork ...'[13]

The eighth sentence of the Creed adds yet another aspect to the Father-Son relationship; here, the theme is not the birth of the Son from the Father; rather, the continued working of the Son is referred to: 'Since that time [that is, since his victory over death] he [Christ] is the lord of the heavenly forces upon earth and lives as the fulfiller of the fatherly deeds of the ground of the world.'

At the moment, we are mainly concerned with the second part of the sentence; for that, too, we find corresponding motifs in the Epistles, which express how the Son leads the working of the Father into the future, in fact as 'the fulfiller of the fatherly deeds of the ground of the world.'*

Let us think back for a moment to the Trinity Epistle, in which Christ is called the 'spirit-word' which wields through the whole world — which is also what is said about the *logos* in John's Prologue. However, this fundamental statement is subject to much differentiation in other texts; how does the Christ work as 'spirit-word' in the different realms of the world?

We find words which make this statement more concrete in, for example, the Ordination Service: his working is 'mighty in spirit' through all 'cycles of time'; in his creating, he 'bears' the eternal being of the Father — again a wonderful image for the Father-Son relationship; he works in such a way that 'eternal spirit-light' can be wrested from the darkness of earth-existence (here the relationship of the Christ to the Spirit God is shown, as it is also to be found in the Michaelmas Epistle: the 'heavenly light' must not vanish in the earthly light; and at Christmas the light of the Spirit streams with 'healing grace' into earth night and into 'sense darkness').

The working of the cosmic Christ, 'mighty in Spirit,' also comes to expression in the Act of Consecration of Man; at the

---

* Compare, for instance, John 5:17.

end of the transubstantiation it is said that he works in the world's becoming, creating, healing and ensouling it — the three verbs may indicate once more that in Christ the triune Godhead is present — and that through the Son, the Father fulfils the revelation of His being in the 'ordering of space' and the 'course of time.'

In the Offering we have already found the corresponding expression about the Spirit who permeates the 'widths of space' and the 'depths of time.'

The Communion takes this idea further: The cosmic Christ 'bears' and 'orders' the life of the world, and he does it as he receives it from the Father — and, at the same time, he works into the future of the earth, healing, 'making whole,' through the power of the Spirit.

Gathering together these statements about the cosmic Christ once more, we can say: like a mature, future-bearing power, he proceeds from the all-wielding and all-blessing working of the Father — like a sun bestowing life and light. In fact, understood spiritually, the image of the sun and its light is an expression for the world power of Christ which creates and bestows the outer light, and which gleams in the sun-chariot and shines in the bow of colour.

'Mighty in Spirit,' the Christ wields through the world as the creative 'spirit-word,' with a power which embraces heaven and earth — bearing and ordering, healing and ensouling the eternal being of the Father which he receives from Him as the 'life of the world,' and calling forth eternal spirit-light out of the darkness of earth. He works as the spirit of the widths of space, the depths of time in the revelation of the Father within the ordering of space and the course of time.

THE RE-ENLIVENING OF THE DYING EARTH EXISTENCE

We did not quote in full the second sentence of the Creed previously, since we were primarily concerned with the second half, the statement about the Father-Son relationship. The complete sentence runs as follows: 'Christ, through whom men attain the re-enlivening of the dying earth-existence, is to this divine being as the Son born in eternity.'

Let us now turn to the 're-enlivening of the dying earth-existence.' Something of this was already reflected within some of the themes discussed earlier. Where there was mention of ensouling and of making whole, of bearing and ordering, of the working of the light in the darkness through the working of the cosmic Christ, then this refers, above all, to earth-existence and to mankind itself from whom, however, the consequences of the Fall have then also spread to the entire cosmos.[14]

Incidentally, the statement about the dying earth-existence does not occur in any old forms of the Creed; the renewed Creed contains much that can serve a deepening understanding of Christianity — for example, in the new Creed is shown for the first time the full significance of the cosmic Christ for the evolution of the earth: no less than six times does the word 'earth' recur in various expressions in the Creed, in one place we find the term 'matter' as well.

Two further sentences from the Creed belong to the motif of the dying earth-existence and its permeation with new life: the sentence about the overcoming of death and the Ascension sentence which we will discuss a little later on; they run as follows: 'Then he overcame death after three days. Since that time he is the Lord of the heavenly forces upon earth ...'

These two sentences, too, show a clear advance in knowledge and understanding of the Christ over against previous formulations of the Creed: 'risen from the dead, ascended to heaven' was the wording until now. The new Creed is much more concrete; it emphasizes the fact that, in Christ, death has been conclusively defeated, overcome; and mankind can share in this, little by little.

Let us again complement this sentence by taking other texts into consideration. In the Ascension Epistle, for instance, we speak of Christ's death and 'conquest of death,' at Michaelmas of the 'deed of life and death' which took place on Golgotha; at St John's Tide we hear how Christ has 'borne' life from death, and, finally, at Easter it is said that he has 'risen unto' us human beings as the 'meaning of the earth.'

In the sacrament of Confirmation we also find more on this theme: Christ — it says there — died, so that human souls can live; and, as if this statement were not enough, it is immediately repeated in varied form: he has overcome death to save the life of the human soul.

In addition, the further motifs of the Easter Epistles are heard here — the sacrament of Confirmation is always celebrated in the Easter season. Through Christ, the human soul which was dead lives anew; the human Self which was dark begins to shine again; the human spirit which would have remained closed and isolated can open itself to new developments and experiences through the Risen One whom it is granted us to feel as the 'Vanquisher of Death.'

Naturally, the references to the death-conquering power of the Christ also come to the fore in those ritual acts which accompany the death of a person: in the 'Last Anointing,' at the funeral and in the words which are spoken as a special prayer in the Act of Consecration for the dead.

The 'Last Anointing' indicates to us the 'strong soul life' of Christ which has the might to conquer all death and to lead beyond earthly existence into other realms of existence 'through all cycles of time.'

The Burial is totally united with the fact of resurrection. At its centre is the Gospel statement of Christ just before the raising of Lazarus: 'I am the resurrection and the life. Whoever fills himself with my power through faith, he will live even when he dies.' (John 11:25) In the Burial we are looking to the Risen One who, through his death, has overcome the 'death of soul' which threatened Man — may his strength, says the text, stream towards the deceased; he has been able to win 'eternity' for us human beings.

And finally, in the Act of Consecration of Man which we celebrate in memory of someone who has died, Christ is called 'wakener of the dead' and 'leader of souls.' He can guide the deceased beyond the gate of death into the Father's 'cycles of life,' into 'deathless life.' Here the soul finds the realm which it called its 'home'; here Christ can open the 'eye of the soul' for beholding the divine-spiritual world and its beings, and for living and working with them.

Even now we have not exhausted all the themes which belong in this context. We see that the central event of Christianity is reflected in an extraordinarily rich and varied way in the wording

159

of the Services; all this is relevant if we want to understand what is meant, concretely, by the re-enlivening of the dying earth-existence through Christ.

But we have already seen: Christ's 'conquest of death' does not only refer to mankind on earth; he is not only the 'bringer of salvation' for us, able to redeem us from all that is one-sided in earth-existence. At Easter it becomes apparent that the new life of Christ also takes hold of the earth and even the universe — the aura of the earth begins to shine like a sun, the spiritual forces of the earth take part in the upturn of Christ's life; and, more still: the Easter Epistle says expressly that the cosmic Christ 'offers' his resurrection powers, not only to the earth but also to the 'worlds afar'; that must surely mean that he lets them stream towards the spiritual cosmos and so lays the basis not only for the future of the earth but also for the cosmos — 'advancement of the world,' as the ninth sentence of the Creed has it; here, this means advancement of 'worlds,' not only of the earthly world.

At this point we have an aspect before us which also appears with somewhat different words in the Advent Epistle; in that, there is mention of the decline of creation — the outer sun, the bow of colour will 'fade,' as the Gospel also says: 'Heaven and earth will pass away.' (Luke 21:33) That is to say, not only the earth but also 'heaven' are heading towards their end. But out of this 'twilight of worlds' a new world is to arise: the outer world which is coming to an end can be renewed through the 'Word' which wields, 'God-like.' After the words about the decline of heaven and earth, the Gospel continues in the same sense: '... but my words will not pass away,' which surely also means that in the words of Christ there is the power to create future.

At this point, the reader may recall the outlook on the future which we were able to form in connection with the imagery of John's Apocalypse, the future Jerusalem (see p.128): 'See, I make all things new!' (Rev.21:5) — this is what is uttered to us from the mouth of the cosmic Christ. And we were able to fill out these images with more substance through the insights of anthroposophy (see p.128ff). All this is in the background as we here contemplate the cosmic effects of Christ's deed of sacrifice and its significance for the world's future development.

We are led yet a step further when we now look at the Ascension text itself: 'Since that time he is the Lord of the heavenly forces upon earth ...'

These heavenly forces have been working since the Mystery of Golgotha in a great variety of ways. To begin with, let us turn our attention to the motifs in the Ascension Epistle which relate to this; Christ's 'elevation' to the heavenly spheres is mentioned, and how from there, where he 'abides' with the Father, he transfigures 'earthly being' with 'heavenly being' and bestows his 'blessing' on 'earthly being'; on the other hand, it is also said that he 'embodies' something of the 'earthly being' in the 'heights.'[15]

So, two movements are engendered through Christ's Ascension: he carries something upwards from the earth, spiritualizing it and 'embodying' it in heaven; but he also allows some of the forces of heaven to stream back to the earth — blessing, transfiguring. In this mediating function between heaven and earth, between earth and heaven, he is 'the Lord of the heavenly forces upon earth.'

In nature, the earth receives the benefit of this mediation between below and above through the clouds; they are formed by water which rises from the earth and is then permeated in the heights by the light and warmth of the sun; returning as rain, it bestows 'blessing' and life on the earth.

When the Ascension Epistle repeatedly refers to the 'realm of the clouds' to which the Christ ascends, then, spiritually, this refers to a sphere mediating between the 'heights' of the divine world and the earth, similar to the one which exists externally in nature: the sphere of the clouds which surrounds the earth (see Note 6.9).

From here, the view opens once again upon the central event of the altar, which we have already considered several times: the transubstantiation of bread and wine in the Act of Consecration of Man. We said that the bread and the wine are 'raised' towards Christ in this Act; the offering and the prayer of the congregation carry the earthly substances a little way beyond the everyday-earthly: even quite outwardly, the priest lifts up the bread and the wine at the altar, in prayer and offering, thus expressing the inner movement through an outer one. The other aspect of the event is that the power of the 'ascended' Christ streams down upon the earthly substances, blessing and hallowing them — 'transfiguring' them, as it were; this becomes visible to the clairvoyant eye — as we have already indicated — since bread and wine light up with a sunlike aura.[16] In this way the 'Lord of the heavenly forces upon earth' becomes full, living reality, not least in the altar-event; he who, in 'bestowing blessing' on 'earthly being,' 'transfigures' it and 'embodies' earthly being (here represented by bread and wine) into himself, that is to say: makes it his body and blood.

But we also see the heavenly forces rising and descending in human destiny; they are present, too, in human struggles and striving — we saw this when we were looking at the wording of the Marriage Sacrament. In the life-community of marriage, in which human destiny is to be worked through in joys and sorrows, Christ's 'deed of sacrifice' can transform 'work of earth' into 'work of spirit'; this means that what human beings work through in community can be taken up by the resurrection-power of Christ, be transformed and so shaped that it is there 'for the good and happiness' of all mankind, as the end of the Marriage Sacrament says.

The Baptism, too, points to 'heavenly forces upon earth'; as we have already seen, the 'sending' of human souls from the pre-natal, heavenly community of spirits to the 'community of earth' takes place through Christ; in this way, he himself helps to form and make effective the heavenly forces which every child brings to earth at birth. For ultimately — and this, too, we can glean from the Sacrament of Baptism — the human soul has, in fact, come into being through Christ, it has sprung from 'the creative Word of God'; so the human soul is profoundly at one with the heavenly forces, with Christ, when, at birth, it descends to earth.

It is in accord with this fundamental fact (and we have already discussed it in connection with the Services which accompany dying and death) that at the end of human life, Christ, the 'leader of souls' and 'wakener of the dead' leads the soul back into post-mortem existence, there to open up the realms of 'deathless life' for her — just as he sends the soul from the pre-natal, divine world to the earth.

Now, another sentence from the renewed Creed also belongs

to this: 'In death he became the helper of the souls of the dead who had lost their divine nature'; this formulation, too, is an advance on the old form of the Creed. There it simply says succinctly: 'descended to hell'; the sentence only acquires concrete substance in the new wording.

At the end of this section let us try to gather up the details and summarize without going over all the motifs again. The 're-enlivening of the dying earth-existence' comes to our awareness in four different areas: in 'earthly being,' in the cosmos, in the Sacrament and in humanity on earth.

This re-enlivening radiates out from Christ's overcoming of death, his 'conquest of death,' his 'deed of life and death' on Golgotha; we have seen in how varied a way this fundamental statement of Christianity is expressed in the different texts. For earth-existence, the Easter fact means that the aura of the earth begins to shine and the life-forces of the earth receive an uplift. The newly gained higher life on earth is offered up to the cosmos by Christ, so as to include the cosmos, too, in the 'continuance of the world'; with that, apocalyptic future prospects are opened up: through the cosmic Christ, the hope of a coming, God-permeated future world is set against the decline of heaven and earth.

Then, in the Ascension Epistle, we are made aware of the mediating work of the cosmic Christ between heaven and earth, earth and heaven: in the Sacrament, in the 'transubstantiation' of bread and wine into the body and blood of Christ, we saw a concrete instance of this mediating, blessing, hallowing and transfiguring working of the 'lord of the heavenly forces.' And — a few examples out of many — we looked at these motifs in human destiny: in Marriage and Baptism and in the Acts which accompany the death of a person; here Christ has the power to turn 'work of earth' into 'work of spirit' — for the 'good and happiness' of all mankind, he is able to lead souls at birth down from the divine world, and at death back to that world and to open up 'deathless life' for them.

So in these many-sided, far-reaching motifs, too, we encounter the whole 'fullness' of the Christ-life.

THE RELATIONSHIP OF THE CHRIST TO MAN

In conclusion, let us deal with a third aspect which, however, in some respects links on to motifs from the last section, namely that of Christ becoming Man and his existence within Man's innermost being. 'In Jesus the Christ entered as man into the earthly world,' says the third sentence of the Creed. What motifs from the wordings of the Services can we find to deepen our experience of this sentence?

In the first instance, there are the statements of the Christmas Epistles: Christ has 'appeared in he realm of earth,' and has 'chosen the earthly body' in which to 'dwell.' The expression 'earthly body' is ambiguous; it can refer to the human body in which Christ 'lived among us' (Prologue to John's Gospel), but it can equally well mean the 'body' of the earth itself which he made his own through death and resurrection, so that in a certain sense it has become 'his body'; as John's Gospel also says: 'He who eats my bread treads on me with his feet.' (John 13:18) And finally, the expression 'earthly body of Christ' can be taken to refer to the mystery of the transubstantiation of bread and wine on the altar; for here the bread (and, correspondingly, the wine) are again 'chosen' by Christ as his 'earthly body'; he accepts the bread as his 'body.'

At the same time, however, these motifs of the earthly incarnation of Christ now take on an immediate connection with us human beings. The 'creator word,' 'drawing near,' seeks — so the Christmas Epistle continues — to 'touch' us with its healing power, 'warm' our speaking and strengthen our willing: the events of two thousand years ago did not end Christ's becoming man; rather, it intends to advance further in each individual human being. 'Not I, but the Christ in me,' these are the words with which Paul already in his day responded to Christ's movement towards Man and into the innermost core of each human being; and in the Act of Consecration of Man we hear many times: 'Christ in you,' 'Christ in us.'

And here we must also take up again the significant motif from the Advent Epistle: the activity of the 'Divine Strength of Worlds' which finds its outer expression in nature in the 'gleaming of the chariot of the sun' and the shining 'bow of colour' —

this activity advances further as a 'word of time to come' which begins to 'speak' in the innermost place of the human soul; in our sensing of the cosmic Christ there arises within us a dawning awareness of a future 'becoming of man'; we perceive a 'picture of man's becoming,' but therein the working of God is 'veiled'! We have already drawn attention to the boldness of this statement earlier;[17] it is only comprehensible and acceptable if we have regard to Christ's efforts really to 'dwell' in human beings (see John 14:23); and, of course, this means that he engages with the development of human beings, that he 'veils' his divine becoming in human becoming, but on the other hand also takes some of our 'errors' into his 'divine soul' with 'grace and favour,' 'redeeming' them, and in his turn 'sheltering' them, as the wording says immediately afterwards. At Advent we thus find the embracing aspect of Christ's relationship to Man, for, as we have already seen, after the decline of heaven and earth, the 'becoming of God' within Man ultimately leads to a new, God-permeated world of the future.

The central motif of Christ becoming man is introduced at Advent with far-reaching statements, leading towards the cosmic; following on from the Christmas season, Epiphany (January 6 and the following four weeks) takes up the theme of God becoming man once more and links it to the cosmic aspect: namely in the image of the 'star' which appears from 'the bounds of worlds' and becomes the 'world star of grace' for us human beings; its light is to show us the 'right way' of salvation; in it, salvation shines for us with divine love and warmth. When we place ourselves into the light of this 'star of grace,' when we let the 'light' of our own heart go out towards it, then 'life in Christ' can arise within us. So the Epiphany season brings the cosmic image of the star close to the innermost being of Man and to human destiny and thus rounds off harmoniously the motifs which appear in Advent and at Christmas; these three festive seasons belong together intimately; the unifying motif is Christ's becoming man and his relationship to Man's inner nature.

This motif also comes to the fore in its most fundamental form in the second part of the 'trinitarian' Epistle: Christ — it says — 'creates in us,' and, what is more, in all our soul's creating; that is an echo of the statement of the Advent Epistle. But in the trinitarian Epistle, this statement is widened: in truth, our existing is his creating, indeed our very life is his 'creating life.' The relationship of Christ to Man is as profound as that — we have touched on this before; and we have already called to mind Paul's words to the Athenians: 'He is not far from each one of us, for in him we live and weave and have our being ... we are his offspring.' (Acts 17:27f).

We have now established that this original relationship of Man to Christ is, in fact, the precondition for Christ being able to 'dwell' within Man, that is, that this relationship is not doomed to remain one-sided and unconscious, coming only from Christ, but that it can become ever more conscious, desired by Man himself and also carried and formed by him: in this way, 'life in Christ' can arise within us.

We will just mention one last saying from the trinitarian Epistle; we 'feel,' it says, the divine Son when we become 'aware' of Christ 'in our humanity.' This statement is really only comprehensible against the background of what we have dealt with so far; for mankind is created and formed by the cosmic Christ and has an existential relationship to him. But the expression 'our humanity' also has another meaning; it does not only indicate that which unites all human beings into 'humanity,' but also that which is characteristically human in every human being, that which enables us to be human, as distinct from animal or angel: our 'humanity.' If we take this meaning into consideration, then the sense of the sentence we have quoted is: we only have to be deeply enough aware of Christ in our true humanity, then, through him, we can feel the divine, the 'divine Son' in us. This statement represents an enhancement of all previous motifs.

We have saved the ultimate and highest until last in this section. We will go back to the Christmas Epistle once more and now turn our attention to a word which appears very rarely and sparingly in our texts, and just for that reason is all the more precious: it is the word Love.

In one place we have already heard it sound in the centre of the Act of Consecration of Man, immediately before the priest kneels down at the altar for the transubstantiation of bread and wine; in this solemn moment our gaze is turned to Christ; we strive to unite fully with him, sensing his presence, hoping for his presence; how do we grasp his being? Through love; for he himself is all love; his being is love; he is the divine Son who 'has his being in love'; his love is the background for the transubstantiation which takes place immediately afterwards. It is his all-embracing love which takes hold of the earthly substances, transforms them and so makes them into bearers of eternal salvation for us human beings.

We should have in mind this revelation of his being by Christ when, at Christmas, love is spoken of in the Epistle — but now as a power that is to go forth from us human beings towards God; through the appearing of the 'Word' in an earthly body, we can 'know the divine with our sight' on earth, says the Epistle, and thereby the love of our hearts 'for the unseen' can be 'kindled.'

The appearance of the divine on earth is a deed of love, of the love of God for us human beings: this is the core of the Christmas message; but from our hearts we can respond to this message: may our beholding of Christ as man and the all-embracing love which is brought to us through this Incarnation kindle our love in answer to him who 'first loved us.' (1John 4:19) With that our most profound relationship to Christ has been declared.

Now, however, another motif is linked to this theme of our love to God, a motif which places us human beings into the great cosmic context of the world-beings: with this love of ours — the text continues — we may join in offering with the great sacrifice of the angelic beings, whose nine stages right up to the Cherubim and Seraphim are invoked at Christmas; we may join in their mighty 'song of sacrifice' through which the world's becoming receives its impulses. But this means that our love to God is the motivation, the germ, which makes it possible for us to begin moving up into the ranks of beings who bear and create worlds; through love for the divine our offering attains the power to join with that of the spiritual beings and with that of Christ, from which — as is already stated in Advent and developed further at Easter — a new creation and also a new heaven (cosmos) is ultimately to come forth. So this section, too, closes with the apocalyptic view of the 'new Jerusalem.'

What is the outcome if we now try briefly to summarize the motifs from this third section, too? The theme was Christ's becoming man and his relationship to Man's inner being; we mentioned:

— that Christ has 'chosen' the 'earthly body' in order to 'dwell' in a human being; in order to make the earth his own as his 'body'; and finally also, ever and again, to take on and accept bread and wine as his body, his blood.

And we saw how, going beyond his Incarnation back then, the cosmic Christ continues to seek us human beings, and that the core, the spur of this seeking is his all-embracing love; at Christmas we feel the 'healing creator word' 'drawing near'; it is to 'touch' us and 'permeate' us and lead us to 'Christ in us,' 'Christ in me.'

This motif is introduced at Advent:

— the divine strength of worlds, which has come to expression in the external creation, begins to speak anew within Man;

— after this, a new becoming begins, in which the becoming of God lives, full of grace;

— within the decline of the old, this new becoming leads to a new creation through the Word which 'wields, God-like.'

At Epiphany, this Advent and Christmas proclamation is rounded off:

— the 'World star of Grace' appears from the 'bounds of worlds,' in order — we add here — to warm the human heart in love and thereby show us the way of 'salvation';[18]

— the 'spirit light of worlds' is met by the 'light of prayer' in our hearts, and, in the meeting of the two, 'life in Christ' can 'arise' in us human beings.

Finally, we turned to the basic motifs of the trinitarian Epistle, which remind us of the fundamental relationship of every human being to Christ: of His original and present 'life,' and how we may be 'aware' of the Son, the cosmic Christ, in our 'humanity.'

All this we can embrace as concrete, comprehensive and relevant love of Christ towards us human beings, a love by which our love can be kindled; when human love and divine love unite in offering, a germ begins to form of a new creation which is to take in heaven and earth: we human beings may join in the mighty 'song of sacrifice' of the nine angelic spheres, and thereby begin to be raised up to the level of the beings who give the world its impetus and impulses.

OVERVIEW

At the end of this chapter we can once more bring to mind how the great fullness which lives in the working of the cosmic Christ lies condensed within the individual sentences of the Creed: these sentences are like seeds which conceal forces, but which can also unfold them — we have tried to unfold some of these 'seed forces' here. Referring to the Creed we can now say once more in summary:

The cosmic Christ:

— is 'as the Son born in eternity';
— through him, men attain 'the re-enlivening of the dying earth-existence';
— for he 'overcame death after three days';
— since that time he is 'the Lord of the heavenly forces upon earth and lives as the fulfiller of the fatherly deeds of the ground of the world';
— thereby he is also 'the helper of the souls of the dead';
— all this is founded on the fact that, in Jesus, he 'entered as man into the earthly world';
— and that he desires to continue becoming Man in each one of us.

But what does the working of the cosmic Christ in and with us human beings ultimately lead to? We can now express it in conjunction with what we have said so far, by turning to three of the last sentences of the renewed Creed which we have only quoted in outline so far: 'He [the Christ] will in time unite for the advancement of the world with those whom, through their bearing, he can wrest from the death of matter.'

We have already taken note that this sentence refers to the worlds in which human beings become involved through Christ. In the next, eleventh, sentence of the Creed, the motif 'Christ in us' is given yet another formulation: 'Communities whose members feel the Christ within themselves may feel united in a church to which all belong who are aware of the health-bringing power of the Christ.'

The one Church of Christ has always been referred to as the 'body' of Christ (Paul, Letter to the Ephesians) — here we have the fourth aspect of the 'earthly body' of Christ of which we spoke earlier; but what might be meant by: 'feeling the Christ within us'? Must it not above all mean: feeling his love and loving him? Then the central Christmas motif lights up which joins us to the realms of the angels — the angelic realms which serve the Christ would belong to the one Church of Christ.

About what is said in the eleventh sentence, the twelfth and last sentence says: 'They may hope for the overcoming of the sickness of sin, for the continuance of man's being and for the preservation of their life destined for eternity.'

And perhaps we can add — each according to his capability — 'Yea, so it is.'

7. Finding the cosmic Christ in us

Only a small number of people nowadays will be able to say about themselves that they have been given a conscious relationship to Christ as a gift, maybe as the fruit of a religious upbringing, as a natural faculty of their inner life or as a result of the guidance of destiny. Indeed, it happens not infrequently that, after a long life of religious seeking, people have to confess: I have not found an inner, personal relationship to Christ! We will now try to put forward a number of thoughts which perhaps may prove helpful in this context.

Every human's relationship to Christ

As we have seen, the relationship to Christ is already given with the Creation; the Creation of Man does not only happen 'through' Christ himself, we are also formed 'out of' his being and 'towards' him; this statement is true of Man in an even deeper sense than of the other beings in creation; for Man is at the same time created as the divine 'image' — but, on the other hand, the image, the 'icon' of God, is also Christ himself (for further explanation of this see p.41 and also Note 3.15).

So there is already a deep connection to Christ simply in our being human; in the 'trinitarian' Epistle which is read in the Act of Consecration of Man during the four seasons of the year without festivals, it is said of Christ that his creating is our existence and also that 'his creating life' is our life. Is it possible to conceive of a more profound relationship to Christ?

Initially, however, this relationship remains completely unconscious; it is given for every human being — whether or not they know it, whether or not they have ever heard anything about Christ — simply by the fact that they are human. Yet even more is said in the two sentences from the Epistle: the (cosmic) Christ did not only work into the creation of Man and shape our humanity, he also lives and works now in this his creation, bearing and sustaining it — as Paul says to the Athenians: 'In him we live and weave and have our being!' (Acts 17:28).

But our unconscious relationship to Christ has yet another side. It is hinted at in the words: 'Christ died for all human beings.' (2Cor.5:15) About this, too, we have already spoken: the death and the resurrection of Christ are of significance for all human beings — regardless of their denomination, independent of their knowledge of Christianity. The resurrection of Christ is a re-enlivening power for the 'dying earth-existence' and for mankind; therefore, in the Confirmation it is said of Christ that he died 'that the souls of men can live.' Without the deed of Christ, the consequences of the Fall would long ago have led to the extinction of human existence on the earth. It is thanks to the working of Christ that I am able to live as a human being on the earth.

And a fourth and last thing belongs here, too; we spoke of it in connection with Baptism: it is Christ who sends the human soul 'from the community of spirit to that of earth' — just as, at the gate of death, he also receives Man and leads him back into the spiritual world. So my present human destiny also relates to him.

We can therefore speak of a fourfold, natural and unconscious relationship of every human being to Christ; I can say to myself that I owe my humanity to Christ:

— through my own origin which is to be found in his divine being;

— through his life which continues to bear and sustain my life, indeed goes on creating it anew;

— through his 'deed of life and death' on Golgotha which protects me against the deadly consequences of the Fall within the 'dying earth-existence';

— through the fact that he has sent me into my destiny on earth, invisibly accompanies me through it and, in death, leads me back into the divine world.

Towards the end of his life, Rudolf Steiner expressed in a wonderful way how we can sense our relationship to Christ. He speaks of the physical sun, from which we receive warmth and light:

in the same way, he [the human being] must live towards the spiritual sun, Christ, who has united his existence

172

with that of the earth; in a living way he must receive
into his soul what corresponds to warmth and light in the
spiritual world. He will feel himself permeated by
'spiritual warmth' when he experiences the 'Christ in
me.' Feeling this, he will say to himself: 'This warmth
leads you back to the divine from which you stem
originally.' And in this feeling within Man, the
experience in and with the Christ will merge in innermost
warmth of soul with the experience of genuine and true
humanity. 'Christ gives me my humanity,' that will be
the fundamental feeling which wafts and wells through
the soul. (GA 26, November 3, 1924).

HOW NEAR TO US IS CHRIST?

We can transform what has been described here into a dawning
religious awareness. We can try to feel: I have a profound,
existential relationship to Christ; it is this which is the actual
basis of my humanity. Thereby we make the transition from an
unconscious relationship to Christ, given by nature, to one which
is conscious and personal — and in future everything will depend
on this, if Man is to endure through the storms and perils of
existence. We must not remain at the level of an unconscious
relationship to Christ.

Here the fact that Christ became man takes on an especially
profound significance for us, for the meaning of this Incarnation
is that he has come near to us in all our human experiences, in
joy and sorrow, in despair and certainty, in the heights and
depths of our life. Christ becoming man only has meaning when
it is a reality for us, not only back then but also today. That is
also the significance of the words from the Gospel of Matthew
which indicate how close he is to all his human brothers on
earth: 'What you did for the least of my brothers, that you did for
me!' (Matt.25:40).

If these are not just beautiful, sentimental, illusory words, if
they are a reality, then that must point to the human bond
between Christ and every human being on earth, which, in a
mysterious way, permeates our earthly destiny. But that means it
is right for us to conceive of his nearness, his personal presence,

as humanly deep and close — yes, we are permitted to form a picture of him as of a person who is very close to us, profoundly and intimately, warmly related. We may bring to mind the most intimate, human closeness which we know in our life, the deepest understanding, heart to heart, the warmest intimacy, when we want to feel the closeness and depth of our relationship to Christ.

And more than that: even this most profound attachment to another human being is surpassed by the bond we have with Christ in the depths of our being. On the one hand, it stems from the facts upon which his closeness to us is based; but it can slowly enter our consciousness when we imagine him humanly close, with a degree of closeness which surpasses everything which we otherwise know of closeness between human beings.

Here we can draw upon a comparison with our bodily existence: there are two forces which continuously sustain our bodily life without our devoting even the slightest consciousness to them, namely breathing and heartbeat. If our heart were not unceasingly active within our body, so that the blood can course through the veins every moment of the day or night; and if the stream of our breath did not without fail let new, fresh forces of life flow into us with the air, then we would not be able to live another moment. These two forces are untiringly at work within us, even if we pay no attention to them. They sustain us from the first to the last moment of our existence: not for nothing do we speak of the first and last breath and of the moment when the heart stands still.

In a similar way the life of Christ sustains and carries us every moment of our lives, whether we know it or not. It is so close and profoundly present in us that we do not even suspect its nearness and depth. And when, as we said at the beginning, some people confess at the end of their lives: all my life I sought for the Christ, yet I did not find him — we may ask: in which direction did you look? Did you seek an overwhelming experience as an encounter with Christ? Did you look outwards in your search for Christ? Is it not that he was very close to you precisely in all this searching and questioning? Should you perhaps change the direction of your gaze, and notice that he is already by you, in you and with you, so closely and intimately at one with you that you do not even suspect it?[1]

A beautiful legend tells of this closeness of our relationship with Christ. A man has died and looks back on his life where he notices that the footprints he left behind on earth are accompanied by other footprints. He asks Christ, who appears to him in this moment after death, about these tracks. 'I accompanied you throughout your whole life,' says Christ. Then the man observes that over some of the most difficult stretches of his path there is only one track visible. 'And what happened during those hard times when I needed you most? Where were you then?' he asks. Christ replies: 'There I was carrying you.'

DYING AND BECOMING

This little story brings to expression something of Christ's power to accompany destiny. Earlier when we were discussing Passiontide we became aware that it is especially in the pain, suffering and despair of our existence, in the death-experiences which we have to go through, that he remains humanly united with us; that it is just in these experiences that we can grow beyond ourselves. For the reason that they are full of pain and despair for us is that we have not yet developed the forces in our soul which enable us to withstand and master these moments. If we were able to rise above such times of pain they would not cause us the anguish and suffering which in fact they do. They demand higher and more profound forces of us than we have so far developed in our soul; and that is precisely the reason why they become fruitful in our destiny. They call on us to bring forth from the deeper levels of our existence something which we do not as yet possess, but which lies dormant in us as hidden potential; something which only becomes active in us when we bring it to light in us and which actually makes us stronger through the fact that we create it within ourselves. Nietzsche formulated this in the famous saying: 'Whatever does not kill me makes me stronger!'

In reality, however, such moments are of still deeper significance; for they bring us near to those powers with which Christ himself had to wrestle. In such experiences of suffering and of inner death-experiences, he is able to impart some of his own suffering, his own death-experience to our soul. Here we can think of the expression coined by Goethe: 'Die and become!' Our own 'dying and becoming' unites with the death and resurrection of Christ. Through such experiences he plants a seed of the actuality of his resurrection into our own death-experiences. Only against this background do we understand what is actually meant by: 'I am in your midst all the days until the completion of earthly time.'

So when we seek a personal and conscious relationship to the Christ, we may conceive of him as this humanly close and at one with us; we may allow ourselves to think of him as a human being, as a human brother. And with a divine-human closeness which surpasses all human closeness.

Once again we think of the words of Rudolf Steiner: this closeness is, at the same time, warmth, and this warmth is in reality love, and this love is creative and bestowing — it leads to the feeling: 'Christ gives me my humanity,' he confirms me in my innermost being, he loves me as I am.

This is how we direct our inner perception towards his human closeness: 'He loved us first!,' says John in his First Letter. People who have had a conscious encounter with Christ have been overwhelmed by the power of this love. And while we may not ourselves have had such a conscious Christ-encounter, yet we can and may imagine his closeness as love and acceptance of our being. Down the ages, this has been the actual essence of the Christ-experience. It was, at the same time, the experience of the 'Christ in me,' which Paul formulates in the saying: 'Not I, but Christ in me.' This saying comes from the Letter to the Galatians, where the full text runs:

> It is not I who live, but Christ lives in me. The life which
> I have now in my earthly incarnation I have through
> devotion and faith in the Son of God who loves me and
> has given himself for me. (Gal.2:20).

Christ and the universe

In our approach to the question of a personal relationship to Christ we began with the experience of 'Christ in me,' the most profound closeness to Christ. For most people today this is probably the most likely way by which to approach a real Christ-experience. Yet it must not be forgotten that within this quite personal, humanly close experience of Christ, another, very different experience lies concealed: the feeling and experience of his cosmic greatness and width. For Christ's saying: 'See, I am in your midst all the days until the completion of earthly time' is accompanied by another which refers to his cosmic greatness and width: 'All creative power in heaven and on the earth has been given me!' (Matt.28:18-20) The double aspect of the Christ-experience is expressed magnificently in these two statements: his human closeness — 'I am with you' — and his cosmic power — 'All creative power in heaven and on the earth has been given me.'

So the personal Christ-experience has a cosmic aspect. We can clarify this for ourselves in a picture: There are streets which run dead straight towards the horizon; sometimes such streets have trees planted along both sides, like a boulevard of trees. When we are standing at the beginning of such a street, we see the nearest trees and everything else there very clearly and well defined. It is all very close to us. And yet we notice that this proximity has within it a wide perspective which passes over into the horizon in the distance and vanishes, as it were, into the cosmic widths.

Thus there are two feelings concealed within the experiencing of Christ; initially, it is the feeling of a bond, a union with him; but then this nearness opens out into a wider, cosmic dimension, we learn to feel the nearness as something divine. Divine means: transcending our human status, all-embracingly great. The being of the divine is not constrained, as is our human existence, not limited to a single point in space. As soon as we bring to mind that of course Christ is not only close to us but to every human being, we are led towards this all-embracing divine, which it is certainly far beyond our immediate capacity to imagine. Our human existence, being contracted into a point, as it were, is touched by the nearness of Christ. But because this is also true for every other human being, we see at the same time the comprehensive, the divine aspect of the revelation of his being.

Actually, this twofold experience is also already present in my experience of another human being. However well we believe we know someone, we will always have to say to ourselves: Even though I feel that I know him, I have only grasped a small part of his real, deeper being. For within every human being there is something infinitely rich and comprehensive, which, however, can only come to expression to a very limited extent in current destinies. Heraclitus is right when he says: 'You will never fathom the limits of the soul, though you traverse every street; so deep is its *logos*.' In such a saying the cosmic aspect of every human being comes to expression. Otherwise, how could Man really be 'an image of God' in his true being? Affinity with a human being, then, already contains a 'cosmic aspect,' even if at first we can only dimly surmise it. How much more so will this be with the experience of the nearness of Christ: in this nearness he is, after all, at the same time the cosmic Christ with 'all power in heaven and on the earth.'[2]

Looking at this cosmic dimension of Christ, we can bring different 'levels' to mind. Firstly, there is his affinity with all human souls, with birth and death, with their earthly destinies: Christ is the 'leader of souls,' the 'immortal brother' of mortal human beings.[3]

Secondly, there is the sphere in which he works with the earth and nature-beings, with the cycle of the year, with flowering, growth, thriving, ripening, fruiting and decay, with day and night: here he is the 'Lord of the elements,' the 'Lord of the heavenly forces upon earth.'

Thirdly, he is united with the earth itself; he has become the 'Spirit of the earth' and has wrested the rulership of the earth from the adversary powers through the fundamental conquest of death and the ongoing transformation of evil; in this way he is the 'conqueror of death,' as we might formulate it, with reference to the Creed.

We have, therefore, already three realms which extend into ever greater widths and depths. But beyond that, the view expands past human beings, nature and the earth into the 'cosmos' itself, which — as we have seen — with its planets and fixed stars is the external representation of the hierarchical, spiritual beings; this realm, too, is 'subject' to him, in the sense of the saying: 'To me has been given all power in heaven and on earth' — or according to Paul: 'In the name of Jesus the knees of all beings should bow, in the heavens, on the earth and in the depths of existence.' (Phil.2:10).

Ultimately, though, the being of the cosmic Christ leads

beyond all other beings and worlds to the realm of the Trinity, back to the Father: here he is the *'Logos* of God,' the 'divine Son.'

These stages are like a 'spiritual ladder' whose rungs lead up to ever greater heights and widths; it is the affinity of Christ:
— with all human beings;
— with the nature beings of the earth;
— with the earth itself;
— with the planetary spheres;
— with the world of the fixed stars; and finally
— with the realm of the Godhead.

In all these realms he 'fulfils all in all,' as Paul says, that is to say: he leads all evolution to completion, to fulfilment, so that future arises out of it — the New Jerusalem.

The double aspect of the experience of Christ: his nearness and his cosmic greatness, comes to expression in the Act of Consecration of Man; it begins with the experience of the nearness of Christ, in that it asks that our heart be filled with the life of Christ. But then the further stages of the Act of Consecration lead from the experience of the nearness of Christ, the 'Christ in us,' to the experience of the cosmic greatness of Christ. In the last part of the Act of Consecration, in the Communion, Christ is addressed in his cosmic role: he has the 'authority' to bear and to order the life of the world. We have already mentioned that just this most intimate moment of Communion, the receiving of his 'body' and his 'blood,' also bears within it the experience of his cosmic greatness.

Here we may add another motif; we encounter it in the Act of Consecration, right at the beginning of the Communion as a word of Christ himself: he 'stands,' it says there, 'at peace with the world.' This utterance about 'peace with the world' is immediately repeated twice and thereby forms the impressive entrance into the Communion, which then ascends to the cosmic greatness of Christ in the manner indicated.

The significance of this entrance-motif becomes clear when we compare it with the old text of the Mass at this place; in that, there is as yet no mention of 'peace with the world': 'Lord Jesus Christ, you said to your Apostles: I give you peace ...' Here, then, the peace is bestowed upon the Apostles (in accordance with John 14:27), not upon the world.

Now one may ask; what is it that makes it possible for the Christ to speak in this extended cosmic form about his peace today? The answer must be: his Second Coming. Today that exerts a greater and more comprehensive power for peace than two thousand years ago, when peace could only be granted to those human beings who were close to him.[4]

Yet we are bound to ask: If that is to be more than merely a 'beautiful saying' — how is this peace with the world to be understood? Does he 'stand at peace' with this world which is full of strife and hatred, war and destruction, misery and despair ...? Does the cosmic Christ with his peace float in blessed self-sufficiency above this world, ignoring its need and misery?[5]

That could never be so. If he really has remained with the earth and humanity, then not least with their need and their misery; and then this 'standing at peace with the world' can only mean that it is precisely in conflicts that he is spiritually present for human souls, suffers in them, strives and strengthens the longing for true peace, purifies it and does not let it perish; in the midst of the landscapes of death in our world he sows seeds of a future world which will arise in souls when the fruit of all suffering is revealed.

So with this word of peace from Christ we actually unite with the world as it is today; his peace does not go out to just a few human beings — he turns towards humanity and the earth, and thereby achieves a cosmic dimension, as it were. This cosmic dimension is maintained until the end of the Communion, where the word of peace from the beginning is now spoken to each individual communicant, and where each individual, being a 'piece of the world,' takes the body and blood of Christ into himself — on behalf of many — as a germ of the future.

In conclusion, we may mention one last aspect. We have spoken of the experience of the cycle of the year and of how the experiencing of the cosmic Christ is always like a sympathetic vibration within that experience. As, step by step, we unite ourselves with the Act of Consecration through the year and with the experiences of the Christian festive seasons, the Christ-nearness offers itself to us ever new, in a real, profound human-divine presence. As the poet Novalis says, he becomes 'our food and our drink.' But this experience in the festive seasons of the year also alternates between the nearness of Christ and his cosmic breadth: in Advent he comes close to us; and the festive seasons which follow — Christmas-Epiphany-Passiontide — intensify by stages into an ever more intimate union of the Christ with us. In this process we even experience — in Passiontide — how he unites with our bodily nature, not only with our soul and spirit. Then, of course, at Easter his cosmic greatness breaks through, which, in turn, intensifies by degrees until St John's Tide and Michaelmas. Here we can begin to have an inkling of the reality of the saying of Christ to his disciples: 'I live, and you shall share in this life!' (John 14:19).

In this way, our uniting with the experience of the Act of Consecration through the cycle of the year becomes a living incentive for us to ponder and contemplate his nearness and his cosmic greatness, and to let it live in us.

Wider prospects

The relationship to Christ and the upward glance to the cosmic dimension of Christ must not become stuck for us today as inner experiences of the soul alone, nor as purely mystical experiences of nature and humanity: they have to take on concrete forms of life; we can gradually become aware of the all-permeating life of Christ in all that exists around us and in what we ourselves are. On the other hand, though, we see that this 'existence' is increasingly endangered, for the Adversaries have by no means given up their hope of ultimately seizing hold of the destiny of mankind and the earth for themselves; rather, they continue to escalate their efforts to achieve this end. Therefore we will be seeking those ways in our life and in our work which lead us onto the side of Christ.

The task which is here before us again extends into different spheres. In the first instance it concerns the question (and ultimately everything else depends on the answer to it): can we break through to a 'view' of the world, a *Weltanschauung*, which enables us to speak of a 'spiritual dimension' of existence (for that is what the 'cosmic' dimension of Christ is) in a way which is genuine and which is honestly answerable to thinking? This question became very pertinent for us when we considered the universe: if what modern astronomy, astrophysics, and so on, have to say really is everything that there is to say, then it is fatuous to go on speaking about a 'cosmic' dimension of Christ.

In fact, though, this question touches everything: everything that surrounds us, and also what we ourselves are and what concerns our destiny. For there, too, we only ever grasp the 'external' side with our ordinary consciousness, not the actual essence; the realm in which we would encounter the presence and working of spiritual beings and, ultimately, the existence of the cosmic Christ, is generally hidden from us.

And so we return to the fundamental questions which we outlined at the beginning of this book and which we have touched on repeatedly. We were not in a position to deal with them in detail here, but had to refer the reader to anthroposophy. My conviction — that it is only from there that these fundamental questions can be solved — is the basis for the present work.

The positive answer given by anthroposophy to the fundamental questions makes significant further steps possible. They lead:

— to a deepening of one's 'world-view' in all spheres of life;

— to concrete incentives for spiritual schooling;

— to significant insights into religious questions; among other things, these insights have also contributed to a renewal of the whole of religious life (in The Christian Community). We spoke of this at length in Chapters 5 and 6;

— to thought-provoking ideas for all questions of life; for understanding and coping with destiny, for daily conduct and the striving for morality and humanity;

— to fundamental social questions;

— and finally to new impulses in all important spheres of present-day culture and civilization, especially in education and curative education, medicine and pharmacology, agriculture and nutrition, in all artistic realms (including eurythmy), in all scientific disciplines, including natural science, in the social and commercial fields through the idea of the 'threefolding of the social organism' and through the founding of the Anthroposophical Society.

We have previously referred to the danger of a too generalized talk about the cosmic Christ, which in the end is 'pantheistic' (see p.34). In our concrete sphere of work, and in the particular questions which every sphere of work brings with it, we are called upon to forge ahead to specific insights and answers, for instance in the study of Man in education or medicine, in the world of the nature beings etc.; for there we have before us the most varied realms, beings and their mutual interaction, to which we cannot do justice by mere generalized talk about the cosmic Christ. We must be more precise in our language so as to take account of the infinite multiplicity of the beings of the world; and it must become concrete for the tasks which have to be tackled in the different professions; and for this there are — as we have said — significant impulses for all spheres, arising out of anthroposophy.

Our upward glance to the cosmic Christ can stimulate us and give us strength to take hold of these impulses; when we sense — feel — recognize: within the multiplicity of beings I also encounter Him — Him, thanks to whom I live. Then I will try, in the daily conduct of my life, to be on His side. The real aim of this book has been to inspire such an attitude of heart and mind.

Notes

References to Rudolf Steiner's works are normally given with their GA *(Gesamtausgabe)* bibliographical number.

CHAPTER 1

1.1 In the year 325, the dogma of the complete identity of the Son with the Father was formulated at the council of Nicaea — in opposition to Arius who denied this identity of being. This dogma was to lead to many difficulties of comprehension, since all statements that had to be made about Christ in particular — for example his becoming Man, his death — raised questions about the universal validity of the dogma of the absolute identity of being.

1.2 In his book *On being a Christian,* Hans Küng discusses the question of the Resurrection in detail. For him it is clear that what matters is not 'the empty tomb' but the 'identical personal reality' and 'no continuity of the body'; what may have become of the human body of Jesus of Nazareth is no longer of any interest. With that, however, the central statement of the event of the Resurrection has been abandoned — despite all the further ingenious arguments.

Gerd Lüdemann *(The Resurrection of Jesus)* comes to a similar conclusion: 'Easter faith is an experience in the spirit ... it has nothing to do with the resuscitation of the corpse of Jesus, for that decayed and remained in the tomb.'

In a general way it must be said that a real understanding of the Resurrection probably is only possible on the basis of the fundamental insights of anthroposophy.

1.3 In *On Being a Christian,* Hans Küng discusses the question of the pre-existence of Christ, and denies it. The pronouncement of John's Prologue: 'In the beginning was the Word ... and the Word became flesh and lived among us ...' (John 1) is pushed aside as 'theological reflection.' With that, the view to the cosmic dimension of Christ is totally obscured.

1.4 This is presumably also how the basic statement of Eugen Drewermann is to be understood: Jesus' message is to set us free and heal us from the anxieties and fears of the world.

1.5 See Fritjof Capra, *The Tao of Physics.*

1.6 For an introduction, see H.-W. Schroeder, *Die Christengemeinschaft — Entstehung, Entwicklung, Zielsetzung.*

From the available literature I will only mention the following titles:

Friedrich Rittelmeyer, *Briefe über das Johannesevangelium.*
—, *Christus.*
—, *Ich bin.*
Emil Bock, *Das Evangelium.*
—, *The Three Years.*
—, *The Childhood of Jesus.*
Rudolf Frieling, *Christologische Aufsätze.*
—, *New Testament Studies.*
—, *The Essence of Christianity.*
Dieter Lauenstein, *Der Messias.*
Erdmut-Michael Hoerner, *Christus und die Erde.*
Irene Johanson, *Christuswirken in der Biographie.*
Wilhelm Kelber, *Christ and the Son of Man.*
Rudolf Meyer, *Die Wiedergewinnung des Johannesevangeliums.*
Barbara Nordmeyer, *Leben mit Christus.*
Christoph Rau, *Das Matthäus-Evangelium.*
—, *Struktur und Rhythmus im Johannes-Evangelium.*

Further references to specific titles will be found in the relevant chapters and notes; to the work of Rudolf Steiner especially in Chapter 5.

1.7 A first introduction to the life and work of Rudolf Steiner is presented in:
Childs, *Rudolf Steiner: his Life and Work.*

Easton, *Rudolf Steiner: Herald of a New Epoch.*
Easton, *Man and World in the Light of Anthroposophy.*

1.8 Incidentally, Teilhard de Chardin bases his view of the evolution of the world on a similar idea; this is shown by Johannes Hemleben in *Teilhard de Chardin:*

This human 'I-point' is at the same time the 'fulcrum' of the entire evolution. It is here, in the noosphere, that the divergence reaches its highest point and its ultimate aim. Evolution turns into involution, divergence is succeeded by convergence. From the moment when this critical point was reached within anthropogenesis, the tendencies towards separation in the course of evolution begin to be overcome. For Teilhard, the epitome of the converging power, the power which puts creation together again, is Jesus Christ, the cosmically working world-principle. His will and his Being gathers the scattered world in again, as it were, and leads it back to its origin, to the Godhead. That which was in the beginning works now and will be there at the end: Alpha and Omega — 'I am the Alpha and the Omega, thus speaks the Lord, our God, who is and who was and who is coming, the Pantocrator' (Rev.1:8). At this point, Teilhard the mystic takes over from the palaeontologist. Now he goes on to develop the 'Omega-theology' of the future of the earth and Man, in which all anthropogenesis becomes christogenesis, and anthropology becomes a particular branch of Christology.

1.9 Compare Rudolf Frieling, *The Essence of Christianity;* Rudolf Steiner, *Das Mysterium des Bösen;* Emil Bock, *Genesis* (especially the chapters on 'The Fall' and 'Job'); Emil Bock, *The Apocalypse of St John.*

1.10 Later, we shall be speaking of the connection between the sun and Christ; at this level, Christ identifies himself, as it were, with the angelic beings who are active on the sun, in the same way as he later identifies himself with mankind, becomes Man.

The angelic beings who are active on the sun are far higher than Man — by four stages, in fact; they are the 'Exousiai,' called 'Spirits of Form' by Rudolf Steiner; they are identical with the 'Elohim' of the biblical story of Creation (see Steiner's *Genesis, Secrets of the Biblical Story of Creation,* GA 122).

Christ's identification with the beings on the sun is also the background, among other things, to a remark in the Gospel of Matthew: '... he taught as one in whom the creative powers themselves are at work (literally: as one having *exousia*); not in the usual style of the scribes.' (Matt.7:29).

We also have to explain that when we speak of 'sun-beings' we are not returning to old mythological world-conceptions; rather, it is the other way about: the old knowledge of 'sun-gods' (for instance Osiris, Helios, Apollo), who must then be classified as higher angel-beings, can be included again in a new conception of the cosmos.

1.11 The sense of responsibility for the future can surely only be strengthened in each individual human being when he or she knows that all earthly-material existence also has a spiritual side which ultimately is dependent upon the life and the creating of the cosmic Christ.

This has been developed in concrete terms by the founding of 'biodynamic agriculture' through Rudolf Steiner; it employs effective methods of maintaining and enhancing the life of the earth by taking account of the cosmos in a right way.

1.12 In the New Age movement, the expression 'the dawning of the age of Aquarius' is used; this term has entered the consciousness of a great number of people. Here we could draw attention to the anthroposophical view of the so-called cultural epochs and the beginning of an 'age of light' since 1899.

See Rudolf Steiner, *The Reappearance of Christ in the Etheric,* GA 118, Lecture March 13, 1910.

CHAPTER 2

2.1 A brief survey of the use of the expression 'cosmic' in this connection:

Although the motif as such is widespread in the history of Christianity, the expression 'cosmic Christ' was first used in the USA by Prof. G. Stevens of Yale Divinity School in *The Christian Doctrine of Salvation* (1905). In the following year it was also used by J.W. Buckingham of the Pacific Theological Seminary, Berkeley, in *Christ and the Eternal Order.* In England, the expression was first used by W.R. Inge in 1907. Teilhard de Chardin took up the expression and used it more than thirty times in his early writings (1916–24). During the last ten years of his life, and also in his last essay *'Le Christique,'* Chardin also uses the synonyms *'Christus Universalis,' 'Super-Christus,' 'Christus-Omega,' 'Christus-Evolutor.'*

And Andreas Rössler writes (p.112):

In Teilhard's Creed he says: 'I believe that the universe is an evolution. I believe that the evolution is striving in the direction of the spirit. I believe that the spirit comes to fulfilment in personality. I believe that the fulfilment of the personal is the universal Christ.' The cosmic Christ is the point Omega in which everything will culminate and be suffused with divine love. But the Christ can only be the summit and aim of cosmic evolution because he also is the origin, the deepest driving force and continual motor of this whole evolution. He can only redeem and gather to himself the spiritual beings because he is also the foundation and the basis of their life, the heart of matter itself. The cosmic Christ guarantees the future gathering together of all spiritual forces in love. He is the surety that no effort on behalf of the kingdom of God is lost.

2.2 The Orthodox Church has not followed the Western course in this respect, either; having regard to the early Greek teachers of the Church, it has preserved a certain relationship to the cosmic Christ. The orthodox Easter liturgy can furnish a classic example of this: 'Now everything is filled with light — Heaven, Earth and the realm of death. All creation celebrates the Resurrection of Christ in which it is founded.' (quoted in Jürgen Moltmann, *The Way of Jesus Christ*).

And, as we have already seen, redemption and the rejoicing in victory does not only relate to Man; joining with the joy of our resurrection is also the joy over the

transfiguration of the entire world, over the abolition of
the realm of decay, over the redemption of all creation
and the onset of the realms of life. And the spiritual eye
looks with fervour towards the future glory — to that
'wonderful freedom of the children of God' in which all
creation will have a part. So the Resurrection is an event
of cosmic significance, and through it the world, as much
as Man, is lit up by the heavenly glory already now,
although in a concealed way as yet, and it has attained a
new, high dignity: for it has already taken into itself the
germ of immortality. Christ — so sings the Eastern
Church — 'has risen as God in glory from the grave and
thereby he has awakened the world also,' 'giving life to
the world,' 'he has enlightened the whole world, all
creation,' 'by the glory of his coming and by his cross he
has enlightened the ends of the world,' he has 'made the
earthly one with the heavenly.' 'O wonder of wonders!
How came the life of the universe to taste death? Only
because it wanted to enlighten the world.'

Thus the whole world, all creation, is urged to rejoice
and to praise the Lord: 'Rejoice, O creation, and bloom
like a lily! For Christ has risen from the dead, as God!
Where, O Death, is now your sting? Where is your
victory, O Hell?' 'Let the heavenly beings rejoice and the
earthly jubilate, for the Lord has worked strength with his
arm: he has trampled death under foot through death.'
'All creation and the prophets sing a song of victory to
you, rejoicing.' 'The ends of the world jubilate because of
your rising from the dead.' (From Nikolaus von
Arseniew, *Ostkirche und Mystik,* p.13f. The quotations are
from liturgical texts.)

2.3   In Chapter 5 we shall discuss this in detail and quote the
most important passages. For the moment, we mention here his
fundamental book *Occult Science* (GA 13).

An interesting perspective on the question of the origin of the
universe is offered by the so-called 'anthropic principle' which
is widely debated nowadays:

Furthermore, the so-called anthropic fertility of the

universe is increasingly under discussion. What is meant by this is the discovery that the scientifically describable structure of the cosmos appears to show a degree of fine tuning which makes life and the evolution towards Man possible, whereas quite insignificant alterations of nature constants would suffice to make both impossible (anthropic principle). For example, Barrow and Tippler pointed out that the nuclear energy values for beryllium and carbon have to be exactly what they are in order to make life possible. They also mention the remarkable physical properties of water and the concentration of oxygen in the earth's atmosphere which, for the existence of life on the basis of carbon compounds, is indispensable, and which are dependent upon precisely poised balances of the natural constants. (Klaus Strobach, *Vom 'Urknall' zur Erde,* p.199.)

2.4 The Christian Community was founded in 1922 by in the main Protestant theologians led by Friedrich Rittelmeyer, and with the advice and help of Rudolf Steiner. For the account by H.-W. Schroeder, see Note 1.6 above.

2.5 In addition to the literature of The Christian Community mentioned in Note 1.6 above, the following can be referred to: Friedrich Benesch, *Vorträge und Kurse.* Volumes 2 and 3.

2.6 Although Moltmann, as far as I can see, goes far beyond the usual theological ideas, both as regards the extent and the differentiation of his conceptions, when he regards the cosmic Christ as the 'redeemer of evolution.' He speaks of 'cosmic Christology' (and of 'reconciliation of the entire cosmos with Christ,' with reference to Col.1:20), but what is meant is only the earth with nature and mankind. And although Moltmann says: 'Christ's domain is the whole of creation, the visible as well as the invisible, that is to say all realms which surround mankind and in which Man has a share, and also those realms which are far from human beings because they remain inaccessible for them, as, for example, the heavens, the worlds of the divine powers,' this is not developed in concrete detail.

Moltmann also has something to say about Teilhard de Chardin; delicately he touches on the fact that Teilhard saluted the invention of the atom bomb and also the event of Hiroshima in a way which to us now is incomprehensible, indeed alarming: in them he saw something which would have a positive effect in the evolution he hoped for.

What is more: with Teilhard, too, the talk of the 'cosmic' or 'universal' Christ remains pale and vague as regards the actual cosmos, the universe — important as the impetus has otherwise been which he has given to the conception of the universal activity of Christ. With their development of the 'noosphere,' the dying into the 'Omega-point,' his ideas do essentially relate to earth and mankind.

We shall try to go beyond that; see Chapter 5, especially from p.130ff.

2.7 With regard to world evolution (earth and cosmos), see *inter alia* R. Steiner's *Occult Science* (GA 13). On astronomy, the zodiac, world of the fixed stars, planets — their origin, their relationship to Man, to spiritual beings, and so on — there are numerous lectures by Steiner; a selection, for example, in *Man and the World of Stars* (GA 219).

2.8 It may appear nonsensical from an astronomical point of view that the sun and the moon are here numbered among the planets. We cannot here explain why, from another point of view, it can be absolutely right and meaningful; we include this view in our description without further explanation and direct the reader to the literature indicated in Note 2.7 above.

The same applies to the concept 'planetary sphere,' which implies that the body of the planet could be regarded as only a kind of 'marker' of a great realm which surrounds the earth spherically; it is true also of the view that the earth again appears (geocentrically) in the midpoint of these planetary spheres, which, incidentally, by no means invalidates the heliocentric conception of the universe. It would equally be necessary to give reasons why Uranus, Neptune and Pluto are not being counted among these seven 'planets.'

2.9 The highest angel beings reach beyond the planetary spheres:

Angels — Moon sphere
Archangels — Venus sphere
Archai — Mercury sphere
Exousiai — Sun sphere
Dynameis — Mars sphere
Kyriotetes — Jupiter sphere
Thrones — Saturn sphere

But then:

Cherubim — world of fixed stars and Zodiac
Seraphim — beyond the world of fixed stars

As regards the ordering of the realms of the angels, their names, their relationship to the Godhead above them, see H.-W. Schroeder, *Mensch und Engel.*

2.10 H.-W. Schroeder, *Der Mensch und das Böse,* in particular the chapter: 'Die tieferen Folgen des Sündenfalls.'

2.11 In many places, Rudolf Steiner — despite his fully realistic assessment of future crises — has encouraging words with regard to the eventual overcoming of evil; for example:

The world impulse which prepares for this [that is, the future] says the following to its disciples: people speak of good and evil and do not know that in the design of the world it is necessary for evil, too, to reach its peak, so that those who have to overcome this evil employ their strength in overcoming evil in such a way that an all the greater good shall ultimately come to light ... so the good would not be as great a good if it did not grow through overcoming evil. Love would not be as intense if it did not have to become so great a love that it could overcome even the wickedness in the face of evil human beings ... therefore you should not think that evil is not part of the plan of creation. It is part of it, so that one day the greatest good may come about through it. (R. Steiner, *The Apocalypse,* GA 104. Lecture 8.)

2.12 Teilhard was a medical orderly during the war; it was during his time at the front, 'in mud and blood,' that his work appeared, in which, probably for the first time, his mystical experience of the world becomes clear. I quote first from the essay 'The Picture,' in the contemplation of which the vision of Christ appears:

> The fact remains that as I allowed my gaze to wander over the figure's outlines I suddenly became aware that these were *melting away:* they were dissolving, but in a special manner, hard to describe in words. When I tried to hold in my gaze the outline of the figure of Christ, it seemed to me to be clearly defined; but then, if I let this effort relax, at once these contours and the folds of Christ's garment, the lustre of his hair and the bloom of his flesh, all seemed to merge as it were (though without vanishing away) into the rest of the picture. It was as though the planes which marked off the figure of Christ from the world surrounding it were melting into a single vibrant surface whereon all demarcations vanished.
>
> It seems to me that this transformation began at one particular point on the outer edge of the figure; and that it flowed on thence until it had affected its entire outline. This at least is how the process appeared to be taking place. From this initial moment, moreover, the metamorphosis spread rapidly until it had affected everything.
>
> First of all I perceived that the vibrant atmosphere which surrounded Christ like an aureole was no longer confined to a narrow space about him, but radiated outwards to infinity. Through this there passed from time to time what seemed like trails of phosphorescence, indicating a continuous gushing-forth to the outermost spheres of the realm of matter and delineating a sort of bloodstream or nervous system running through the totality of life.
>
> The entire universe was vibrant! And yet, when I directed my gaze to particular objects, one by one, I found them still as clearly defined as ever in their undiminished individuality. (From *Hymn of the Universe,* p.40f).

In the second essay 'The Monstrance,' the beholding of the host widens into a cosmic perspective:

So, through the mysterious expansion of the host, the whole world had become incandescent, had itself become like a single giant host. One would have said that, under the influence of this inner light which penetrated it, its fibres were stretched to breaking-point and all the energies within them were strained to the utmost. And I was thinking that already in this opening-out of its activity the cosmos had attained its plenitude when I became aware that a much more fundamental process was going on within it.

From moment to moment sparkling drops of pure metal were forming on the inner surface of things and then falling into the heart of this profound light, in which they vanished; and at the same time, a certain amount of dross was being volatilized: a transformation was taking place in the domain of love, dilating, purifying and gathering together every power-to-love which the universe contains. (From *Hymn of the Universe,* p.45f).

2.13 In the Preface to his book, *The Tao of Physics,* Fritjof Capra writes:

Five years ago, I had a beautiful experience which set me on a road that has led to the writing of this book. I was sitting by the ocean one late summer afternoon, watching the waves rolling in and feeling the rhythm of my breathing, when I suddenly became aware of my whole environment as being engaged in a gigantic cosmic dance. Being a physicist, I knew that the sand, rocks, water and air around me were made of vibrating molecules and atoms, and that these consisted of particles which interacted with one another by creating and destroying other particles. I knew also that the Earth's atmosphere was continually bombarded by showers of 'cosmic rays', particles of high energy undergoing multiple collisions as they penetrated the air. All this was familiar to me from my research in high-energy physics, but until that moment I had only experienced it through graphs, diagrams and mathematical theories. As I sat on that beach my former experiences came to life; I 'saw' cascades of energy coming down from outer space, in which particles were created and destroyed in rhythmic pulses; I 'saw' the atoms of the elements and those of my body participating in this cosmic dance of energy; I felt its rhythm and I 'heard' its sound, and at that moment I knew that this was the Dance of Shiva, the Lord of Dancers worshipped by the Hindus.

2.14 Rupert Sheldrake, *A New Science of Life.*

2.15 Lecture by Capra in the Catholic Academy in Bavaria. Oct 17, 1987. Quoted in H. Bürkle, *New Age.*

2.16 Horst Bürkle writes:
The demands of the New Age movement for a so-called 'change of paradigm' relate to insights which have been won by physical science in the sphere of nuclear research ... the New Age physicist Fritjof Capra now goes a decisive step further. For him, this physical thought-model provides the scientific proof for a positively religious overvaluation of these interconnections. The substance of concrete religious revelations, such as those known to Christianity, are thereby relegated by him to the partial, and therefore the temporary ... seeking timeless and nameless experience of all this, he finds the answer in the mysticism of the Far East. Quite consistently, he gives one of his books the title *The Tao of Physics.* The fact is that all this actually is not about religion but about a kind of metaphysics of nature. Oriental religiosity helps the physicist of the New Age movement to give a religious gloss to the harmonizing interweaving of the part-phenomena within the whole. (From 'Die Unterscheidung der Geister,' in Horst Bürkle, *New Age,* p.114ff.)

2.17 An example of harsh criticism from the philosophical-scientific side:

> New Age authors like Fritjof Capra and Marilyn Ferguson
> have abstracted a metaphysics of the whole from it, in
> which everything is connected with everything else, and,
> it follows, nothing is impossible any more. For the reader
> interested in the scientific world view, only this much is
> of importance: the representatives of the New Age can
> appeal neither to the results of quantum physics nor to the
> philosophical-theoretical statements of the authors of
> quantum theory when they advance their peculiar
> coupling of spirit and matter. Whether the taoist texts
> permit these conclusions is for Sinologist to judge. (From
> Bernulf Kantscheider, *Von der mechanistischen Welt zum
> kreativen Universum,* p.100.)

2.18 In how naive and undifferentiated a way physical concepts are transferred to religious notions can be seen from the following example:

> Great scientists become ecstatic about the complexity of
> reality — about the power which lies hidden behind the
> cosmic energy. They see the immense total organism as
> being held together by a unitary Founder. Without
> subscribing to any particular confession they develop
> deep religious feelings; but what they confess to is not so
> much religion as a cosmic spirituality, such as was
> demonstrated in his own life by Albert Einstein, for
> example.
>
> The dynamic principle of self-organization in the
> universe is active in every part of it as it is in the whole.
> Without a name and without an image. And yet: God is
> the name which the various religions have found to save
> it from namelessness, to raise it into our consciousness
> and to let us celebrate it in practical life ... for everyone
> who has once experienced the secret which we call God,
> everything is a way, and each single being is a sacrament
> and a gate to an encounter with Him. (From L. Boff, *Von
> der Würde der Erde,* p.48f.)

2.19 Teilhard comes very near to this mistake when he says: 'Through his incarnation, Christ indwells the world ... is rooted in the world, right into the heart of the tiniest atom.' *(Collected Works,* Vol.6.)

And elsewhere: 'Christ works physically around us, so as to order everything. Without disturbing them, he continuously ensouls all movements of the earth ... from the last vibration of the atom to the highest mystical contemplation.' *(My Universe* in *Science and Christ).*

Others express similar views:

'I am the core of every atom, every nucleus and its inner radiance. I am all of that, and as I unfold myself, he unfolds: I am you, and you are I ... Christ is in all things and all people.' (David Spangler, *New Age.)*

Schiwy appears to concur with such ideas, calling them 'Johannine.' And Matthew Fox writes of 'the image of God in every atom and every galaxy.'

In contrast, see Wolfgang Kilthau, 'Das "menschliche Atom." Zum Verlauf einer okkulten Strömung im 20. Jahrhundert' in *Das Goetheanum,* July 18, 1993; and also 'New Age und das menschliche Atom' in *Die Drei,* Supplement 3, November 1990.

2.20 Teilhard de Chardin reflects upon this danger of pantheism as follows:

> Everything around us is physically 'Christified', and everything ... can become progressively more fully so.
>
> In this 'pan-Christism', it is evident, there is no false pantheism ... Because our omega, Christ, is placed at the upper term of conscious spiritualisation, his universal influence far from dissociating, consolidates; far from confusing, differentiates; far from allowing the soul to wallow in a vague, supine union, it drives it ever higher along the hard and fast paths of action. The danger of false pantheisms has been removed, and yet we retain the irreplaceable strength of the religious life that the pantheists unjustly claim as their own.
>
> All around us, Christ is physically active in order to control all things. From the ultimate vibration of the atom to the loftiest mystical contemplation; from the lightest

breeze that ruffles the air to the broadest currents of life
and thought, he ceaselessly animates, without disturbing,
all the earth's processes. (*My Universe* in *Science and
Christ* p.59.)

One can discern that various views of the unity — or the
manifoldness — of the world are one-sided, tending either in a
'luciferic' or an 'ahrimanic' direction: everything is one and
ultimately the same; everything is fragmented into an infinite
number of details. If, in thought, we can bring into relationship
with each other what is justified in each of these one-sided views,
we will be led rightly into the sphere of the cosmic Christ.

2.21 To this, Matthew Fox (*The Coming of the Cosmic Christ*)
says without any differentiation:

The Eucharist, for example, could be greatly de-trivialized
if Christians would learn that the body of Christ which
they eat and drink really is the factual eating and drinking
of the cosmic body and blood of the divine which is
present in every atom and every galaxy of our universe ...
what could root us more firmly, what could be more
intimate, local and erotic than eating and drinking? And if
Jesus Christ is the crucified mother earth, then the eating
and drinking in the Eucharist is the eating and drinking of
the wounded earth ...

We are all nourishment for one another. 'Take and eat,
for this is my body.' The body which we eat is no longer
confined to the loaf of bread, whether leavened or
unleavened, but the bread is seen for what it is: a
cosmological gift, two billion years old, a present from
earth, air, fire and water, from photosynthesis and sun,
from the supernovae and the original fiery spheres. The
ingenuity to be able to make bread out of wheat and earth
and to harvest grapes is itself a gift of the waves of light
and the waves of the brain which enabled human
consciousness to arrive at such ideas.

The Eucharist represents a complete vindication of the
cosmic Christ's desire for intimacy with Man, that is to
say, the cosmic Christ must be consumed, eaten. At such
a moment the entire creation is present, at such a festive

gathering nothing and no one is excluded from this truly cosmic event.

In many respects one could agree with Fox here, although it would at the same time be clear that 'body' and 'blood' can, in the sacrament, fully achieve the degree of reality which, even with earnest daily effort, can only be striven for. Already Paul, after all, makes it a condition for the 'worthy' receiving of communion that right 'distinctions' are made (1Cor.11:26ff).

CHAPTER 3

3.1 In *Saint Paul,* Emil Bock shows in detail that the so-called conversion of Paul actually corresponds in a new way to the experience of initiation in the ancient mysteries.

In his letters, Paul repeatedly speaks of supersensible experiences: 1Cor.11:23, 2Cor.12:2–4, Gal.1:16, Eph.6:12.

Rudolf Steiner speaks frequently on this subject, for instance, in *Heilfaktoren für den sozialen Organismus (Healing of the Social Organism),* GA 198, lecture of April 2, 1920.

3.2 In the New Testament it is generally Christ's proclamation that is meant when the 'word of God' is mentioned, for example in the Parable of the Sower: 'The seed is the word *(logos)* of God' (Luke 8:11); nevertheless, the meaning 'Christ' frequently shines through, quite explicitly in 2Pet.3:5, Heb.11:3, Acts 19:13.

3.3 This is shown beautifully in Wladimir Lindenberg, *Die heilige Ikone.* As a motto for his book, Lindenberg quotes Dionysius the Areopagite:

The picture, however, full of grace, allows the Christian to partake of the holiness of the archetypal image, and itself becomes a mystery. It is an image of the invisible and has the power to raise the beholding of the visible into a vision of the divine.

3.4 Here Paul uses words for higher angels. In my book *Mensch und Engel,* I have described the nine ranks of the angels with their Greek and/or Hebrew names, together with their (varying) translations. What is referred to here are the 'thronoi,' 'kyriotetes'

(World Guides), 'archai' (World Powers), and 'exousiai' (Revealers). The translation given here in parenthesis is based on that by Emil Bock.

3.5 In his book *Saint Paul,* Emil Bock has shown that Paul is not promoting a doctrine of predestination, such as has played so disastrous a role in Christianity (Augustine, Calvin, and so on). The same applies to the famous passage in Romans 8.

3.6 It has already been mentioned that, in accordance with Genesis 1, the 'Elohim' (a Hebrew plural, that is, 'gods') are the creators (see Note 1.10) — but according to John 1 it is the *Logos,* that is to say, Christ. The contradiction is resolved when one considers: the Elohim are the 'sun-beings' (Exousiai) among whom Christ has arrived in the course of his cosmic descent, and to whom he appeals to become creatively active at this stage; that also becomes clear from the fact that the Elohim create through the 'word.' Seven times we hear: '... and God (Elohim) said ...' This also explains: 'Let us make man in our image, after our likeness ...' (Gen.1:26).

The connection between Christ and Yahweh is described by Rudolf Steiner as follows:

What is the significance of the revelations to Moses? They signify that that which was drawing near to the earth as the Christ Being first showed himself as in a reflection, as in a mirror. Let us imagine a spiritualized version of the event which we perceive on the moon every night when the moon is full. When we look up to the full moon we see the rays of the sun reflected back to us, mirrored. It is sunlight which streams towards us there; only, we call it moonlight because it appears reflected from the moon. Whom was it that Moses saw in the burning bush and fire on Mount Sinai? It was the Christ. But just as one does not see the sunlight on the moon directly, but reflected, so he saw Christ in a reflection. And just as we call sunlight 'moonlight' when we see it reflected from the moon, so Christ was called Yahweh or Jehovah in those days. So Yahweh or Jehovah is in fact the reflection of Christ before he himself

201

appeared on the earth. In this way the Christ made himself known, indirectly, to the human being who, as yet, was not able to behold him in his very essence; just as the sunlight makes itself known on an otherwise dark night through the moon beams. Yahweh or Jehovah is the Christ, seen not directly but indirectly, as reflected light. (From *The Gospel of St Luke,* GA 114. Lecture of Sept 21, 1909.)

3.7 Interestingly, this component acquires particular succinctness in the Stoa (see p.92). The *Theologisches Begriffslexikon zum Neuen Testament* says:

In this mode of thinking, the *Logos* is the expression for the order and teleological harmony of the world ... it is the principle which gives form to the cosmos, permeating matter. In that the world is perceived as a unity and as an unfolding of the *Logos,* the *Logos* is invested with a high degree of spiritualization.

3.8 With this, the spirit-aspect of the *Logos* is touched on at the same time. In the threefoldness of Word — Life — Light, as we encounter it in John's Prologue, something of the divine Trinity of Father — Son — Spirit also appears.

3.9 'To the individual human egos ...' Here I follow the translation by Emil Bock (correspondingly Rudolf Steiner: 'the individual human beings, the "ego human beings"'). The Greek text here says: *eis ta idia* and *hoi idioi* respectively; the primary meaning of *ta idia* is 'home,' but then also 'property, ownership.' John wants to say that, in coming to Man, the 'true light' seeks out that which belongs to it, its home, where it is truly 'at home' and has 'property rights' — but the tragedy is that human beings meanwhile have become *hoi idioi,* that is 'selves' who want to 'own' themselves: in other words: 'ego people.' So the brilliant play on the words *idia* and *idioi* at one and the same time indicates the nearness of the human ego to Christ and the tragedy of the ego-development which in its first stage leads to egoism.

3.10 Nowadays, the 'Childhood Gospels' (Matt.1 and 2, Luke 1 and 2) are dismissed as invention. That they are anything but that has been shown by Emil Bock in *The Childhood of Jesus*.

Eugen Drewermann at least attempts to rescue the eternal content of the images.

3.11 In *Background to the Gospel of St Mark* (GA 124), Steiner discusses the cosmic aspect of the 'Temptation' of Christ among the 'animals' after the Baptism.

3.12 Further motifs from John's Gospel: 'He who comes from above, towers above all ... the One who comes from the heavenly world exceeds all others ...' (John 3:31). The cosmic descent of Christ which we have described is being indicated here. 'Whoever hears the word that I speak, and places his trust in Him who sent me, he has life beyond the cycles of time ...' (John 5:24). In this saying, the future life of Man is associated with the 'word' of Christ. This life is to be 'beyond time,' that is, it will itself take its course in a cosmic dimension.

From the abundance of possible quotations, just one more — from the dispute with the Jews, in Chapter 8: 'From the days before Abraham was [born], I existed as the I-AM!' (John 8:58). The 'I' of Christ is in existence before all human creation: this, too, an indication of the cosmic dimension.

3.13 This theme appears from another aspect in the Letter to the Colossians:

> By stripping the primal powers and the creator-spirits of
> their might which had become darkened, he made them
> emerge with power into the light and made them subject
> to his triumphant revelation. (Col.2:15).

The power of the cosmic beings to strive asunder into multiplicity, indeed into lawlessness and chaos, came above all from the mights of the spiritual world who resisted the divine, that is: the beings of the Adversaries. Here, then, it becomes clear that the raising of Christ has also put a stop to these Powers, so that, in the end, they, too, shall be woven into the community of the cosmic aims.

Something similar is probably meant by the obscure saying in the First Letter of Peter: 'And in the spirit he also went and brought the proclamation to the spirits in prison, who once closed themselves off from the will of God ...' (3:19).

A quotation from Peter's address in the Acts of the Apostles goes beyond the motif of Christ being 'exalted,' although it does include a reference to the Ascension of Christ: '... when he will be sent to you, too, who is to come to you: the Christ Jesus. The sphere of the heavens must shelter him until the time when all existence is led back to its origins.' (Acts 3:20f).

Here Christ is thought of as 'occupying' heaven, and, linked to that, is the future prospect that he will come again and restore the true order of all things. However, that second part of the quotation takes us beyond this section of the book; we will return to it later.

3.14 Particular attention should be drawn to the following, among other passages, in his address in Athens:

The divine Being who created the cosmos and all
beings who are within it, the Lord of heaven and
earth, does not live in temples built with hands ... in
Him we live and weave and have our being ... (Acts
17:24,27).

Again, before King Agrippa, Paul describes his Damascus-experience: 'In the midday hour, O King, I saw on the way a light from heaven, brighter than the sun itself, which shone around me and my companions.' (Acts 26:13).

3.15 It was a central aspect of Paul's proclamation that human beings have an inner ('mystical') share in the death, resurrection and higher life of Christ, already during their earthly existence. This is summed up in the famous saying which we have already quoted — in contracted form: 'Not I, but Christ in me' — and which continues: 'I am crucified with Christ. So it is not I who live, but Christ lives in me. The life which I have now in my earthly incarnation I have through devotion and faith in the Son of God who loves me and has given himself for me.' (Gal. 2:19–21, 3:27; compare 2Cor.5:15, Eph.1:18–20, Phil.3:10f, Col. 2:12–14, Rom.6:3, 4:1, 1Pet.2:24, 3:21).

3.16 Here, as also in the case of other letters whose 'genuineness' is considered doubtful, we take the view that there are valid and good reasons why they are part of the canon of the New Testament, and that they stem from the broad stream of positive, early-Christian revelation. Questions concerning authorship etc. resolve themselves when one bears in mind that other states of soul and consciousness obtained in those days, and that there were therefore also other possibilities of receiving genuine inspirations; so it was absolutely feasible to speak and write 'in the spirit of' Paul, Peter etc. In view of this, earthly authorship was of secondary importance.

Further passages about cosmic transformation at the end; first of all again: 'All that is in the heavens and on the earth shall be ... united into one being in Christ.' (Eph.1:10).

But in the First Letter to the Corinthians, Paul goes far beyond this:

> Then comes the goal, when he gives the world which has united itself with him to the divine Father, and brings to nought the Mights, Revealers and the World Powers.
>
> He must be the Lord of destiny until he has forced all enemies under his feet. As the last enemy, death is brought to nought, then he really has subjected the whole cosmos to the tread of his foot ... When everything has become completely subject to him, then he himself, the Son, will subordinate himself to the One who has made everything subject to him, so that God is everything in everything. (1Cor.15:24–28).

Here we once more encounter a motif which we came across in a previous section of the book: in Christ lives the power to gather the cosmos together again, which has become prey to the powers of the Adversaries and is falling apart. In addition, Paul here includes the power of death which has permeated all creation since the Fall: death, too, is to be made powerless. In the First Letter to the Corinthians, Paul discusses this motif with an eye to Man; but if we consult Romans 8, we see that he also means the transformation of those forces of death which exist in the rest of creation. This is true also for Corinthians, which continues:

> At the sound of the trumpet the dead shall be called to

life as imperishable beings, and we shall all be
transformed; for that which now bears decay must clothe
itself with imperishable being, and that which now bears
mortality must clothe itself with immortal being. But
when that which now bears decay has been clothed with
imperishable being, and when that which is mortal now
has been clothed with immortality, then the word will be
fulfilled which is written: Death is destroyed by the
victory of life. Death, where is your victory? Death,
where is your sting?

The sting of death is sin, and sin exercises its power
through the Law. Let us thank God who has given us the
victory of life through Jesus Christ, our Lord.
(1Cor.15:51–57).

For the sake of completeness, another passage, the beginning
of which we have already quoted:

Whoever is in Christ, in him begins the new creation. All
that is old has passed away; see, something new has come
into being. All this has been caused by God who has
transformed us back towards Himself in Christ, and has
commissioned us to carry out the priestly service of
transformation. God worked through Christ and,
transforming it, He raised the world back to Himself. No
longer did He look upon its errors, but in our midst He
instituted the creative word of transformation.
(2Cor.5:17–19).

3.17 We cannot substantiate this in detail here; let us just say
that in the fourth and fifth chapters of the Apocalypse we
encounter the realm of the divine creator powers — the 'seven
creator-spirits' are specifically mentioned; among them belongs
the cosmic Christ as the actual centre, here in the image of the
Lamb. In bygone ages, mankind had a quite different relationship
to animals: in Egypt, for example, even the highest gods could
appear in animal guise; the Zodiac, the 'circle of animals,' among
the fixed stars was the expression of exalted spiritual beings.
Something was still experienced of the profound wisdom and
power which is imaged in the earthly animals.

3.18 Here let us again call to mind that quotation from Peter's address in the Acts of the Apostles, already cited: 'When he will be sent to you, too, who is to come to you: the Christ Jesus. The sphere of the heavens must shelter him until the time when all existence is led back to its origins.' (Acts 3:20f) This hints, as it were, at the ultimate perspective for the future of the world; it even extends beyond the Revelation to John, for in the Apocalypse it is left open what will happen to the powers and beings who cannot advance to the New Jerusalem. Will they remain eternally lost?

In Peter's address we now see before us the prospect that 'the true order of all existence' will be restored through the cosmic working of Christ. This conception of the restoration of all things, the so-called *apokatastasis panton,* was held in early Christianity, for instance by Origen. He even emphasized that the powers of the Adversaries, too, would be included in this restoration of the original order.

This, then, would present us with the farthest aim of the cosmic working of Christ, as it is shown us in these words from the Acts of the Apostles; having, indeed, already been sounded in Paul's words to the Corinthians in the First Letter, fifteenth chapter: '... so that God is everything in everything.' This hope for the most distant future is allied to the view of the cosmic existence of Christ (see also Note 5.16).

3.19 Some other Psalms which, in a similar way, see divine working in creation: Ps.19: 'The heavens are telling;' Ps.8: 'how majestic is thy name in all the earth!' Ps.148: 'he commanded and they were created;' Ps.65: 'Thou visitest the earth and waterest it, thou greatly enrichest it;' Ps.24: 'The earth is the Lord's and the fullness thereof,' and so on.

Compare Rudolf Frieling, *Hidden Treasures in the Psalms.* On the theme 'creation as garment,' see also Heb.1:10–12.

3.20 This plays a role, especially in 'feminist' literature, since *ruach* (Hebrew = 'spirit, breath, life-force, wind/storm') is feminine (as is Greek *sophia* = wisdom). For that reason, *ruach* is often translated into German in a feminine version, that is, 'spiritess.' It occurs almost four hundred times in the Old Testament.

The differentiation of being within the working of the Godhead can be characterized in three directions as follows:

Father — being and substance

Son — existence: life/creating/becoming

Spirit — consciousness: meaning/light/aim

Compare H.-W. Schroeder, *Dreieinigkeit und Dreifaltigkeit.*

CHAPTER 4

4.1 The change in human consciousness during the course of evolution, from 'natural clairvoyance' to present-day self-awareness, is described by Rudolf Steiner in many places, for instance: *Cosmic Memory* (GA 11), *Occult Science* (GA 13).

Against the background of the history of philosophy: *The Riddles of Philosophy* (GA 18).

4.2 On the old clairvoyance and imaginative consciousness:
A life of soul did once exist, in which human beings
were not so dependent upon such external impressions, in
which they had an old, dreamlike clairvoyance. At that
time, images arose clairvoyantly within them, which
reproduced and expressed an outer reality, but not the
kind of outer reality which we nowadays have around us.
Everything which we have around us in the way of plants
and animals, air and water, clouds and mountains — all
this was not yet surrounded by boundaries for mankind at
that time; at most, people then saw things as if through a
mist. At that time, human beings looked up to the next
realm through their dreamlike, twilight consciousness, to
the realm of the angels. At a yet higher stage of consciousness they looked up to the realm of the archangels
and to the realm of the Spirits of Personality. In the same
way that we nowadays look at the realm of the minerals,
so human beings in those days looked up to the hierarchies which they perceived in their dreamlike, twilight
consciousness ... Only slowly and by degrees was
perception turned towards the merely external world. The
portal to the spiritual world was closed. (R. Steiner,
GA 118. Lecture of Feb 20, 1910.)

4.3   From Note 4.2 above it can be seen that early humanity was able to look up clairvoyantly to the most varied spiritual beings; it must be understood, however, that in the spiritual world there are no such things as boundaries or 'isolation' as they are given for us with the earthly-material body; yet in the realm of the air this is already different: for example, we breathe the same air as other people (in a closed room) and are not able there to separate ourselves off. With this in mind, it becomes comprehensible when we are told that spiritual beings can permeate one another mutually, and that thereby higher beings (the cosmic Christ) can work within lower beings as in a spiritual 'body-form.' This makes the relationship of Christ to the 'sun-gods' and 'creator-gods' multiform and complex.

4.4   Quoted from Pierre Grimal (ed.) *Mythen der Völker.*
   The connection with the 'carpenter's son' Jesus is surely more than a mere coincidence; on the other hand, 'literary dependence' — which would usually be suggested in such a case — would hardly come into question; in which case we would here have before us a classic instance of how archetypal images win through: as mythical sayings, but reflected as earthly facts in the deeds of Christ.

4.5   Quoted from *Die Schöpfungsmythen.*
   Compare Gen.2:7: 'Then the Lord God formed man of dust from the ground ...' Werner H. Schmidt remarks: 'The verb used, *jasar,* to form, refers to the activity of a potter (compare Gen. 2:19, Jer.18:1–6, Isa.45:9, 29:16 *et al.)* ' and cites a list of Egyptian, Mesopotamian, Babylonian and Greek parallels *(Die Schöpfungsgeschichte der Priesterschrift).* Here, then, it would be possible to think in terms of 'literary dependence.' A more obvious explanation suggests itself, however; namely, that the clairvoyant seeing of like facts (for instance the creation of Man) produces like or similar images; the differences which arise would be caused by the different 'spiritual position' of the seers, just as an earthly landscape, viewed from different positions (mountain, valley; summer, winter; day, night etc.) also has to be described in different ways. On the subject of Mystery terminology, see also Eph.1:13, 6:19 and Col.1:28, 4:3.

4.6 Welburn cites the following passages: Mark 4:10–12; 4:34, Matt.11:27; Luke 10:22, 9:1–6, 10:1–16, 12:2–12, Matt.9:35–10:4, Mark 6:7–11, 8:31–33, 9:30–50, 10:32–45, 13:5–23,26,27, 14:18–21, 26–31.

4.7 The increasing flood of books about the Essenes and Qumran is evidence of a growing public interest. See also Rudolf Steiner, *The Gospel of St Matthew* (GA 123) on the Essenes and Jeshu ben Pandira; and Emil Bock, *Cäsaren und Apostel,* especially Chapter 4 and the appendix, in which evidence from antiquity and the recent finds are discussed.

4.8 Welburn writes:
The book covers a wide field, and is not addressed to specialists. Where it relies on new interpretations of material discovered at Nag Hammadi or elsewhere, I have published more detailed scholarly accounts establishing my position. The material from the *Apocalypse of Adam* is analysed in my article published in W. Haase and H. Temporini (eds.), *Aufstieg und Niedergang der römischen Welt,* Part II, vol. 25.4, Berlin and New York 1988; the details of Gnostic cosmology are reconstructed in my articles in the journals *Vigiliae Christianae* (1978) and *Novum Testamentum* (1981); the background of the Gospel of Philip is the theme of another contribution to *Aufstieg und Niedergang der römischen Welt,* the still forthcoming Part II, vol. 22. *(op. cit.* p.viii.)

4.9 Kurt Rudolph, *Gnosis:*
For the Gnostic, then, the entire world-system, the cosmos, is a system of compulsion which he can therefore construe as 'darkness,' 'death,' 'deception,' 'badness.' 'The cosmos is the fullness of the bad.' *(Corp. Herm.* VI,4) It owes its origin to inferior powers, hostile to God; they especially harass human beings who find themselves in this 'housing' without easily finding ways and means of escaping from it.
The gnostic conception of the origin of the world is formulated in a concise way, stripped of mythological

colouring, in the (Valentinian) Gospel of Philip: 'The
cosmos came into being through a lapse. For he who
created it wanted to create it imperishable and immortal.
He lapsed, and did not achieve what was hoped for. For
the cosmos did not become imperishable, and he who had
created the cosmos was not imperishable.' (Nag
Hammadi-Codex II, 3, 123, 2–9).'

4.10 Welburn *(Beginnings of Christianity,* p.215ff) puts forward
further interesting points of view about the Resurrection.

Fundamental is Rudolf Steiner, *From Jesus to Christ* (GA 131).
See also Emil Bock, *The Three Years;* also *Das Evangelium.*

4.11 According to anthroposophical conceptions, the notion of
the 'harmony of the spheres' is absolutely based on reality: in
certain realms, the *logos* intensifies from 'speaking' to 'sounding'
and to 'tones.' In the prologue to *Faust,* Goethe says: 'The sun
sounds in its ancient way ...', and at the beginning of Part II: '...
what an uproar the light brings [at sunrise]!'

Rudolf Steiner describes the connection with the cosmic Christ
in, for example, *Christ and the Human Soul* (GA 155), lecture of
July 16, 1914.

CHAPTER 5

5.1 Further passages about this: GA 215, Sep 8, 1922; GA 220,
Jan 13, 1923; GA 232, Dec 2, 1923; GA 233, Dec 27, 1923. The
subject is mentioned in various ways in GA 93a, 74, 97, mainly
in discussion of the Prologue to John's Gospel; among these, GA
103 and 112 (lectures on John's Gospel).

5.2 On the theme 'Christ and the sun,' see, among many:
GA 26, Nov 3, 1924; GA 112, June 24, 1909; GA 113, Aug 28,
1909; GA 114, Sep 21, 1909; GA 209, Dec 25, 1921; GA 215,
Sep 12, 1922; GA 226, May 17, 1923; GA 239, April 5, 1924
and May 25, 1924; GA 240, Aug 27, 1924.

5.3 This raises the question of the 'inspiration' of the evangelists. That the evangelists were in possession of spiritual schooling

(Mystery-background) is described by Rudolf Steiner in various ways in his lectures about the gospels (see Note 5.4 below), especially GA 131 and 136 (the gospels were written out of inspiration, only one has to go back to their original texts: GA 136, April 11, 1912. Similarly: GA 139, Sep 24, 1912). In GA 137, June 10, 1912, can be found an indication of the relevant paths of initiation.

5.4 The most important 'gospel cycles' by Rudolf Steiner: GA 103 and 112 (John); 114 (Luke); 117 and 123 (Matthew); 124 and 139 (Mark); see also GA 131 *(From Jesus to Christ)*.

5.5 Origen can be mentioned as testimony to this:
Therefore, for the sake of understanding who the Christ is, John does not only describe the descent of the Spirit upon Jesus, but, in addition to this coming down, also the remaining of the Spirit in Jesus. For it is written that John said: 'He who sent me to baptize said: he on whom you see the Spirit descend and remain, he it is who will baptize with Holy Spirit and with fire.' He does not only say: 'He on whom you see the Spirit descend' — for it will certainly also have descended upon others — but: 'on whom it descends and remains in him.' *(Commentary on John's Gospel,* XX, 19).
And elsewhere:
Because Jesus bequeaths what he has acquired as a human being, he is the corner stone. Jesus, who also has a share in the divinity of the Son of God, is cleansed by being taken up by him, and then he opens himself to the untouched and guileless dove of the Spirit which unites with him and can never again depart from him. *(Commentary on John's Gospel,* II, 11).

5.6 See E. Bock, *The Three Years.*
On the Transfiguration, see R. Frieling, 'The Transfiguration on the Mountain,' Chapter 17 in *New Testament Studies.*
On the Resurrection, see Note 4.10, also Note 5.7 below.

5.7   The lecture cycle *From Jesus to Christ,* (GA 131) to which we draw attention here, is among the important foundations for an understanding of the nature of the Resurrection Body. Here, Rudolf Steiner describes in detail the nature of the original spiritual body of Man, its destruction through the Fall and through being permeated with matter, and its renewal through Christ.

5.8   In this context, Rudolf Steiner also uses the word 'atom':

> ... They [the spiritual beings whose leader is the Christ]
> will be able to instil into Man other thoughts than that
> there are only material atoms; for they will be able to
> teach Man that substance is permeated by the spirit of
> Christ, right into the smallest particles of the world ...
> [see quotation on p.121.]

Here the question arises as to how the concepts 'substance,' 'atom,' 'matter' are employed by Steiner — sometimes in very different ways, according to the context. Fundamental statements about the atom are to be found in GA 93 in the appendix as 'special notice,' in which early remarks on this topic are re-printed, which lead towards a spiritual understanding of the atom-concept.

Compare also our discussion of Teilhard de Chardin and others, regarding a naive notion of the connection between Christ and matter (see p.34f; also Note 2.19 above).

5.9   Steiner says:

> But on this earth, such ritual acts as proceed from a right
> grasp of the spiritual world will also take place ... By
> virtue of the fact that these ritual acts are carried out,
> elemental-spiritual beings are invoked into the realm of
> these ritual acts ... they are invisible to the outer eye. But
> a time will come when everything which now fills with
> matter the minerals, the plants, the animals, the clouds,
> that which works in wind and weather, will have
> vanished. The earth's covering of plants will have
> disappeared, will have become dust in the universe, as
> will obviously also the utensils which are used in these
> ritual acts. But what has been invoked as elemental

spiritual beings into the realm of the ritual acts will remain; when this earth approaches its fulfilment, that will be within the earth in just as perfect a form as, in autumn, the seeds of next year lie hidden within the plant. And just as the withered and dry leaves fall from the plant, so everything there is in the kingdoms of the minerals, the plants and the animals will crumble into the universe. And, like a seed for the future, the elemental beings, who by then will have perfected themselves, will be there, living on into the Jupiter-existence. (GA 216, Sep 29, 1922).

5.10 This contradicts other statements which speak of Man's eternal union with Christ. The contradiction is resolved when we bear in mind that reality has different stages: it was in order to reach not only the spiritual-soul core of Man but also that which the human soul experiences every day on earth, that what is indicated here had to take place.

5.11 The relationship of Christ to Man is described from ever new perspectives by Rudolf Steiner: Christ is found in the depths of the soul: GA 156, Dec 27, 1914. Personal relationship to Christ: GA 155, July 12, 1914. Christ became 'acquainted with death' for the sake of Man: GA 155, July 16, 1914. It is only through Christ that Man becomes a 'complete soul': GA 155, July 16, 1914. Spiritual fertilization of the inner human being: GA 155, May 24, 1912. 'Putting on' Christ: GA 127, May 3, 1911.

5.12 On this topic, too, many lectures could be cited, among others: GA 107, Oct 23, 1908. The effects of Man's relationship to Christ on earth continue after death: GA 140, Oct 26, 1912 and Jan 21, 1913.

Experience of Christ — at the moment of death: GA 176, Aug 28, 1917. Guide after death: GA 227, Aug 26, 1923. Christ makes possible a relationship between the living and the dead: GA 172, Nov 26 and 27, 1916.

5.13 To complement the theme 'Christ died for all human beings,' we must here draw attention to the continuation of the lecture already quoted (GA 224 on p.118f). The enlivening of the physical bodies through the Resurrection occurred in the past, but it will wane if Man does not gradually find his own awake and conscious access to Christ:

> For this Mystery of Golgotha took place in order to supply the physical human body with new forces, to, as it were, renew mankind on earth, to refresh them to the degree to which it is necessary to rejuvenate them. That happened. And it made it possible for human beings to find bodies on earth into which they can also incarnate for a certain, still very far-reaching length of time. But thereby human beings initially only pass through such rejuvenated earthly bodies as spiritual-soul beings; they can appear on earth again and again ...

However, the Christ-impulse is not only meant to be of significance for Man's body, but also for his spirit and his soul.

> For that to take effect, it is necessary that human beings confess out of knowledge to the substance of the Mystery of Golgotha. So the right spiritual effect of the Mystery of Golgotha can only proceed from a right acknowledgement of the substance of the Mystery of Golgotha ...
>
> That is the image of the Festival of Whitsun: the spirit-soul of Man is permeated with the power which understands the Mystery of Golgotha, the sending of the Holy Spirit. Christ fulfilled his deed for all mankind. He has sent the Spirit to each individual who is to understand this deed, to each single human individual, so that the human spirit-soul can find access to the deed which is for all mankind. Man must acquire the Christ-mystery inwardly in his spirit and soul through the Spirit.
> (GA 224, May 7, 1923; compare GA 226, May 17 and 20, 1923).

5.14 See also the lecture 'Erbsünde und Gnade,' (Original Sin and Grace), GA 127, May 3, 1911.

Because anthroposophy is repeatedly accused of teaching 'self-redemption,' let me refer the reader to: *Christentum — Anthroposophie — Waldorfschule,* Stuttgart 1987; and Andreas Binder *Wie christlich ist die Anthroposophie? Standortbestimmung aus der Sicht eines evangelischen Theologen.* Stuttgart 1990.

5.15 Rudolf Steiner speaks of Man's collaboration towards the future 'Jupiter' in: General GA 134, Dec 31, 1911; GA 104, June 26 and 30, 1908. Morality: GA 127, March 6, 1911; GA 275, Jan 3, 1915. Vocational work: GA 172, Nov 6, 1916. Art: GA 94, May 28, 1906; GA 110, April 18, 1909.

5.16 The 'return' of all things was spoken of in early Christianity, by Origen, for example:

This 'falling away' is complemented exactly by the return of the whole world to the spirit, as described in detail by Origen in his early work *Peri Archon,* and also in his *Commentary on John's Gospel.* There, Origen so elaborated the ideas of the New Testament as they are indicated in the Acts of the Apostles and in the First Letter to the Corinthians, Chapter 15, that he could show how the entire world is led back to its original state — a teaching which later is only promulgated by him through hints, but which now belongs to the 'heresies' which have to be extirpated ...

For a man like Origen it was simply not possible to think that it could be worthy of God to create a world, form a human being, then banish him from Paradise and save some, but let others burn in an eternal fire of Hell. Therefore Origen was of the view that ultimately everything will return to God, so that the 'middle phase,' that is, our entire world-evolution, is the 'interim stage' in which that whole vast drama is played out which includes the evolution of evil, its working, the consequences thereof; but also Christ's deed of redemption and its healing effects. As Origen says in his Psalm commentary: 'See, Lord, you know everything, the last and the first. What lies between the two is passed over in silence, because it is evil which occupies the interim. For in the beginning it did not exist, and at the end it will no longer be.' (Quoted from Reinhard Wagner, *Die Gnosis von Alexandria.*)

The idea of the 'return of everything' links on to Peter's second address (Acts 3:21); see H.-W. Schroeder, *Der Mensch und das Böse,* the chapter titled, 'Erlösung des Bösen?' (see also Note 3.18 above).

5.17 It has always been said (having in mind Col.2:15) that the exalted Christ subdues the rebellious cosmic powers: 'By stripping the primal powers and the creator-spirits of their might which had become darkened, he made them emerge with power into the light and made them subject to his triumphant revelation.' Here we have to bear in mind that there are hierarchical angel-beings associated with Ahriman and Lucifer. Some of them also have cosmic dimensions, and they, too, are to be included in the continuation of worlds.

5.18 In the lecture series *The Bridge between Universal Spirituality and the Physical Constitution of Man* (GA 202, Dec 4, 1920), Steiner considers in more detail the complicated relationship that exists between thinking and sense-perception on the one hand and willing on the other, with regard to the unfolding of the forces indicated here. How artistic and religious life help to shape the future of the cosmos is described in GA 276, June 8, 1923.

CHAPTER 6

6.1 Genuine meditation, though, also works more deeply into the human forces of soul and life; the same applies to regular prayer and to taking part in communal worship.

6.2 See Rudolf Frieling, 'Agape — Divine Love in the Fourth Gospel' in *New Testament Studies.*
Some other passages from John 15:12,17: 'As the Father has loved me, so I have loved you' (15:9). 'Whoever truly loves me bears my word [literally: my *logos]* in himself, and my Father will love him, and we will come to him and dwell with him for ever' (14:23). As Frieling shows, this motif is developed by stages to the end, to Christ's question to Peter: 'Do you love me?' The deep significance of this question, which of course cannot be meant formally, 'rhetorically,' is revealed in the discussion

of 'Love and Freedom' in Frieling's book. Incidentally, these two words appear close together in the centre of the Act of Consecration.

6.3 Perhaps one can imagine that the dark events in which mankind is embroiled at present also cast gloomy shadows onto the earth and darken it more and more in the course of the year; every year at Easter, the Christ breaks through this darkness and irradiates and transforms it with resurrection-power. Compare Note 6.8 below.

6.4 'Epistle' (Lat. *epistola* = letter): in the old Mass, the first of the two readings which are generally taken from a letter of one of the Apostles. In that place in the Act of Consecration we now have the 'Seasonal Prayers' which are also 'letters,' as it were — from the Christ who is present. They are his particular 'message' to the congregation at a given festive season.

6.5 The far-reaching questions in this connection have still to be thoroughly worked through and presented. Friedrich Benesch has taken first steps in this direction in *Vorträge und Kurse.*

6.6 Far-reaching reflections on the Christian festive seasons have been made by Rudolf Steiner, for instance:

In the age of the consciousness soul, human consciousness would be completely benighted over against the spirit-world if the consciousness soul were not able to grow strong enough to look back upon its divine-spiritual origins with insight. But if it can do that, it finds the world-*logos* as the entity which can guide it back. It permeates itself with the mighty image which reveals what took place on Golgotha.

And the beginning of this understanding is to grasp in love the World's Holy Night which is remembered festively every year. For the consciousness soul grows strong when, initially taking intellectuality into itself, it allows love to enter into this coldest of soul-elements; that warm love which flows at its most exalted when it is directed towards the Jesus child who appears on earth in the World's Holy Night. Then a human being has allowed the most sublime earthly spirit-fact (which was at the same time physical fact) to work upon his soul; he has begun to take the Christ into himself ...

To guide the human heart towards these great cosmic relationships: that is the right content of that festive remembrance which approaches Man every year when he contemplates the World's Holy Night. If that kind of love lives in the human heart, it warms the cold light-element of the consciousness soul. If it did not experience this warming, then Man would never achieve its permeation with spirit. He would perish in the chill of his intellectual consciousness, or he would have to remain in a spiritual life which does not advance to evolution of the consciousness soul. He would then have to linger at the stage of development of the intellectual- or mind soul.

But in its essence the consciousness soul is not cold. It only appears so at the beginning of its development, because at that stage it can only reveal its affinity with light, not yet the world-warmth out of which, after all, it originates.

To feel and experience Christmas in this way can make the soul aware: how the glory of the divine-spiritual beings, revealing their images in the widths of the stars, is proclaimed before Man, and how Man is set free in his earthly abode from the powers who want to distance him from his origins. (GA 26, Christmas 1924).

This motif is developed further by Rudolf Steiner in the next instalment (New Year 1925). In GA 175, Steiner describes the unconscious encounter of every human soul with Christ, which takes place during sleep in the Holy Nights (Feb 20, 1917).

6.7 See also GA 175, Feb 20, 1917 (Note 6.6 above): during the time of Epiphany 'until the time of Easter, conditions are particularly favourable for bringing to our consciousness Man's encounter with the Christ Jesus ...'; during that time, he 'walks beside us, as it were ... he now approaches us most closely.'

6.8 The topicality of every Easter festival is described by Rudolf Steiner, for example in the 'Easter Imagination' (GA 229, Oct 7, 1923):

> The Mystery of Golgotha did not only occur once as a unique event. Certainly, it had to take place as a unique event in the circumstances of earth; but this event, this Mystery of Golgotha, is renewed in a certain way for Man every year ... This is the figure of Christ as he appears every year in Spring, how we must picture him to ourselves: standing on what is earthly, what is to become ahrimanic; conqueror of death, risen from the grave, the Resurrected One raising himself to transfiguration — to transfiguration which comes about by transmuting what is luciferic into the earthly beauty of Christ's countenance. Thus the Christ, coming into view in his resurrection-form, is beheld as the Easter Appearance between what is ahrimanic and what is luciferic.

Compare also GA 223, March 31, 1923: that which is 'sun-like ... which unites with the Christ-power radiating out from the earth.'

6.9 At the end of the Gospel of Luke it becomes clear that the 'blessing' of Christ is bound up with the Ascension: 'And he led them out to near Bethany and raised his hands and blessed them. And while he was blessing them (literally: in blessing them), he vanished from their sight [and was taken up into heaven].' (Luke 24:50f).

On the subject of Ascension (and especially regarding 'the cloud') see Friedrich Benesch, *Ascension,* and H.-W. Schroeder, *Von der Wiederkunft Christi heute.*

6.10 To this belongs also what we expounded in Chapter 5. The intimacy and one-ness with Christ is present in a very particular way in the small child; for the development of walking — speaking — thinking in the first three years of life proceeds from the being of Christ who says: 'I am the way — the truth — the life.' (see GA 15, first and second lecture).

6.11 The 'Creed' of The Christian Community is as follows:
An almighty divine being, spiritual-physical, is the
ground of existence of the heavens and of the earth who
goes before his creatures like a Father.

Christ, through whom men attain the re-enlivening of
the dying earth-existence, is to this divine being as the
Son born in eternity.

In Jesus the Christ entered as man into the earthly
world. The birth of Jesus upon earth is a working of the
holy Spirit who, to heal spiritually the sickness of sin of
the bodily nature of mankind, prepared the son of Mary
to be the vehicle of the Christ.

The Christ Jesus suffered under Pontius Pilate the
death on the cross and was lowered into the grave of the
earth.

In death he became the helper of the souls of the dead
who had lost their divine nature; then he overcame death
after three days.

Since that time he is the Lord of the heavenly forces
upon earth and lives as the fulfiller of the fatherly deeds
of the ground of the world.

He will in time unite for the advancement of the world
with those whom, through their bearing, he can wrest
from the death of matter.

Through him can the healing Spirit work.

Communities whose members feel the Christ within
themselves may feel united in a church to which all
belong who are aware of the health-bringing power of the
Christ;

they may hope for the overcoming of the sickness of
sin
for the continuance of man's being
and for the preservation of their life
destined for eternity.
Yea, so it is.

6.12 The image of the 'chariot' as a conveyance for God also
appears in the Old Testament: '... [thou] makest the clouds thy
chariot' (Ps.104:3); compare Isa.66:15; Jer.4:13, *et al.*

6.13 In Genesis 1, the 'firmament' (Lat. = mainstay, support) separates above and below; the conception here is that everything sensory in the cosmos has a boundary where the realm of divine beings proper is established 'beyond the spheres of the fixed stars.'

6.14 In the Gospel this is seen in the 'cosmic reactions' — the sun growing dark, and so on — at Christ's death on the cross.

6.15 The word 'embodies' [or 'incorporates'] appears at the end of *How to Know Higher Worlds* (see the quotation on p.134f), which also deals with the 'embodiment' of the fruits of earthly existence into the supersensible world.

6.16 Perhaps this fact is also the basis for Teilhard de Chardin's vision (see Note 2.12 above). This phenomenon finds outer expression in the Catholic 'monstrance' when the host is displayed on the altar in a circle of rays of gold or silver.

6.17 Earlier theology would have dismissed this as blasphemous (God is perfect; any change in him could only make him less than perfect — otherwise he is not yet perfect). Nowadays this question is being mooted once more.

Wilhelm Maas offers a survey in *Die Unveränderlichkeit Gottes*.

6.18 It is worthy of note that in Rudolf Steiner's *Calendar of the Soul* (GA 40) it is precisely in the four verses belonging to the season of Epiphany that the words 'love' and 'warmth' occur frequently; and the word 'heart' in every one, which otherwise only appears twice in the whole year.

Chapter 7.

7.1 We are not here speaking of supersensible, concrete experiences of Christ, which indeed occur more and more nowadays (see H.-W. Schroeder, *Von der Wiederkunft Christi heute,*) but of the approach of the experience or sensing of the nearness of Christ in normal consciousness.

7.2 On the theme of 'the nearness and distance of Christ': Luther knows that the Ascension is misunderstood if one considers only the material mode of existence, the 'comprehensible bodily mode in which He [Christ] physically walked on earth, taking up and leaving space according to His actual size *(quantitas)* ... He does not exist in such a way ... in heaven ...; since God has no spatial body .... Furthermore [there is] the incomprehensible spiritual mode of existence in which He neither takes nor leaves space, but permeates all creatures according to His will .... Thirdly [there is] the divine heavenly mode, since He is one person with God, whereby all creatures are of course bound to be very much more open and accessible to Him.' He who ascends to heaven sits at God's right hand, but 'God's right hand is everywhere.' 'He has not climbed up to heaven on a ladder or come down on a rope.' Luther speaks of the 'way His [Christ's] divine Being can exist wholly and completely in all creatures, and in each in a special way, even more profoundly, intimately and actually than the creature to himself ...' (Quoted in Rudolf Frieling, *Christianity and Reincarnation,* p.39.)

Here I would draw attention to a lecture by Rudolf Steiner, in which he states that Christ is the only spiritual being who can be found in the cosmos and within the soul (mystically). (GA 113, Aug 28, 1909).

7.3 These words occur in the ritual acts of The Christian Community: 'leader of souls' in the wording heard in the Act of Consecration in memory of one who has died; 'immortal brother of mortal men' in the burial Service for children.

7.4 Christ strengthens and extends the forces with which he accompanies humanity's path through the centuries. In our time this is shown by an intensified 'presence' of Christ, which we also call his 'second coming.' The being and effectiveness of the renewed Mass, the Act of Consecration of Man, flows from this 'fact' (Lat. *factum* = deed) of his return.

See H.-W. Schroeder, *Die Wiederkunft Christi heute.*

7.5 The peace which the angels proclaim at Christmas ('peace on earth') is as yet still a hope and a promise; the peace of the Resurrected One is the outcome of suffering and death, has been wrested from the event of Golgotha and therefore does not need to draw back from Man's experiences of suffering and death; the prime example of this is the experience of the early Christian martyrs.

Bibliography

Arseniew, Nikolaus von, *Ostkirche und Mystik,* Munich 1943.
Augstein, Rudolf, *Jesus — Menschensohn,* Munich/Gütersloh/ Vienna 1972.
Balthasar, Hans Urs von, *Theologik Band II. Die Wahrheit Gottes,* Einsiedeln 1985.
Bateson, Gregory, *Mind and Nature,* New York 1979.
Benesch, Friedrich, *Ascension,* Floris, Edinburgh 1978.
Benesch, Friedrich, *Vorträge und Kurse.* Volumes 2 and 3, 'Christliche Feste,' Stuttgart 1993/94.
Besant, Annie, *Esoteric Christianity,* Theosophical Publishing House, London 1910.
Bock, Emil, *The Apocalypse of St John,* Floris, Edinburgh 1996.
—, *Cäsaren und Apostel,* Urachhaus, Stuttgart 1983.
—, *The Childhood of Jesus,* Floris, Edinburgh 1997.
—, *Das Evangelium. Betrachtungen zum Neuen Testament,* Urachhaus, Stuttgart 1995.
—, *Genesis,* Floris, Edinburgh 1983.
—, *Saint Paul,* Floris, Edinburgh 1993.
—, *The Three Years,* Floris, Edinburgh 1994.
Boff, Leonardo, *Von der Würde der Erde,* Düsseldorf 1994.
Buckingham, J.W. *Christ and the Eternal Order.*
Bürkle, Horst, (ed.) 'Die Unterscheidung der Geister,' in *New Age — Kritische Anfragen an eine verlokkende Bewegung,* Düsseldorf 1988,
Capra, Fritjof, *The Tao of Physics,* Fontana, London 1975.
Chardin, Teilhard de *Collected Works,* Vol.6.
—, *Hymn of the Universe,* Fontana, London 1970.
—, *Science and Christ,* Collins, London 1968.
Childs, Gilbert, *Rudolf Steiner: his Life and Work,* Floris Books, Edinburgh 1995.
Easton, Stewart, *Man and World in the Light of Anthroposophy,* Anthroposophic Press, New York 1975.

—, *Rudolf Steiner: Herald of a New Epoch,* Anthroposophic Press, New York 1980.

Fox, Matthew, *The Coming of the Cosmic Christ. The Healing of Mother Earth and the Birth of a Global Renaissance,* Harper and Row, San Francisco 1988.

Frieling, Rudolf, *Christianity and Reincarnation,* Floris, Edinburgh 1977.

—, *Christologische Aufsätze,* Urachhaus, Stuttgart 1982.

—, *The Essence of Christianity,* Floris, Edinburgh 1989.

—, *Hidden Treasures in the Psalms,* Floris, Edinburgh 1967.

—, *New Testament Studies,* Floris, Edinburgh 1994.

Grimal, Pierre, (ed.) *Mythen der Völker,* II, Fischer Taschenbuch 779.

Hemleben, Johannes, *Teilhard de Chardin,* Rowohlt, Hamburg.

Hildegard of Bingen, *Welt und Mensch,* Trans. Heinrich Schipperges, Salzburg 1965.

—, *Der Mensch in der Verantwortung,* Trans. Heinrich Schipperges, Salzburg 1972.

Hoerner, Erdmut-Michael, *Christus und die Erde,* Urachhaus, Stuttgart 1985.

Johanson, Irene, *Christuswirken in der Biographie,* Urachhaus, Stuttgart 1992.

Kantscheider, Bernulf, *Von der mechanistischen Welt zum kreativen Universum. Zu einem neuen philosophischen Verständnis der Natur,* Darmstadt 1993.

Kelber, Wilhelm, *Christ and the Son of Man,* Floris, Edinburgh 1997.

—, *Die Logoslehre von Heraklit bis Origines,* Urachhaus, Stuttgart 1976.

Knitter, Paul, *Ein Gott — viele Religionen,* Munich 1988.

Küng, Hans, *On being a Christian,* SCM Press, London 1974.

Kuschel, Karl-Josef, *Born Before All Time?,* SCM Press, London 1992.

Lauenstein, Dieter, *Der Messias. Eine biblische Untersuchung,* Urachhaus, Stuttgart 1971.

Lindenberg, Wladimir, *Die heilige Ikone,* Urachhaus, Stuttgart 1987.

Lüdemann, Gerd, *The Resurrection of Jesus,* SCM Press, London 1994.

Maas, Wilhelm, *Die Unveränderlichkeit Gottes. Zum Verhältnis von griechisch-philosophischer zu christlicher Gotteslehre,* Munich/Paderborn/Vienna 1978.

Meyer, Rudolf, *Die Wiedergewinnung des Johannesevangeliums,* Urachhaus, Stuttgart 1962.

Moltmann, Jürgen, *The Way of Jesus Christ,* SCM, London 1990.

Nordmeyer, Barbara, *Leben mit Christus. Betrachtungen zum Johannes-Evangelium,* Urachhaus, Stuttgart 1981.

Panikkar, Raimundo, *The Unknown Christ of Hinduism,* London.

Rahner, Karl, *Theological Investigations Vol V,* Darton, Longman and Todd, London.

Rau, Christoph, *Das Matthäus-Evangelium. Entstehung — Gestalt — Essenischer Einfluss,* Urachhaus, Stuttgart 1976.

—, *Struktur und Rhythmus im Johannes-Evangelium,* Urachhaus, Stuttgart 1972.

Rittelmeyer, Friedrich, *Briefe über das Johannesevangelium,* Urachhaus, Stuttgart 1954.

—, *Christus,* Urachhaus, Stuttgart 1950.

—, *Ich bin. Reden und Aufsätze über die sieben 'Ich-bin' Worte des Johannes Evangeliums,* Urachhaus, Stuttgart 1992.

Rössler, Andreas, *Steht Gottes Himmel allen offen? Zum Symbol des kosmischen Christus,* Stuttgart 1990.

Rudolph, Kurt, *Gnosis,* T&T Clark, Edinburgh 1993.

Schiwy, Günther, *Der kosmische Christus. Spuren Gottes ins Neue Zeitalter,* Munich 1990.

Schöpfungsgeschichte der Priesterschrift, Die, Neunkirchener Verlag 1993.

Schöpfungsmythen, Die, Einsiedeln/Zurich/Cologne 1964.

Schroeder, Hans-Werner, *Die Christengemeinschaft — Entstehung, Entwicklung, Zielsetzung,* Urachhaus, Stuttgart 1990.

—, *Dreieinigkeit und Dreifaltigkeit. Vom Geheimnis der Trinität.* Urachhaus, Stuttgart.

—, *Der Mensch und das Böse,* Urachhaus, Stuttgart 1990.

—, *Mensch und Engel,* Urachhaus, Stuttgart 1988.

—, *Von der Wiederkunft Christi heute,* Urachhaus, Stuttgart 1991.

Sheldrake, Rupert, *A New Science of Life,* Blond and Briggs, London 1981.

—, *The Rebirth of Nature: New Science and the Revival of Animism,* Century, London 1993.

Sheldrake, Rupert and Matthew Fox, *Natural Grace,* Bloomsbury, London 1997.

Schütze, Alfred, *Vom Wesen der Trinität,* Stuttgart 1980.

Schütze, Alfred, *The Enigma of Evil (Das Rätsel des Bösen,* Stuttgart 1969.

Spangler, David, *New Age.*

Steiner, Rudolf, GA *(Gesamtausgabe,* Complete Works, No.) 10. *Wie erlangt man Erkenntnisse der höheren Welten?* [*How to Know Higher Worlds,* Anthroposophic Press, New York 1994].

—, GA 11. *Aus der Akasha-Chronik.* [*Cosmic Memory,* Rudolf Steiner Publications, New York 1959].

—, GA 13. *Die Geheimwissenschaft im Umriß.* [*Occult Science: An Outline,* Rudolf Steiner Press, London 1979].

—, GA 15. *Die geistige Führung des Menschen und der Menschheit.* [*The Spiritual Guidance of the Individual and Humanity,* Anthroposophic Press, New York 1992].

—, GA 18. *Die Rätsel der Philosophie.* [*The Riddles of Philosophy,* Anthroposophic Press, New York 1973].

—, GA 26. *Anthroposophische Leitsätze.* [*Anthroposophical Leading Thoughts,* Rudolf Steiner Press, London 1985].

—, GA 40. *Anthroposophischer Seelenkalender.* [*The Calendar of the Soul,* Anthroposophic Press, New York 1988].

—, GA 93a. *Grundelemente der Esoterik.* [*Foundations of Esotericism,* Rudolf Steiner Press, London 1982].

—, GA 97. *Das christliche Mysterium,* Rudolf Steiner Verlag, Dornach 1981.

—, GA 102. *Das Hereinwirken geistiger Wesenheiten in den Menschen.* [*The Influence of Spiritual Beings upon Man,* Anthroposophic Press, New York 1982].

—, GA 103. *Das Johannes-Evangelium.* [*The Gospel of St John,* Anthroposophic Press, New York 1988].

—, GA 104. *Die Apokalypse des Johannes.* [*The Apocalypse of St John,* Rudolf Steiner Press, London 1977].

—, GA 110. *Geistige Hierarchien und ihre Widerspiegelung in der physischen Welt.* [*The Spiritual Hierarchies and the Physical World,* Anthroposophic Press, New York 1996].

—, GA 112. *Das Johannes-Evangelium im Verhältnis zu den drei anderen Evangelien.* [*The Gospel of St John and its Relation to the other Gospels,* Anthroposophic Press, New York 1982].

—, GA 114. *Das Lukas-Evangelium*. [*The Gospel of St Luke*, Rudolf Steiner Press, London 1988].

—, GA 118. *Das Ereignis der Christus-Erscheinung in der ätherischen Welt.* [*The Reappearance of Christ in the Etheric*, Anthroposophic Press, New York 1983].

—, GA 122. *Die Geheimnisse der biblischen Schöpfungsgeschichte.* [*Genesis, Secrets of the Biblical Story of Creation*, Rudolf Steiner Press, London 1982].

—, GA 123. *Das Matthäus-Evangelium.* [*The Gospel of St Matthew*, Rudolf Steiner Press, London 1985].

—, GA 124. *Exkurse in das Gebiet des Markus-Evangeliums.* [*Background to the Gospel of St. Mark*, Rudolf Steiner Press, London 1968].

—, GA 127. *Erbsünde und Gnade.* [*The Concepts of Original Sin and Grace*, Rudolf Steiner Press, London].

—, GA 129. *Weltenwunder, Seelenprüfungen und Geistesoffenbarungen.* [*Wonders of the World, Ordeals of the Soul, Revelations of the Spirit*, Rudolf Steiner Press, London 1983].

—, GA 130. *Die Ätherisation des Blutes.* [*The Etherisation of the Blood*, Rudolf Steiner Press, London 1985].

—, GA 131. *Von Jesus zu Christus.* [*From Jesus to Christ*, Rudolf Steiner Press, London 1991].

—, GA 143. *Erfahrungen des Übersinnlichen. Die drei Wege der Seele zu Christus*, Rudolf Steiner Verlag, Dornach 1994.

—, GA 148. *Das Fünfte Evangelium.* [*The Fifth Gospel*, Rudolf Steiner Press, London 1995].

—, GA 152. *Vorstufen zum Mysterium von Golgatha.* [*The Four Sacrifices of Christ*, Anthroposophic Press, New York 1981].

—, GA 155. *Christus und die menschliche Seele.* [*Christ and the Human Soul*, Rudolf Steiner Press, London 1972].

—, GA 156. *Okkultes Lesen und okkultes Hören.* [*Occult Reading and Occult Hearing*, Rudolf Steiner Press, London 1975].

—, GA 161. *Wege der geistigen Erkenntnis und der Erneuerung künstlerischer Weltanschauung*, Rudolf Steiner Verlag, Dornach 1980.

—, GA 170. *Das Rätsel des Menschen.* [*The Riddle of Humanity*, Rudolf Steiner.Press, London 1990].

—, GA 174b *Die geistigen Hintergründe des Ersten Weltkrieges*, Rudolf Steiner Verlag, Dornach 1994.

—, GA 175. *Bausteine zu einer Erkenntnis des Mysteriums von Golgatha.* [*Building Stones for an Understanding of the Mystery of Golgotha,* Rudolf Steiner Press, London 1985].

—, GA 181. *Erdensterben und Weltenleben. Anthroposophische Lebensgaben. Bewußtseins-Notwendigkeiten für Gegenwart und Zukunft,* Rudolf Steiner Verlag, Dornach 1991.

—, GA 198. *Heilfaktoren für den sozialen Organismus,* Rudolf Steiner Verlag, Dornach 1984.

—, GA 202. *Die Brücke zwischen der Weltgeistigkeit und dem Physischen des Menschen.* [*The Bridge between Universal Spirituality and the Physical Constitution of Man,* Anthroposophic Press, New York 1979].

—, GA 207. *Anthroposophie als Kosmosophie,* I. [*Cosmosophy,* Vol.I, Anthroposophic Press, New York 1985].

—, GA 209. *Nordische und mitteleuropäische Geistimpulse,* Rudolf Steiner Verlag, Dornach 1982.

—, GA 211. *Das Sonnenmysterium und das Mysterium von Tod und Auferstehung,* Rudolf Steiner Verlag, Dornach 1986.

—, GA 215. *Die Philosophie, Kosmologie und Religion in der Anthroposophie.* [*Philosophy, Cosmology and Religion,* Anthroposophic Press, New York 1984].

—, GA 216. *Die Grundimpulse des weltgeschichtlichen Werdens der Menschheit.* [*Supersensible Influences in the History of Mankind,* Rudolf Steiner Press, London 1956].

—, GA 219. *Das Verhältnis der Sternenwelt zum Menschen und des Menschen zur Sternenwelt.* [*Man and the World of Stars,* Anthroposophic Press, New York 1982].

—, GA 220. *Lebendiges Naturerkennen. Intellektueller Sündenfall und spirituelle Sündenerhebung,* Rudolf Steiner Verlag, Dornach 1982.

—, GA 221. *Erdenwissen und Himmelserkenntnis.* [*Earthly Knowledge and Heavenly Wisdom,* Anthroposophic Press, New York 1991].

—, GA 222. *Die Impulsierung des weltgeschichtlichen Geschehens durch geistige Mächte.* [*The Driving Force of Spiritual Powers in World History,* Steiner Book Centre, Vancouver 1983].

—, GA 223. *Der Jahreskreislauf als Atmungsvorgang der Erde und die vier grossen Festeszeiten.* [*The Cycle of the Year,*

Anthroposophic Press, New York 1988; *Michaelmas and the Soul Forces of Man,* Anthroposophic Press, New York 1982].

—, GA 224. *Die menschliche Seele in ihrem Zusammenhang mit göttlich-geistigen Individualitäten,* Rudolf Steiner Verlag, Dornach 1992.

—, GA 226. *Menschenwesen, Menschenschicksal und Welt-Entwickelung.* [*Man's Being, his Destiny and World Evolution,* Anthroposophic Press, New York 1984].

—, GA 230. *Der Mensch als Zusammenklang des schaffenden, bildenden und gestaltenden Weltenwortes.* [*Man as Symphony of the Creative Word,* Rudolf Steiner Press, London 1991].

—, GA 231. *Der übersinnliche Mensch, anthroposophisch erfasst.* [*Supersensible Man,* Anthroposophical Publishing Company, London 1961].

—, GA 318. *Das Zusammenwirken von Ärzten und Seelsorgern.* [*Pastoral Medicine,* Anthroposophic Press, New York 1987].

—, GA 344. *Vorträge und Kurse über christlich-religiöses Wirken,* III, Rudolf Steiner Verlag, Dornach 1994.

—, *Das Mysterium des Bösen,* ten lectures (ed. M. Stalisch), Stuttgart 1993.

Stevens, G. *The Christian Doctrine of Salvation,* 1905.

Strobach, Klaus, *Vom 'Urknall' zur Erde. Werden und Wandlung unseres Planeten im Kosmos,* Melsungen 1983.

Theologisches Begriffslexikon zum Neuen Testament Wuppertal 1979.

Tillich, Paul, *Systematic Theology,* Vol.3, SCM Press, London 1997.

Tippler, Frank, *The Physics of Immortality,* Pan Macmillan, London 1996.

Wagner, Reinhard, *Die Gnosis von Alexandria. Eine Frage des frühen Christentums an die Gegenwart,* Stuttgart.

Welburn, Andrew, *The Beginnings of Christianity,* Floris, Edinburgh 1991.

—, *The Mysteries: Rudolf Steiner's writings on spiritual initiation,* Floris, Edinburgh 1997.

Index of biblical references

Index

The Beginnings of Christianity

*Essene mystery, Gnostic revelation
and the Christian vision*

Andrew Welburn

*Readers interested in the origins of Christianity and its hidden
esoteric current will find this an outstandingly interesting
scholarly study.* **David Lorimer**

*... belongs in the library of anyone with more than a casual
interest in matters gnostic and Essene.* **Gnosis**

Recent work on the Dead Sea Scrolls and other ancient documents has provided much new knowledge of the early Christian
Church and the messianic sects in the Holy Land around the time
of Christ. These texts reveal that early Christianity had a powerful esoteric current, which is also reflected in the New Testament
writings of Mark, Paul and above all John.

During the early centuries after Christ, Gnostic Christians tried
to preserve this tradition, using the archaic Mysteries as a way to
knowledge *(gnosis)* of higher cosmic truths. The Gnostic sects
were finally suppressed by an authoritarian Church which would
not tolerate deviation from the established Christian teachings.

Andrew Welburn reveals a kinship between our own age and
the early Christians, and shows how we now have the chance to
rediscover the spiritual world and meaning of the early years of
the Christian era. He has further developed these themes in his
companion book, *Gnosis, the Mysteries and Christianity*, which
contains many of the actual texts discussed in *The Beginnings of
Christianity*.

Floris Books